SAINT MARY'S COLLEGE OF CALIFORNIA
COLLEGIATE SEMINAR 002

WESTERN TRADITION I

THIRD EDITION

Printed in the United States of America

ISBN-13: 978-1-50669-760-4

Cover Photo: "Dante Running from the Three Beasts" by William Blake, 1824–1827). National Gallery of Victoria, Melbourne.

Acknowledgments:

pp. 1–12: From *Five Dialogues* by Plato, translated by GMA Grube. Copyright © 2002 by Hackett Publishing Company, Inc. Reprinted by permission of the publisher.
pp. 13–37: From *The History of the Peloponnesian War* by Thucydides, translated by Rex Warner, with an introduction and notes by M. I. Finley (Penguin Classics 1954, revised edition 1972). Translation copyright © 1954 by Rex Warner. Introduction and Appendices copyright © 1972 by M. I. Finley. Reprinted by permission of Penguin Books Ltd.
pp. 38–68: From *On the Nature of the Universe* by Lucretius, translated by R. E. Latham, revised with an introduction by John Goodwin (Penguin 1951, 1994). Translation copyright © R. E. Latham, 1951. Revisions, introduction and notes copyright © John Goodwin, 1994.

pp. 76–92: From *Meditations* by Marcus Aurelius, translated by Martin Hammond. Copyright © 2006. Reprinted by permission of Penguin Books Ltd.

pp. 93–97: Scripture texts in this work are taken from the *New American Bible*, revised edition © 2010, 1991, 1986, 1970 Confraternity of Christian Doctrine, Washington, D.C. and are used by permission of the copyright owner. All Rights Reserved. No part

530 Great Road
Acton, MA 01720
800-562-2147
www.xanedu.com

Contents

Collegiate Seminar Goals and Outcomes

Collegiate Seminar Vision Statement

The Collegiate Seminar Program seeks to engage Saint Mary's students in a critical and collaborative encounter with the world of ideas as expressed in great texts of the Western tradition in dialogue with and exposure to its encounter with other traditions. Thereby students become part of the Great Conversation. The Program seeks to help them develop as curious, thoughtful members of an intellectual community. Designed to serve the College's goals of a liberal education, the Program strives to put students in possession of their powers to think clearly, critically, and collaboratively, and articulate their ideas effectively—powers that will serve them for the rest of their lives.

Goals of the Collegiate Seminar Program

The Collegiate Seminar Program fosters a genuine sense of collegiality and intellectual community by providing an authentic forum for students to meet and partake of a common experience—the reading and discussion of shared texts under the guidance of faculty from all disciplines. Its participants engage in collaborative dialogue with texts whose ideas shape our world. Through careful reading, shared inquiry, and writing, students improve their skills of analysis and communication. During this process students will develop increased appreciation for these great ideas, and grow in their intellectual curiosity, becoming life-long learners and thinkers. Students will be exposed to a variety of ways of knowing, encouraged in their search for meaning, and learn to accept ambiguity while aiming for clarity.

Seminar Specific Learning Outcomes

As a result of their participation in the Collegiate Seminar Program, students will grow in their ability to:

1. Understand, analyze, and evaluate challenging texts from different genres and periods.
2. Comprehend the intellectual threads that connect works both backward and forward through history.

3. Relate the works studied to their own experience and to notions of authentic humanity.
4. Reflect on prior knowledge and assess one's own process of learning.

Critical Thinking

Critical thinking within Seminar is grounded on the processes of analysis, synthesis and evaluation necessary to read with understanding. Through careful reading, listening, and reflection, which lead to a solid understanding of the texts, critical thinking allows students to make perceptive insights and connections between texts, Seminars and ultimately their life experiences. Critical thinking within Seminar also includes skills that allow for sound judgments to be made when multiple, competing viewpoints are possible. Seminar is a place where reading critically is transformed and integrated into a habit of mind, providing students with the tools to question the authority of the text and the foundations of their own assumptions. In short, critical thinking allows students to recognize, formulate and pursue meaningful questions, which are not only factual but also interpretive and evaluative, about the ideas of others as well as their own.

Critical Thinking Learning Outcomes

As a result of their participation in the Collegiate Seminar Program, students will grow in their ability to:

1. Distinguish the multiple senses of a text (literal and beyond the literal).
2. Identify and understand assumptions, theses, and arguments that exist in the work of authors.
3. Evaluate and synthesize evidence in order to draw conclusions consistent with the text. Seek and identify confirming and opposing evidence relevant to original and existing theses.
4. Ask meaningful questions and originate plausible theses.
5. Critique and question the authority of texts, and explore the implications of those texts.

Written and Oral Communication

A mind is not truly liberated until it can effectively communicate what it knows. Thus the Collegiate Seminar Program seeks to develop strong written and oral communication skills in its students. Students will develop skills that demonstrate an understanding of the power of language to shape thought and experience. They will learn to write and speak logically, with clarity, and with originality, and grow in their intellectual curiosity through the process of writing.

Written and Oral Communication Learning Outcomes

As a result of their participation in the Collegiate Seminar Program, students will grow in their ability to:

1. Recognize and compose readable prose, as characterized by clear and careful organization, coherent paragraphs and well-constructed sentences that employ the conventions of Standard Written English and appropriate diction.
2. Recognize and formulate effective written and oral communication, giving appropriate consideration to audience, context, format, and textual evidence.
3. Analyze arguments so as to construct ones that are well supported (with appropriate use of textual evidence), are well reasoned, and are controlled by a thesis or exploratory question.
4. Use discussion and the process of writing to enhance intellectual discovery and unravel complexities of thought.

Shared Inquiry

Shared inquiry is the act of reasoning together about common texts, questions, and problems. It is a goal of Collegiate Seminar to advance students' abilities to develop and pursue meaningful questions in collaboration with others, even in the context of confusion, paradox, and/or disagreement. Through the habits of shared inquiry students will carefully consider and understand the perspectives and reasoned opinions of others, reconsider their own opinions, and develop rhetorical skills.

Shared Inquiry Learning Outcomes

As a result of their participation in the Collegiate Seminar Program, students will grow in their ability to:

1. Advance probing questions about a common text or other objects of study.

2. Pursue new and enriched understandings of the texts through sustained collaborative inquiry.
3. Reevaluate initial hypotheses in light of evidence and collaborative discussion with the goal of making considered judgments.
4. Engage in reflective listening and inclusive, respectful conversation.

Honor Code and Seminar

The Student Honor Council (of academic 2004–2005) has requested that all Seminar sections discuss the proper use of other persons' opinions in Seminar classes. The Governing Board of Collegiate Seminar proposes the following list of good practices:

Authentic engagement in seminar classes requires that—

1. Students read only the assigned texts in preparation;
2. Students give their own thoughts about the assigned readings;
3. Students do not introduce opinions of experts into the conversation;
4. Student essays present the student's own thoughts on the agreed-upon topic;
5. Instructors advise whether and how essays should respond to, use, or cite opinions which other students have voiced in class.

(CSGB, 5/19/04)

Collegiate Seminar Guidelines for Grading Oral Participation

The following criteria shall be considered in evaluating the oral participation of seminar students:

- Good listening and close attention to the discussion.
- Frequency of contribution to discussion.
- Quality of contributions in terms of forwarding the conversation.
- Clear evidence of reflection upon the reading.
- Ability, with respect to the reading, to describe, propose insights, analyze, see alternatives, compare, and evaluate.
- Ability to counter questions and/or challenge other discussants (including the seminar leader) respectfully.
- Seriousness of engagement, degree of interest in the ideas under discussion, and spontaneity.
- Sense of responsibility for the group's understanding of the text and for the progress of the conversation.

Seminar leaders and students are encouraged to use these criteria to evaluate perfomance as follows:

The student who earns a grade of "A" for oral participation is one who:

1) Is rarely if ever absent from class and is likely to inform the instructor in advance.
2) Is always excellently prepared and demonstrates her/his preparation by consistently offering text-related contributions throughout the discussion.
3) Is self-motivated, entering the discussion with pertinent and useful contributions as appropriate.
4) Is engaged and active in pursuing questions and in testing opinions.

5) Regularly forwards the discussion by drawing comparisons, analyzing problems and questions, offering opinions on interpretations, and responding critically and respectfully to the contributions of others.
6) Listens with active interest to the comments of others; questions others in an effort to understand not only what they are saying but also the reasons and implications of what they are saying.
7) Takes responsibility for the "health and well-being" of the seminar.

The student who earns a grade of "B" for oral participation is one who:

1) Is rarely, if ever, absent from class and is likely to inform the instructor in advance.
2) Is nearly always well prepared and demonstrates her/his preparation by often offering text-related contributions to the discussion.
3) Is often self-motivated, entering the discussion with pertinent and useful contributions as appropriate.
4) Is sometimes engaged and active, sometimes more passive, in pursuing questions and in testing opinions.
5) Sometimes forwards the conversation, sometimes takes a less active role, supporting or questioning the more positive contributions of others.
6) Listens with active interest to the comments of others.
7) Does not obstruct or retard the "health and well being" of the seminar.

The student who earns a grade of "C" for oral participation is one who:

1) Is seldom absent from class.
2) Is generally prepared and demonstrates her/his preparation by offering text-related contributions at some point in the discussion.
3) Regularly contributes to discussion but takes a follower's rather than a leader's role in forwarding the conversation.
4) Listens respectfully to the comments of others.
5) Does not obstruct or retard the "health and well-being" of the seminar.

The student who earns a grade of "D" for oral participation is one who:

1) May be absent from class more than three or four times per semester.
2) May be unprepared for discussion or fail to demonstrate preparation by pertinent text-related contributions to the discussion.
3) Often does not contribute, even as a follower, in the seminar discussion.
4) May fail to listen to others; may engage in disruptive "side conversations."
5) May obstruct or retard the "health and well-being" of the seminar.

The student who earns a grade of "F" for oral participation is one who:

1) May be often absent from seminar.
2) Is unprepared for the majority of classes.
3) Rarely, if ever, contributes to the discussion.
4) Does not listen to others or follow the course of the discussion; may engage in disruptive behavior.
5) May obstruct or retard the seminar.

Saint Mary's College Grading Standards

Collegiate Seminar Program

Seminar 02/14

	***The C essay** is competent, exhibiting no serious or frequent deficiencies.*	***The B essay** is strong in most areas.*
Thesis/ Purpose/ Controlling Idea	The C essay addresses the topic and offers a thesis. The thesis, however, may not explore the topic with sufficient complexity or take on a significant intellectual challenge.	The B essay exhibits intellectual engagement. It has a narrowly focused thesis, with a clear sense of purpose and audience. It explores the topic in some depth and with some complexity.
Structure, Organization, and Development	The C essay offers support for its thesis; however, this support may not be evaluated or analyzed thoughtfully, or may tend toward plot summary. The C essay has an introduction, body, and conclusion, generally unified paragraphs, and transitions between paragraphs. However, it may proceed formulaically or mechanically. (e.g. listing examples). The conclusion may not move much beyond the initial thesis.	The B essay proceeds logically and offers appropriate support for its thesis. It is a generally unified essay, with a clear introduction, coherent paragraphs, and effective transitions. Its conclusion does not merely restate the argument, but attempts to draw together preceding insights in a new way.
Language, Style, and Syntax	The C essay employs readable prose, but the sentences may be simple and lack variety. Language may be overly general and wordy.	In the B essay, sentences are sufficiently varied. Language is generally concise and appropriate.
Grammar, Spelling, Punctuation, Formatting, and Documentation of Sources	The C essay employs generally correct grammar, punctuation, formatting, spelling, and documentation. Errors, however, may be serious enough to detract from the effectiveness of the essay.	The B essay employs generally correct grammar, punctuation, formatting, spelling, and documentation. Errors, when they appear, do not detract from the overall effectiveness of the essay.

The F essay is seriously deficient. It may exhibit a poor grasp of the assignment or a lack of familiarity with assigned texts. It may be deficient in one or more of the following areas: purpose, organization and development, language, and mechanics. It may lack a clear thesis or fail to support its thesis.

	The A essay *excels in all areas.*	***The D essay*** *is deficient in one or more areas.*
	The A essay has a clearly defined, intellectually challenging focus and a strong sense of purpose and audience. It exhibits depth and complexity in its analysis and originality in its thought.	The D essay may lack a clear thesis, or the thesis may be weak or overly general.
	The A essay is distinguished by sound logic. It offers sufficient and appropriate support for the thesis in the form of concrete, specific, and relevant evidence. It is a unified essay that proceeds coherently with an effective introduction, well-developed and unified paragraphs, graceful transitions, and a conclusion that, rather than summarizing previous points, explores the implications of the preceding analysis.	The D essay may fail to provide adequate support for its thesis in the form of textual analysis or other evidence; it may substitute repetition for development or make inaccurate claims. It may lack a clear structure and paragraphs may lack coherence. Transitions may be awkward or nonexistent.
	In the A essay, sentences are skillfully crafted and effectively varied; langauge is fresh, precise, and economical. It maintains a consistent and appropriate tone.	The D essay often lacks variety in sentence structure and suffers from inappropriate diction and akward syntax. Language tends to be vague, imprecise, or rambling.
	The A essay is almost entirely free of errors in grammar, punctuation, formatting, spelling, and documentation.	A D essay is often characterized by grammatical errors such as fragments, comma splices, agreement errors, or inappropriate shifts in tense, voice, mood, or person. It may also be rife with spelling, punctuation, or formatting errors. It may lack documentation or be improperly documented.
Other common features of failing essays are: faulty logic, ineffective organization, incoherent paragraphs, misreadings, incorrect diction, and so many syntactic and grammatical errors that the essay becomes unreadable.		

Kinds of Questions

Questions of Fact

To a question of fact there will be only one answer which can be supported using evidence from the text; this answer may, however, take some effort to discover.

Example: In "The Analogy of the Cave", why do philosophers (those with "beatific vision") appear foolish in the everyday world (such as in the law courts)?

Questions of Interpretation

Your purpose is to make sense of the text. You might ask what conclusions we can draw about the author's meaning, purpose, or basic assumptions. Or you might question the relationship of two statements which seem to be in contradiction. To questions of interpretation, attentive readers can give differing answers, each of which can be supported using evidence from the text.

Example: According to Socrates, the prisoners of "The Analogy of the Cave" are "like us." How does the reading support this view?

Questions of Evaluation

Judge what is presented in the reading. Is what is written true? False? Neither true nor false? Likely? Unlikely? Wrong? Right? Fair? Unfair? Insightful? Obvious? Of course, these categories of judgment (and others like them) are often themselves the very subject of the readings.

Example: Is "The Analogy of the Cave" a good and useful image of human existence? (And what do I mean by "good" or by "useful" or by "image"?)

Chronological Outline of Greek, Roman, and Latin Christian Authors and Historical References

Before Current (Christian) Era (BCE)

1280–1180	Trojan War
753	Founding of Rome
750–620	*Odyssey*
600	Sappho
510	Athenian democratic constitution of Cleisthenes
509	Beginning of the Roman Republic
477	Commencement of Athenian Supremacy
461	Ascendency of Pericles. Aeschylus writes *The Oresteian Trilogy*
440	Sophocles exhibits the *Antigone*, and is made one of the ten Athenian generals in the war with Samos
431	Commencement of the Peloponnesian War
430	Plague at Athens
before 410	Thucydides writes *The History of the Peloponnesian War*
360	Plato writes *Crito*
335–322	Aristotle writes *The Nicomachean Ethics*
322	Suppression of Athenian democracy
300	Euclid teaches geometry in Alexandria
1st century	Lucretius writes *On the Nature of Things* before mid-century
44	Collapse of the Roman Republic and beginning of the Principate
29–19	Virgil writes *The Aeneid*

Current (Christian) Era (CE)

1	Beginning of the Christian Era with the birth of Christ (actually 4 BCE ca.)
1st century	Writing of the New Testament in the last quarter of the century
167	Marcus Aurelius writes *The Meditations*
4th century	Constantinian Revolution (transformation of Roman Empire to a Christian Roman Empire)
398	Augustine writes *The Confessions*
570	Birth of Mohammed
622	Beginning of the Muslim Era
800	Inauguration of the Frankish Carolingian Empire of the Romans
962	The German Empire of the Romans replaces the Carolingian Empire
1048–1122	Reform of the papacy
1265–1274	Thomas Aquinas writes *The Summa Theologica*
Late 12th century	Marie de France writes *The Lais*
1198–1303	Ascendancy of the papacy in Europe
1307–1321	Dante Alighieri writes "Inferno" and "Purgatorio" as part of his *Divine Comedy*
1309–1376	Avignon papacy, or Babylonian Captivity of the papacy
1378–1417	Great Schism of the Western Church
1380–1400	Geoffrey Chaucer writes *The Canterbury Tales*
1395	Julian of Norwich writes *Revelations of Divine Love*
1453	Conquest of Constantinople by the Turks and the fall of the Byzantine Eastern Roman Empire

Western Tradition I

Crito

Plato

About the time of Socrates' trial, a state galley had set out on an annual religious mission to the small Aegean island of Delos, sacred to Apollo, and while it was away, no execution was allowed to take place. So it was that Socrates was kept in prison for a month after the trial. The ship has now arrived at Cape Sunium in Attica and is thus expected at the Piraeus, Athens' port, momentarily. So Socrates' old and faithful friend, Crito, makes one last effort to persuade him to escape into exile, and all arrangements for this plan have been made. It is this conversation between the two old friends that Plato professes to report in this dialogue. It is, as Crito plainly tells him, his last chance, but Socrates will not take it, and he gives his reasons for his refusal. Whether this conversation took place at this particular time is not important, for there is every reason to believe that Socrates' friends tried to plan his escape and that he refused. Plato more than hints that the authorities would not have minded much, as long as he left the country.

G.M.A.G.

SOCRATES: Why have you come so early, Crito? Or is it not still early?

CRITO: It certainly is.

SOCRATES: How early?

CRITO: Early dawn.

SOCRATES: I am surprised that the warder was willing to listen to you.

CRITO: He is quite friendly to me by now, Socrates. I have been here often and I have given him something.

SOCRATES: Have you just come, or have you been here for some time?

CRITO: A fair time.

SOCRATES: Then why did you not wake me right away but sit there in silence?

CRITO: By Zeus no, Socrates. I would not myself want to be in distress and awake so long. I have been surprised to see you so peacefully asleep. It was on purpose that I did not wake you, so that you should spend your time most agreeably. Often in the past throughout my life, I have considered the way you live happy, and especially so now that you bear your present misfortune so easily and lightly.

SOCRATES: It would not be fitting at my age to resent the fact that I must die now.

CRITO: Other men of your age are caught in such misfortunes, but their age does not prevent them resenting their fate.

SOCRATES: That is so. Why have you come so early?

CRITO: I bring bad news, Socrates, not for you, apparently, but for me and all your friends the news is bad and hard to bear. Indeed, I would count it among the hardest.

SOCRATES: What is it? Or has the ship arrived from Delos, at the arrival of which I must die?

CRITO: It has not arrived yet, but it will, I believe, arrive today, according to a message some men brought from Sunium, where they left it. This makes it obvious that it will come today, and that your life must end tomorrow.

SOCRATES: May it be for the best. If it so please the gods, so be it. However, I do not think it will arrive today.

CRITO: What indication have you of this?

SOCRATES: I will tell you. I must die the day after the ship arrives.

CRITO: That is what those in authority say.

SOCRATES: Then I do not think it will arrive on this coming day, but on the next. I take to witness of this a dream I had a little earlier during this night. It looks as if it was the right time for you not to wake me.

CRITO: What was your dream?

SOCRATES: I thought that a beautiful and comely woman dressed in white approached me. She called me and said: "Socrates, may you arrive at fertile Phthia[1] on the third day."

CRITO: A strange dream, Socrates.

SOCRATES: But it seems clear enough to me, Crito.

CRITO: Too clear it seems, my dear Socrates, but listen to me even now and be saved. If you die, it will not be a single misfortune for me. Not only will I be deprived of a friend, the like of whom I shall never find again, but many people who do not know you or me very well will think that I could have saved you if I were willing to spend money, but that I did not care to do so. Surely there can be no worse reputation than to be thought to value money more highly than one's friends, for the majority will not believe that you yourself were not willing to leave prison while we were eager for you to do so.

SOCRATES: My good Crito, why should we care so much for what the majority think? The most reasonable people, to whom one should pay more attention, will believe that things were done as they were done.

CRITO: You see, Socrates, that one must also pay attention to the opinion of the majority. Your present situation makes clear that the majority can inflict not the least but pretty well the greatest evils if one is slandered among them.

SOCRATES: Would that the majority could inflict the greatest evils, for they would then be capable of the greatest good, and that would be fine, but now they cannot do either. They cannot make a man either wise or foolish, but they inflict things haphazardly.

CRITO: That may be so. But tell me this, Socrates, are you anticipating that I and your other friends would have trouble with the informers if you escape from here, as having stolen you away, and that we should be compelled to lose all our property or pay heavy fines and suffer other punishment besides? If you have any such fear, forget it. We would be justified in running this risk to save you, and worse, if necessary. Do follow my advice, and do not act differently.

SOCRATES: I do have these things in mind, Crito, and also many others.

CRITO: Have no such fear. It is not much money that some people require to save you and get you out of here. Further, do you not see that those informers are cheap, and that not much money would be needed to deal with them? My money is available and is, I think, sufficient. If, because of your affection for me, you feel you should not spend any of mine, there are those strangers here ready to spend money. One of them, Simmias the Theban, has brought enough for this very purpose. Cebes, too, and a good many others. So, as I say, do not let this fear make you hesitate to save yourself, nor let what you said in court trouble you, that you would not know what to do with yourself if you left Athens, for you would be welcomed in many places to which you might go. If you want to go to Thessaly, I have friends there who will greatly appreciate you and keep you safe, so that no one in Thessaly will harm you.

Besides, Socrates, I do not think that what you are doing is just, to give up your life when you can save it, and to hasten your fate as your enemies would hasten it, and indeed have hastened it in their wish to destroy you. Moreover, I think you are betraying your sons by going away and leaving them, when you could bring them up and educate them. You thus show no concern for what their fate may be. They will probably have the usual fate of orphans. Either one should not have children, or one should share with them to the end the toil of upbringing and education. You seem to me to choose the easiest path, whereas one should choose the path a good and courageous man would choose, particularly when one claims throughout one's life to care for virtue, I feel ashamed on your behalf and on behalf of us, your friends, lest all that has happened to you be thought due to cowardice on our part: the fact that your trial came to court when it need not have done so, the handling of the trial itself, and now this absurd ending which will be thought to have got beyond our control through some cowardice and unmanliness on our part, since we did not save you, or you save yourself, when it was possible and could be done if we had been of the slightest use. Consider, Socrates, whether this is not only evil, but shameful, both for you and for us. Take counsel with yourself, or rather the time for counsel is past and the decision should have been taken, and there is no further opportunity, for this whole business must be ended tonight. If we delay now, then it will no longer be possible; it will be too late. Let me persuade you on every count, Socrates, and do not act otherwise.

SOCRATES: My dear Crito, your eagerness is worth much if it should have some right aim; if not, then the greater your keenness the more difficult it is to deal with. We must therefore examine whether we should act in this way or not, as not only now but at all times I am the kind of man who listens to nothing within me but the argument that on reflection seems best to me. I cannot, now that this fate has come upon me, discard the arguments I used; they seem to me much the same. I value and respect the same principles as before, and if we have no better arguments to bring up at this moment, be sure that I shall not agree with you, not even if the power of the majority were to frighten us with more bogeys, as if we were children, with threats of incarcerations and executions and confiscation of property. How should we examine this matter most reasonably? Would it be by taking up first your argument about the opinions of men, whether it is sound in every case that one should pay attention to some opinions, but not to others?

Or was that well-spoken before the necessity to die came upon me, but now it is clear that this was said in vain for the sake of argument, that it was in truth play and nonsense? I am eager to examine together with you, Crito, whether this argument will appear in any way different to me in my present circumstances, or whether it remains the same, whether we are to abandon it or believe it. It was said on every occasion by those who thought they were speaking sensibly, as I have just now been speaking, that one should greatly value some people's opinions, but not others. Does that seem to you a sound statement?

You, as far as a human being can tell, are exempt from the likelihood of dying tomorrow, so the present misfortune is not likely to lead you astray. Consider then, do you not think it a sound statement that one must not value all the opinions of men, but some and not others, nor the opinions of all men, but those of some and not of others? What do you say? Is this not well said?

CRITO: It is.

SOCRATES: One should value the good opinions, and not the bad ones?

CRITO: Yes.

SOCRATES: The good opinions are those of wise men, the bad ones those of foolish men?

CRITO: Of course.

SOCRATES: Come then, what of statements such as this: Should a man professionally engaged in physical training pay attention to the praise and blame and opinion of any man, or to those of one man only, namely a doctor or trainer?

CRITO: To those of one only.

SOCRATES: He should therefore fear the blame and welcome the praise of that one man, and not those of the many?

CRITO: Obviously.

SOCRATES: He must then act and exercise, eat and drink in the way the one, the trainer and the one who knows, thinks right, not all the others?

CRITO: That is so.

SOCRATES: Very well. And if he disobeys the one, disregards his opinion and his praises while valuing those of the many who have no knowledge, will he not suffer harm?

CRITO: Of course.

SOCRATES: What is that harm, where does it tend, and what part of the man who disobeys does it affect?

CRITO: Obviously the harm is to his body, which it ruins.

SOCRATES: Well said. So with other matters, not to enumerate them all, and certainly with actions just and unjust, shameful and beautiful, good and bad, about which we are now deliberating, should we follow the opinion of the many and fear it, or that of the one, if there is one who has knowledge of these things and before whom we feel fear and shame more than before all the others? If we do not follow his directions, we shall harm and corrupt that part of ourselves that is improved by just actions and destroyed by unjust actions. Or is there nothing in this?

CRITO: I think there certainly is, Socrates.

SOCRATES: Come now, if we ruin that which is improved by health and corrupted by disease by not following the opinions of those who know, is life worth living for us when that is ruined? And that is the body, is it not?

CRITO: Yes.

SOCRATES: And is life worth living with a body that is corrupted and in bad condition?

CRITO: In no way.

SOCRATES: And is life worth living for us with that part of us corrupted that unjust action harms and just action benefits? Or do we think that part of us, whatever it is, that is concerned with justice and injustice, is inferior to the body?

CRITO: Not at all.

SOCRATES: It is more valuable?

CRITO: Much more.

SOCRATES: We should not then think so much of what the majority will say about us, but what he will say who understands justice and injustice, the one, that is, and the truth itself. So that, in the first place, you were wrong to believe that we should care for the opinion of the many about what is just, beautiful, good, and their opposites. "But," someone might say, "the many are able to put us to death."

CRITO: That too is obvious, Socrates, and someone might well say so.

SOCRATES: And, my admirable friend, that argument that we have gone through remains, I think, as before. Examine the following statement in turn as to whether it stays the same or not, that the most important thing is not life, but the good life.

CRITO: It stays the same.

SOCRATES: And that the good life, the beautiful life, and the just life are the same; does that still hold, or not?

CRITO: It does hold.

SOCRATES: As we have agreed so far, we must examine next whether it is just for me to try to get out of here when the Athenians have not acquitted me. If it is seen to be just, we will try to do so; if it is not, we will abandon the idea. As for those questions you raise about money, reputation, the upbringing of children, Crito, those considerations in truth belong to those people who easily put men to death and would bring them to life again if they could, without thinking; I mean the majority of men. For us, however, since our argument leads to this, the only valid consideration, as we were saying just now, is whether we should be acting rightly in giving money and gratitude to those who will lead me out of here, and ourselves helping with the escape, or whether in truth we shall do wrong in doing all this. If it appears that we shall be acting unjustly, then we have no need at all to take into account whether we shall have to die if we stay here and keep quiet, or suffer in another way, rather than do wrong.

CRITO: I think you put that beautifully, Socrates, but see what we should do.

SOCRATES: Let us examine the question together, my dear friend, and if you can make any objection while I am speaking, make it and I will listen to you, but if you have no objection to make, my dear Crito, then stop now from saying the same thing so often, that I must leave here against the will of the Athenians. I think it important to persuade you before I act, and not to act against your wishes. See whether the start of our inquiry is adequately stated, and try to answer what I ask you in the way you think best.

CRITO: I shall try.

SOCRATES: Do we say that one must never in any way do wrong willingly, or must one do wrong in one way and not in another? Is to do wrong never good or admirable, as we have agreed in the past, or have all these former agreements been washed out during the last few days? Have we at our age failed to notice for some time that in our serious discussions we were no different from children? Above all, is the truth such as we used to say it was, whether the majority agree or not, and whether we must still suffer worse things than we do now, or will be treated more gently, that, nonetheless, wrongdoing or injustice is in every way harmful and shameful to the wrongdoer? Do we say so or not?

CRITO: We do.

SOCRATES: So one must never do wrong.

CRITO: Certainly not.

SOCRATES: Nor must one, when wronged, inflict wrong in return, as the majority believe, since one must never do wrong.

CRITO: That seems to be the case.

SOCRATES: Come now, should one do harm to anyone or not, Crito?

CRITO: One must never do so.

SOCRATES: Well then, if one is oneself done harm, is it right, as the majority say, to do harm in return, or is it not?

CRITO: It is never right.

SOCRATES: Doing people harm is no different from wrongdoing.

CRITO: That is true.

SOCRATES: One should never do wrong in return, nor do any man harm, no matter what he may have done to you. And Crito, see that you do not agree to this, contrary to your belief. For I know that only a few people hold this view or will hold it, and there is no common ground between those who hold this view and those who do not, but they inevitably despise each other's views. So then consider very carefully whether we have this view in common, and whether you agree, and let this be the basis of our deliberation, that neither to do wrong nor to return a wrong is ever correct, nor is doing harm in return for harm done. Or do you disagree and do not share this view as a basis for discussion? I have held it for a long time and still hold it now, but if you think otherwise, tell me now. If, however, you stick to our former opinion, then listen to the next point.

CRITO: I stick to it and agree with you. So say on.

SOCRATES: Then I state the next point, or rather I ask you: when one has come to an agreement that is just with someone, should one fulfill it or cheat on it?

CRITO: One should fulfill it.

SOCRATES: See what follows from this: if we leave here without the city's permission, are we harming people whom we should least do harm to? And are we sticking to a just agreement, or not?

CRITO: I cannot answer your question, Socrates. I do not know.

SOCRATES: Look at it this way. If, as we were planning to run away from here, or whatever one should call it, the laws and the state came and confronted us and asked: "Tell me, Socrates, what are you intending to do? Do you not by this action you are attempting intend to destroy us, the laws, and indeed the whole city, as far as you are concerned? Or do you think it possible for a city not to be destroyed if the verdicts of its courts have no force but are nullified and set at naught by private individuals?" What shall we answer to this and other such arguments? For many things could be said, especially by an orator on behalf of this law we are destroying, which orders that the judgments of the courts shall be carried out. Shall we say in answer, "The city wronged me, and its decision was not right." Shall we say that, or what?

CRITO: Yes, by Zeus, Socrates, that is our answer.

SOCRATES: Then what if the laws said: "Was that the agreement between us, SOCRATES, or was it to respect the judgments that the city came to?" And if we wondered at their words, they would perhaps add: "Socrates, do not wonder at what we say but answer, since you are accustomed to proceed by question and answer. Come now, what accusation do you bring against us and the city, that you should try to destroy us? Did we not, first, bring you to birth, and was it not through us that your father married your mother and begat you? Tell us, do you find anything to criticize in those of us who are concerned with marriage?" And I would say that I do not criticize them. "Or in those of us concerned with the nurture of babies and the education that you too received? Were those assigned to that subject not right to instruct your father to educate you in the arts and in physical culture?" And I would say that they were right "Very well," they would continue, "and after you were born and nurtured and educated, could you, in the first place, deny that you are our offspring and servant, both you and your forefathers? If that is so, do you think that we are on an equal footing as regards the right, and that whatever we do to you it is right for you to do to us? You were not on an equal footing with your father as regards the right, nor with your master if you had one, so as to retaliate for anything they did to you, to revile them if they reviled you, to beat them if they beat you, and so with many other things. Do you think you have this right to retaliation against your country and its laws? That if we undertake to destroy you and think it right to do so, you can undertake to destroy us, as far as you can, in return? And will you say that you are right to do so, you who truly care for virtue? Is your wisdom such as not to realize that your country is to be honored more than your mother, your father, and all your ancestors, that it is more to be revered and more sacred, and that it counts for more among the gods and sensible men, that you must worship it, yield to it, and placate its anger more than your father's? You must either persuade it or obey its orders, and endure in silence whatever it instructs you to endure, whether blows or bonds, and if it leads you into war to be wounded or killed, you must obey. To do so is right, and one must not give way or retreat or leave one's post, but both in war and in courts and everywhere else, one must obey the commands of one's city and country, or persuade it as to the nature of justice. It is impious to bring violence to bear against your mother or father; it is much more so to use it against your country." What shall we say in reply, Crito, that the laws speak the truth, or not?

CRITO: I think they do.

SOCRATES: "Reflect now, Socrates," the laws might say, "that if what we say is true, you are not treating us rightly by planning to do what you are planning. We have given you birth, nurtured you, educated you; we have given you and all other citizens a share of all the good things we could. Even so, by giving every Athenian the opportunity, once arrived at voting age and having observed the affairs of the city and us the laws, we proclaim that if we do not please him, he can take his possessions and go wherever he pleases. Not one of our laws raises any obstacle or forbids him, if he is not satisfied with us or the city, if one of you wants to go and live in a colony or wants to go anywhere else, and keep his property. We say, however, that whoever of you remains, when he sees how we conduct our trials and manage the city in other ways, has in fact come to an agreement with us to obey our instructions. We say that the one who disobeys does wrong in three ways, first because in us he disobeys his parents, also those who brought him up, and because, in spite of his agreement, he neither obeys us nor, if we do something wrong, does he try to persuade us to do better. Yet we only propose things, we do not issue savage commands to do whatever we order; we give two alternatives, either to persuade us or to do what we say. He does neither. We do say that you too, Socrates, are open to those charges if you do what you have in mind; you would be among, not the least, but the most guilty of the Athenians." And if I should say "Why so?" they might well be right to upbraid me and say that I am among the Athenians who most definitely came to that agreement with them. They might well say: "Socrates, we have convincing proofs that we and the city were congenial to you. You would not have dwelt here most consistently of all the Athenians if the city had not been exceedingly pleasing to you. You have never left the city, even to see a festival, nor for any other reason except military service; you have never gone to stay in any other city, as people do; you have had no desire to know another city or other laws; we and our city satisfied you. "So decisively did you choose us and agree to be a citizen under us. Also, you have had children in this city, thus showing that it was congenial to you. Then at your trial you could have assessed your penalty at exile if you wished, and you are now attempting to do against the city's wishes what you could then have done with her consent.

Then you prided yourself that you did not resent death, but you chose, as you said, death in preference to exile. Now, however, those words do not make you ashamed, and you pay no heed to us, the laws, as you plan to destroy us, and you act like the meanest type of slave by trying to run away, contrary to your commitments and your agreement to live as a citizen under us. First then, answer us on this very point, whether we speak the truth when we say that you agreed, not only in words but by your deeds, to live in accordance with us." What are we to say to that, Crito? Must we not agree?

CRITO: We must, Socrates.

SOCRATES: "Surely," they might say, "you are breaking the commitments and agreements that you made with us without compulsion or deceit, and under no pressure of time for deliberation. You have had seventy years during which you could have gone away if you did not like us, and if you thought our agreements unjust. You did not choose to go to Sparta or to Crete, which you are always saying are well governed, nor to any other city, Greek or foreign. You have been away from Athens less than the lame or the blind or other handicapped people. It is clear that the city has been outstandingly more congenial to you than to other Athenians, and so have we, the laws, for what city can please without laws? Will you then not now stick to our agreements? You will, Socrates, if we can persuade you, and not make yourself a laughingstock by leaving the city.

"For consider what good you will do yourself or your friends by breaking our agreements and committing such a wrong. It is pretty obvious that your friends will themselves be in danger of exile, disfranchisement, and loss of property. As for yourself, if you go to one of the nearby cities—Thebes or Megara, both are well governed—you will arrive as an enemy to their government; all who care for their city will look on you with suspicion, as a destroyer of the laws. You will also strengthen the conviction of the jury that they passed the right sentence on you, for anyone who destroys the laws could easily be thought to corrupt the young and the ignorant. Or will you avoid cities that are well governed and men who are civilized? If you do this, will your life be worth living? Will you have social intercourse with them and not be ashamed to talk to them? And what will you say? The same as you did here, that virtue and justice are man's most precious possession, along with lawful behavior and the laws? Do you not think that Socrates would appear to be an unseemly kind of person? One must think so. Or will you leave those places and go to Crito's friends in Thessaly? There you will find the greatest license and disorder, and they may enjoy hearing from you how absurdly you escaped from prison in some disguise, in a leather jerkin or some other things in which escapees wrap themselves, thus altering your appearance. Will there be no one to say that you, likely to live but a short time more, were so greedy for life that you transgressed the most important laws? Possibly, Socrates, if you do not annoy anyone, but if you do, many disgraceful things will be said about you.

"You will spend your time ingratiating yourself with all men, and be at their beck and call. What will you do in Thessaly but feast, as if you had gone to a banquet in Thessaly? As for those conversations of yours about justice and the rest of virtue, where will they be? You say you want to live for the sake of your children, that you may bring them up and educate them. How so? Will you bring them up and educate them by taking them to Thessaly and making strangers of them, that they may enjoy that too? Or not so, but they will be better brought up and educated here, while you are alive, though absent? Yes, your friends will look after them. Will they look after them if you go and live in Thessaly, but not if you go away to the underworld? If those who profess themselves your friends are any good at all, one must assume that they will.

"Be persuaded by us who have brought you up, Socrates. Do not value either your children or your life or anything else more than goodness, in order that when you arrive in Hades you may have all this as your defense before the rulers there. If you do this deed, you will not think it better or more just or more pious here, nor will any one of your friends, nor will it be better for you when you arrive yonder. As it is, you depart, if you depart, after being wronged not by us, the laws, but by men; but if you depart after shamefully returning wrong for wrong and mistreatment for mistreatment, after breaking your agreements and commitments with us, after mistreating those you should mistreat least—yourself, your friends, your country, and us—we shall be angry with you while you are still alive, and our brothers, the laws of the underworld, will not receive you kindly, knowing that you tried to destroy us as far as you could. Do not let Crito persuade you, rather than us, to do what he says."

Crito, my dear friend, be assured that these are the words I seem to hear, as the Corybants seem to hear the music of their flutes, and the echo of these words resounds in me, and makes it impossible for me to hear anything else. As far as my present beliefs go, if you speak in opposition to them, you will speak in vain. However, if you think you can accomplish anything, speak.

CRITO: I have nothing to say, Socrates.

SOCRATES: Let it be then, Crito, and let us act in this way, since this is the way the god is leading us.

Note

1. A quotation from the ninth book of the *Iliad* (363). Achilles has rejected all the presents of Agamemnon for him to return to the battle and threatens to go home. He says his ships will sail in the morning, and with good weather he might arrive on the third day "in fertile Phthia" (which is his home). Socrates takes the dream to mean that he will die, and his soul will find its home, on the third day. As always, counting the first member of a series, the third day is the day after tomorrow.

from *History of the Peloponnesian War*

Thucydides
Translated by Rex Warner

Pericles' Funeral Oration

In the same winter the Athenians, following their annual custom, gave a public funeral for those who had been the first to die in the war. These funerals are held in the following way: two days before the ceremony the bones of the fallen are brought and put in a tent which has been erected, and people make whatever offerings they wish to their own dead. Then there is a funeral procession in which coffins of cypress wood are carried on wagons. There is one coffin for each tribe, which contains the bones of members of that tribe. One empty bier is decorated and carried in the procession: this is for the missing, whose bodies could not be recovered. Everyone who wishes to, both citizens and foreigners, can join in the procession, and the women who are related to the dead are there to make their laments at the tomb. The bones are laid in the public burial-place, which is in the most beautiful quarter outside the city walls. Here the Athenians always bury those who have fallen in war. The only exception is those who died at Marathon, who, because their achievement was considered absolutely outstanding, were buried on the battlefield itself.

When the bones have been laid in the earth, a man chosen by the city for his intellectual gifts and for his general reputation makes an appropriate speech in praise of the dead, and after the speech all depart. This is the procedure at these burials, and all through the war, when the time came to do so, the Athenians followed this ancient custom. Now, at the burial of those who were the first to fall in the war Pericles, the son of Xanthippus, was chosen to make the speech. When the moment arrived, he came forward from the tomb and, standing on a high platform, so that he might be heard by as many people as possible in the crowd, he spoke as follows:

"Many of those who have spoken here in the past have praised the institution of this speech at the close of our ceremony. It seemed to them a mark of honour to our soldiers who have fallen in war that a speech should be made over them. I do not agree. These men have shown themselves valiant in action, and it would be enough, I think, for their glories to be proclaimed in action, as you have just seen it done at this funeral organized by the state. Our belief in the courage and manliness of so many should not be hazarded on the goodness or badness of one man's speech. Then it is not easy to speak with a proper sense of balance, when a man's listeners find it difficult to believe in the truth of what one is saying. The man who knows the facts and loves the dead may well think that an oration tells less than what he knows and what he would like to hear: others who do not know so much may feel envy for the dead, and think the orator over-praises them, when he speaks of exploits that are beyond their own capacities. Praise of other people is tolerable only up to a certain point, the point where one still believes that one could do oneself some of the things one is hearing about. Once you get beyond this point, you will find people becoming jealous and incredulous. However, the fact is that this institution was set up and approved by our forefathers, and it is my duty to follow the tradition and do my best to meet the wishes and the expectations of every one of you.

'I shall begin by speaking about our ancestors, since it is only right and proper on such an occasion to pay them the honour of recalling what they did. In this land of ours there have always been the same people living from generation to generation up till now, and they, by their courage and their virtues, have handed it on to us, a free country. They certainly deserve our praise. Even more so do our fathers deserve it. For to the inheritance they had received they added all the empire we have now, and it was not without blood and toil that they handed it down to us of the present generation. And then we ourselves, assembled here today, who are mostly in the prime of life, have, in most directions, added to the power of our empire and have organized our State in such a way that it is perfectly well able to look after itself both in peace and in war.

'I have no wish to make a long speech on subjects familiar to you all: so I shall say nothing about the warlike deeds by which we acquired our power or the battles in which we or our fathers gallantly resisted our enemies, Greek or foreign. What I want to do is, in the first place, to discuss the spirit in which we faced our trials and also our constitution and the way of life which has made us great. After that I shall speak in praise of the dead, believing that this kind of speech is not inappropriate to the present occasion, and that this whole assembly, of citizens and foreigners, may listen to it with advantage.

'Let me say that our system of government does not copy the institutions of our neighbours. It is more the case of our being a model to others, than of our imitating anyone else. Our constitution is called a democracy because power is in the hands not of a minority but of the whole people. When it is a question of settling private disputes, everyone is equal before the law; when it is a question of putting one person before another in positions of public responsibility, what counts is not membership of a particular class, but the actual ability which the man possesses. No one, so long as he has it in him to be of service to the state, is kept in political obscurity because of poverty. And, just as our political life is free and open, so is our day-to-day life in our relations with each other. We do not get into a state with our next-door neighbour if he enjoys himself in his own way, nor do we give him the kind of black looks which, though they do no real harm, still do hurt people's feelings. We are free and tolerant in our private lives; but in public affairs we keep to the law. This is because it commands our deep respect.

'We give our obedience to those whom we put in positions of authority, and we obey the laws themselves, especially those which are for the protection of the oppressed, and those unwritten laws which it is an acknowledged shame to break.

'And here is another point. When our work is over, we are in a position to enjoy all kinds of recreation for our spirits. There are various kinds of contests and sacrifices regularly throughout the year; in our own homes we find a beauty and a good taste which delight us every day and which drive away our cares. Then the greatness of our city brings it about that all the good things from all over the world flow in to us, so that to us it seems just as natural to enjoy foreign goods as our own local products.

'Then there is a great difference between us and our opponents, in our attitude towards military security. Here are some examples: Our city is open to the world, and we have no periodical deportations in order to prevent people observing or finding out secrets which might be of military advantage to the enemy. This is because we rely, not on secret weapons, but on our own real courage and loyalty. There is a difference, too, in our educational systems. The Spartans, from their earliest boyhood, are submitted to the most laborious training in courage; we pass our lives without all these restrictions, and yet are just as ready to face the same dangers as they are. Here is a proof of this: When the Spartans invade our land, they do not come by themselves, but bring all their allies with them; whereas we, when we launch an attack abroad, do the job by ourselves, and, though fighting on foreign soil, do not often fail to defeat opponents who are fighting for their own hearths and homes. As a matter of fact none of our enemies has ever yet been confronted with our total strength, because we have to divide our attention between our navy and the many missions on which our troops are sent on land. Yet, if our enemies engage a detachment of our forces and defeat it, they give themselves credit for having thrown back our entire army; or, if they lose, they claim that they were beaten by us in full strength. There are certain advantages, I think, in our way of meeting danger voluntarily, with an easy mind, instead of with a laborious training, with natural rather than with state-induced courage. We do not have to spend our time practising to meet sufferings which are still in the future; and when they are actually upon us we show ourselves just as brave as these others who are always in strict training. This is one point in which, I think, our city deserves to be admired. There are also others:

'Our love of what is beautiful does not lead to extravagance; our love of the things of the mind does not make us soft. We regard wealth as something to be properly used, rather than as something to boast about. As for poverty, no one need be ashamed to admit it: the real shame is in not taking practical measures to escape from it. Here each individual is interested not only in his own affairs but in the affairs of the state as well: even those who are mostly occupied with their own business are extremely well-informed on general politics—this is a peculiarity of ours: we do not say that a man who takes no interest in politics is a man who minds his own business; we say that he has no business here at all. We Athenians, in our own persons, take our decisions on policy or submit them to proper discussions: for we do not think that there is an incompatibility between words and deeds; the worst thing is to rush into action before the consequences have been properly debated. And this is another point where we differ from other people. We are capable at the same time of taking risks and of estimating them beforehand. Others are brave out of ignorance; and, when they stop to think, they begin to fear. But the man who can most truly be accounted brave is he who best knows the meaning of what is sweet in life and of what is terrible, and then goes out undeterred to meet what is to come.

'Again, in questions of general good feeling there is a great contrast between us and most other people. We make friends by doing good to others, not by receiving good from them. This makes our friendship all the more reliable, since we want to keep alive the gratitude of those who are in our debt by showing continued goodwill to them: whereas the feelings of one who owes us something lack the same enthusiasm, since he knows that, when he repays our kindness, it will be more like paying back a debt than giving something spontaneously. We are unique in this. When we do kindnesses to others, we do not do them out of any calculations of profit or loss: we do them without afterthought, relying on our free liberality. Taking everything together then, I declare that our city is an education to Greece, and I declare that in my opinion each single one of our citizens, in all the manifold aspects of life, is able to show himself the rightful lord and owner of his own person, and do this, moreover, with exceptional grace and exceptional versatility. And to show that this is no empty boasting for the present occasion, but real tangible fact, you have only to consider the power which our city possesses and which has been won by those very qualities which I have mentioned. Athens, alone of the states we know, comes to her testing time in a greatness that surpasses what was imagined of her. In her case, and in her case alone, no invading enemy is ashamed at being defeated, and no subject can complain of being governed by people unfit for their responsibilities. Mighty indeed are the marks and monuments of our empire which we have left. Future ages will wonder at us, as the present age wonders at us now. We do not need the praises of a Homer, or of anyone else whose words may delight us for the moment, but whose estimation of facts will fall short of what is really true. For our adventurous spirit has forced an entry into every sea and into every land; and everywhere we have left behind us everlasting memorials of good done to our friends or suffering inflicted on our enemies.

'This, then, is the kind of city for which these men, who could not bear the thought of losing her, nobly fought and nobly died. It is only natural that every one of us who survive them should be willing to undergo hardships in her service. And it was for this reason that I have spoken at such length about our city, because I wanted to make it clear that for us there is more at stake than there is for others who lack our advantages; also I wanted my words of praise for the dead to be set in the bright light of evidence. And now the most important of these words has been spoken. I have sung the praises of our city; but it was the courage and gallantry of these men, and of people like them, which made her splendid. Nor would you find it true in the case of many of the Greeks, as it is true of them, that no words can do more than justice to their deeds.

'To me it seems that the consummation which has overtaken these men shows us the meaning of manliness in its first revelation and in its final proof. Some of them, no doubt, had their faults; but what we ought to remember first is their gallant conduct against the enemy in defence of their native land. They have blotted out evil with good, and done more service to the commonwealth than they ever did harm in their private lives. No one of these men weakened because he wanted to go on enjoying his wealth: no one put off the awful day in the hope that he might live to escape his poverty and grow rich. More to be desired than such things, they chose to check the enemy's pride. This, to them, was a risk most glorious, and they accepted it, willing to strike down the enemy and relinquish everything else. As for success or failure, they left that in the doubtful hands of Hope, and when the reality of battle was before their faces, they put their trust in their own selves. In the fighting, they thought it more honourable to stand their ground and suffer death than to give in and save their lives. So they fled from the reproaches of men, abiding with life and limb the brunt of battle; and, in a small moment of time, the climax of their lives, a culmination of glory, not of fear, were swept away from us.

'So and such they were, these men—worthy of their city. We who remain behind may hope to be spared their fate, but must resolve to keep the same daring spirit against the foe. It is not simply a question of estimating the advantages in theory. I could tell you a long story (and you know it as well as I do) about what is to be gained by beating the enemy back. What I would prefer is that you should fix your eyes every day on the greatness of Athens as she really is, and should fall in love with her. When you realize her greatness, then reflect that what made her great was men with a spirit of adventure, men who knew their duty, men who were ashamed to fall below a certain standard. If they ever failed in an enterprise, they made up their minds that at any rate the city should not find their courage lacking to her, and they gave to her the best contribution that they could. They gave her their lives, to her and to all of us, and for their own selves they won praises that never grow old, the most splendid of sepulchres—not the sepulchre in which their bodies are laid, but where their glory remains eternal in men's minds, always there on the right occasion to stir others to speech or to action. For famous men have the whole earth as their memorial: it is not only the inscriptions on their graves in their own country that mark them out; no, in foreign lands also, not in any visible form but in people's hearts, their memory abides and grows. It is for you to try to be like them. Make up your minds that happiness depends on being free, and freedom depends on being courageous. Let there be no relaxation in face of the perils of the war. The people who have most excuse for despising death are not the wretched and unfortunate, who have no hope of doing well for themselves, but those who run the risk of a complete reversal in their lives, and who would feel the difference most intensely, if things went wrong for them. Any intelligent man would find a humiliation caused by his own slackness more painful to bear than death, when death comes to him unperceived, in battle, and in the confidence of his patriotism.

'For these reasons I shall not commiserate with those parents of the dead, who are present here. Instead I shall try to comfort them. They are well aware that they have grown up in a world where there are many changes and chances. But this is good fortune—for men to end their lives with honour, as these have done, and for you honourably to lament them: their life was set to a measure where death and happiness went hand in hand. I know that it is difficult to convince you of this. When you see other people happy you will often be reminded of what used to make you happy too. One does not feel sad at not having some good thing which is outside one's experience: real grief is felt at the loss of something which one is used to. All the same, those of you who are of the right age must bear up and take comfort in the thought of having more children. In your own homes these new children will prevent you from brooding over those who are no more, and they will be a help to the city, too, both in filling the empty places, and in assuring her security. For it is impossible for a man to put forward fair and honest views about our affairs if he has not, like everyone else, children whose lives may be at stake. As for those of you who are now too old to have children, I would ask you to count as gain the greater part of your life, in which you have been happy, and remember that what remains is not long, and let your hearts be lifted up at the thought of the fair fame of the dead. One's sense of honour is the only thing that does not grow old, and the last pleasure, when one is worn out with age, is not, as the poet said, making money, but having the respect of one's fellow men.

'As for those of you here who are sons or brothers of the dead, I can see a hard struggle in front of you. Everyone always speaks well of the dead, and, even if you rise to the greatest heights of heroism, it will be a hard thing for you to get the reputation of having come near, let alone equalled, their standard. When one is alive, one is always liable to the jealousy of one's competitors, but when one is out of the way, the honour one receives is sincere and unchallenged.

'Perhaps I should say a word or two on the duties of women to those among you who are now widowed. I can say all I have to say in a short word of advice. Your great glory is not to be inferior to what God has made you, and the greatest glory of a woman is to be least talked about by men, whether they are praising you or criticizing you. I have now, as the law demanded, said what I had to say. For the time being our offerings to the dead have been made, and for the future their children will be supported at the public expense by the city, until they come of age. This is the crown and prize which she offers, both to the dead and to their children, for the ordeals which they have faced. Where the rewards of valour are the greatest, there you will find also the best and bravest spirits among the people. And now, when you have mourned for your dear ones, you must depart.'

from *History of the Peloponnesian War*

Thucydides

In 427 B.C., having put down a revolt by the city state of Mytilene, the Athenian assembly decided initially to execute all Mytilenian citizens. The next day, the assembly reconsiders.

The Mytilenian Debate

When Salaethus and the other prisoners reached Athens, the Athenians immediately put Salaethus to death in spite of the fact that he undertook, among other things, to have the Peloponnesians withdrawn from Plataea, which was still being besieged. They then discussed what was to be done with the other prisoners and, in their angry mood, decided to put to death not only those now in their hands but also the entire adult male population of Mytilene, and to make slaves of the women and children. What they held against Mytilene was the fact that it had revolted even though it was not a subject state, like the others, and the bitterness of their feelings was considerably increased by the fact that the Peloponnesian feet had actually dared to cross over to lonia to support the revolt. This, it was thought, could never have happened unless the revolt had been long premeditated. So they sent a trireme to Paches to inform him of what had been decided, with orders to put the Mytilenians to death immediately.

Next day, however, there was a sudden change of feeling and people began to think how cruel and how unprecedented such a decision was—to destroy not only the guilty, but the entire population of a state. Observing this, the deputation from Mytilene which was in Athens and the Athenians who were supporting them approached the authorities with a view to having the question debated again. They won their point the more easily because the authorities themselves saw clearly that most of the citizens were wanting someone to give them a chance of reconsidering the matter. So an assembly was called at once. Various opinions were expressed on both sides, and Cleon, the son of Cleaenetus, spoke again. It was he who had been responsible for passing the original motion for putting the Mytilenians to death. He was remarkable among the Athenians for the violence of his character, and at this time he exercised far the greatest influence over the people.[1] He spoke as follows:

'Personally I have had occasion often enough already to observe that a democracy is incapable of governing others, and I am all the more convinced of this when I see how you are now changing your minds about the Mytilenians. Because fear and conspiracy play no part in your daily relations with each other, you imagine that the same thing is true of your allies, and you fail to see that when you allow them to persuade you to make a mistaken decision and when you give way to your own feelings of compassion you are being guilty of a kind of weakness which is dangerous to you and which will not make them love you any more. What you do not realize is that your empire is a tyranny exercised over subjects who do not like it and who are always plotting against you; you will not make them obey you by injuring your own interests in order to do them a favour; your leadership depends on superior strength and not on any goodwill of theirs. And this is the very worst thing—to pass measures and then not to abide by them. We should realize that a city is better off with bad laws, so long as they remain fixed, than with good laws that are constantly being altered, that lack of learning combined with sound common sense is more helpful than the kind of cleverness that gets out of hand, and that as a general rule states are better governed by the man in the street than by intellectuals. These are the sort of people who want to appear wiser than the laws, who want to get their own way in every general discussion, because they feel that they cannot show off their intelligence in matters of greater importance, and who, as a result, very often bring ruin on their country. But the other kind—the people who are not so confident in their own intelligence—are prepared to admit that the laws are wiser than they are and that they lack the ability to pull to pieces a speech made by a good speaker; they are unbiased judges, and not people taking part in some kind of a competition; so things usually go well when they are in control. We statesmen, too, should try to be like them, instead of being carried away by mere cleverness and a desire to show off our intelligence and so giving you, the people, advice which we do not really believe in ourselves.

'As for me, I have not altered my opinion, and I am amazed at those who have proposed a reconsideration of the question of Mytilene, thus causing a delay which is all to the advantage of the guilty party. After a lapse of time the injured party will lose the edge of his anger when he comes to act against those who have wronged him; whereas the best punishment and the one most fitted to the crime is when reprisals follow immediately. I shall be amazed, too, if anyone contradicts me and attempts to prove that the harm done to us by

Mytilene is really a good thing for us, or that when we suffer ourselves we are somehow doing harm to our allies. It is obvious that anyone who is going to say this must either have such confidence in his powers as an orator that he will struggle to persuade you that what has been finally settled was, on the contrary, not decided at all, or else he must have been bribed to put together some elaborate speech with which he will try to lead you out of the right track. But in competitions of this sort the prizes go to others and the state takes all the danger for herself. The blame is yours, for stupidly instituting these competitive displays. You have become regular speech-goers, and as for action, you merely listen to accounts of it; if something is to be done in the future you estimate the possibilities by hearing a good speech on the subject, and as for the past you rely not so much on the facts which you have seen with your own eyes as on what you have heard about them in some clever piece of verbal criticism. Any novelty in an argument deceives you at once, but when the argument is tried and proved you become unwilling to follow it; you look with suspicion on what is normal and are the slaves of every paradox that comes your way. The chief wish of each one of you is to be able to make a speech himself, and, if you cannot do that, the next best thing is to compete with those who can make this sort of speech by not looking as though you were at all out of your depth while you listen to the views put forward, by applauding a good point even before it is made, and by being as quick at seeing how an argument is going to be developed as you are slow at understanding what in the end it will lead to. What you are looking for all the time is something that is, I should say, outside the range of ordinary experience, and yet you cannot even think straight about the facts of life that are before you. You are simply victims of your own pleasure in listening, and are more like an audience sitting at the feet of a professional lecturer than a parliament discussing matters of state.

'I am trying to stop you behaving like this, and I say that no single city has ever done you the harm that Mytilene has done. Personally I can make allowances for those who revolt because they find your rule intolerable or because they have been forced into it by enemy action. Here, however, we have the case of people living on an island, behind their own fortifications, with nothing to fear from our enemies except an attack by sea against which they were adequately protected by their own force of triremes; they had their own independent government and they were treated by us with the greatest consideration. Now, to act as they acted is not what I should call a revolt (for people only revolt when they have been badly treated); it is a case of calculated aggression, of deliberately taking sides with our bitterest enemies in order to destroy us. And this is far worse than if they had made war against us simply to increase their own power. They learned nothing from the fate of those of their neighbours who had already revolted and been subdued; the prosperity which they enjoyed did not make them hesitate before running into danger; confident in the future, they declared war on us, with hopes that indeed extended beyond their means, though still fell short of their desires. They made up their minds to put might first and right second, choosing the moment when they thought they would win, and then making their unprovoked attack upon us.

'The fact is that when great prosperity comes suddenly and unexpectedly to a state, it usually breeds arrogance; in most cases it is safer for people to enjoy an average amount of success rather than something which is out of all proportion; and it is easier, I should say, to ward off hardship than to maintain happiness. What we should have done long ago with the Mytilenians was to treat them in exactly the same way as all the rest; then they would never have grown so arrogant; for it is a general rule of human nature that people despise those who treat them well and look up to those who make no concessions. Let them now therefore have the punishment which their crime deserves. Do not put the blame on the aristocracy and say that the people were innocent. The fact is that the whole lot of them attacked you together, although the people might have come over to us and, if they had, would now be back again in control of their city. Yet, instead of doing this, they thought it safer to share the dangers, and join in the revolt of the aristocracy.

'Now think of your allies. If you are going to give the same punishment to those who are forced to revolt by your enemies and those who do so of their own accord, can you not see that they will all revolt upon the slightest pretext, when success means freedom and failure brings no very dreadful consequences? Meanwhile we shall have to spend our money and risk our lives against state after state; if our efforts are successful, we shall recover a city that is in ruins, and so lose the future revenue from it, on which our strength is based; and if we fail to subdue it, we shall have more enemies to deal with in addition to those we have already, and we shall spend the time which ought to be used in resisting our present foes in making war on our own allies.

'Let there be no hope, therefore, held out to the Mytilenians that we, either as a result of a good speech or a large bribe, are likely to forgive them on the grounds that it is only human to make mistakes. There was nothing involuntary about the harm they did us; they knew what they were about and they planned it all beforehand; and one only forgives actions that were not deliberate. As for me, just as I was at first, so I am now, and I shall continue to impress on you the importance of not altering your previous decisions. To feel pity, to be carried away by the pleasure of hearing a clever argument, to listen to the claims of decency are three things that are entirely against the interests of an imperial power. Do not be guilty of them. As for compassion, it is proper to feel it in the case of people who are like ourselves and who will pity us in their turn, not in the case of those who, so far from having the same feelings towards us, must always and inevitably be our enemies. As for the speech-makers who give such pleasure by their arguments, they should hold their competitions on subjects which are less important, and not on a question where the state may have to pay a heavy penalty for its light pleasure, while the speakers themselves will no doubt be enjoying splendid rewards for their splendid arguments. And a sense of decency is only felt towards those who are going to be our friends in future, not towards those who remain just as they were and as much our enemies as they ever have been.

'Let me sum the whole thing up. I say that, if you follow my advice, you will be doing the right thing as far as Mytilene is concerned and at the same time will be acting in your own interests; if you decide differently, you will not win them over, but you will be passing judgement on yourselves. For if they were justified in revolting, you must be wrong in holding power. If, however, whatever the rights or wrongs of it may be, you propose to hold power all the same, then your interest demands that these too, rightly or wrongly, must be punished. The only alternative is to surrender your empire, so that you can afford to go in for philanthropy. Make up your minds, therefore, to pay them back in their own coin, and do not make it look as though you who escaped their machinations are less quick to react than they who started them. Remember how they would have been likely to have treated you, if they had won, especially as they were the aggressors. Those who do wrong to a neighbour when there is no reason to do so are the ones who persevere to the point of destroying him, since they see the danger involved in allowing their enemy to survive. For he who has suffered for no good reason is a more dangerous enemy, if he escapes, than the one who has both done and suffered injury.

'I urge you, therefore, not to be traitors to your own selves. Place yourselves in imagination at the moment when you first suffered and remember how then you would have given anything to have them in your power. Now pay them back for it, and do not grow soft just at this present moment, forgetting meanwhile the danger that hung over your heads then. Punish them as they deserve, and make an example of them to your other allies, plainly showing that revolt will be punished by death. Once they realize this, you will not have so often to neglect the war with your enemies because you are fighting with your own allies.'

So Cleon spoke. After him Diodotus, the son of Eucrates, who in the previous assembly also had vigorously opposed the motion to put the Mytilenians to death, came forward again on this occasion and spoke as follows:

'I do not blame those who have proposed a new debate on the subject of Mytilene, and I do not share the view which we have heard expressed, that it is a bad thing to have frequent discussions on matters of importance. Haste and anger are, to my mind, the two greatest obstacles to wise counsel—haste, that usually goes with folly, anger, that is the mark of primitive and narrow minds. And anyone who maintains that words cannot be a guide to action must be either a fool or one with some personal interest at stake; he is a fool, if he imagines that it is possible to deal with the uncertainties of the future by any other medium, and he is personally interested if his aim is to persuade you into some disgraceful action, and, knowing that he cannot make a good speech in a bad cause, he tries to frighten his opponents and his hearers by some good-sized pieces of misrepresentation. Then still more intolerable are those who go further and accuse a speaker of making a kind of exhibition of himself, because he is paid for it. If it was only ignorance with which he was being charged, a speaker who failed to win his case could retire from the debate and still be thought an honest man, if not a very intelligent one. But when corruption is imputed, he will be suspect if he wins his case, and if he loses it, will be regarded as dishonest and stupid at the same time. This sort of thing does the city no good; her counsellors will be afraid to speak and she will be deprived of their services. Though certainly it would be the best possible thing for the city if these gentlemen whom I have been describing lacked the power to express themselves; we should not then be persuaded into making so many mistakes.

'The good citizen, instead of trying to terrify the opposition, ought to prove his case in fair argument; and a wise state, without giving special honours to its best counsellors, will certainly not deprive them of the honour they already enjoy; and when a man's advice is not taken, he should not even be disgraced, far less penalized. In this way successful speakers will be less likely to pursue further honours by speaking against their own convictions in order to make themselves popular, and unsuccessful speakers, too, will not struggle to win over the people by the same acts of flattery. What we do here, however, is exactly the opposite. Then, too, if a man gives the best possible advice but is under the slightest suspicion of being influenced by his own private profit, we are so embittered by the idea (a wholly unproved one) of this profit of his, that we do not allow the state to receive the certain benefit of his good advice. So a state of affairs has been reached where a good proposal honestly put forward is just as suspect as something thoroughly bad, and the result is that just as the speaker who advocates some monstrous measure has to win over the people by deceiving them, so also a man with good advice to give has to tell lies if he expects to be believed. And because of this refinement in intellectuality, the state is put into a unique position; it is only she to whom no one can ever do a good turn openly and without deception. For if one openly performs a patriotic action, the reward for one's pains is to be thought to have made something oneself on the side. Yet in spite of all this we are discussing matters of the greatest importance, and we who give you our advice ought to be resolved to look rather further into things than you whose attention is occupied only with the surface—especially as we can be held to account for the advice we give, while you are not accountable for the way in which you receive it. For indeed you would take rather more care over your decisions, if the proposer of a motion and those who voted for it were all subject to the same penalties. As it is, on the occasions when some emotional impulse on your part has led you into disaster, you turn upon the one man who made the original proposal and you let yourself off, in spite of the fact that you are many and in spite of the fact that you were just as wrong as he was.

'However, I have not come forward to speak about Mytilene in any spirit of contradiction or with any wish to accuse anyone. If we are sensible people, we shall see that the question is not so much whether they are guilty as whether we are making the right decision for ourselves. I might prove that they are the most guilty people in the world, but it does not follow that I shall propose the death penalty, unless that is in your interests; I might argue that they deserve to be forgiven, but should not recommend forgiveness unless that seemed to me the best thing for the state.

'In my view our discussion concerns the future rather than the present. One of Cleon's chief points is that to inflict the death penalty will be useful to us in the future as a means for deterring other cities from revolt; but I, who am just as concerned as he is with the future, am quite convinced that this is not so. And I ask you not to reject what is useful in my speech for the sake of what is specious in his. You may well find his speech attractive, because it fits in better with your present angry feelings about the Mytilenians; but this is not a law-court, where we have to consider what is fit and just; it is a political assembly, and the question is how Mytilene can be most useful to Athens.

'Now, in human societies the death penalty has been laid down for many offences less serious than this one. Yet people still take risks when they feel sufficiently confident. No one has ever yet risked committing a crime which he thought he could not carry out successfully. The same is true of states. None has ever yet rebelled in the belief that it had insufficient resources, either in itself or from its allies, to make the attempt. Cities and individuals alike, all are by nature disposed to do wrong, and there is no law that will prevent it, as is shown by the fact that men have tried every kind of punishment, constantly adding to the list, in the attempt to find greater security from criminals. It is likely that in early times the punishments even for the greatest crimes were not as severe as they are now, but the laws were still broken, and in the course of time the death penalty became generally introduced. Yet even with this, the laws are still broken. Either, therefore, we must discover some fear more potent than the fear of death, or we must admit that here certainly we have not got an adequate deterrent. So long as poverty forces men to be bold, so long as the insolence and pride of wealth nourish their ambitions, and in the other accidents of life they are continually dominated by some incurable master passion or another, so long will their impulses continue to drive them into danger. Hope and desire persist throughout and cause the greatest calamities—one leading and the other following, one conceiving the enterprise, and the other suggesting that it will be successful—invisible factors, but more powerful than the terrors that are obvious to our eyes. Then too, the idea that fortune will be on one's side plays as big a part as anything else in creating a mood of over-confidence; for sometimes she does come unexpectedly to one's aid, and so she tempts men to run risks for which they are inadequately prepared. And this is particularly true in the case of whole peoples, because they are playing for the highest stakes—either for their own freedom or for the power to control others—and each individual, when acting as part of a community, has the irrational opinion that his own powers are greater than in fact they are. In a word it is impossible (and only the most simple-minded will deny this) for human nature, when once seriously set upon a certain course, to be prevented from following that course by the force of law or by any other means of intimidation whatever.

'We must not, therefore, come to the wrong conclusions through having too much confidence in the effectiveness of capital punishment, and we must not make the condition of rebels desperate by depriving them of the possibility of repentance and of a chance of atoning as quickly as they can for what they did. Consider this now: at the moment, if a city has revolted and realizes that the revolt cannot succeed, it will come to terms while it is still capable of paying an indemnity and continuing to pay tribute afterwards. But if Cleon's method is adopted, can you not see that every city will not only make much more careful preparations for revolt, but will also hold out against siege to the very end, since to surrender early or late means just the same thing? This is, unquestionably, against our interests—to spend money on a siege because of the impossibility of coming to terms, and, if we capture the place, to take over a city that is in ruins so that we lose the future revenue from it. And it is just on this revenue that our strength in war depends.

'Our business, therefore, is not to injure ourselves by acting like a judge who strictly examines a criminal; instead we should be looking for a method by which, employing moderation in our punishments, we can in future secure for ourselves the full use of those cities which bring us important contributions. And we should recognize that the proper basis of our security is in good administration rather than in the fear of legal penalties. As it is, we do just the opposite: when we subdue a free city, which was held down by force and has, as we might have expected, tried to assert its independence by revolting, we think that we ought to punish it with the utmost severity. But the right way to deal with free people is this—not to inflict tremendous punishments on them after they have revolted, but to take tremendous care of them before this point is reached, to prevent them even contemplating the idea of revolt, and, if we do have to use force with them, to hold as few as possible of them responsible for this.

'Consider what a mistake you would be making on this very point, if you took Cleon's advice. As things are now, in all the cities the democracy is friendly to you; either it does not join in with the oligarchies in revolting, or, if it is forced to do so, it remains all the time hostile to the rebels, so that when you go to war with them, you have the people on your side. But if you destroy the democratic party at Mytilene, who never took any hand in the revolt and who, as soon as they got arms, voluntarily gave the city up to you, you will first of all be guilty of killing those who have helped you, and, secondly, you will be doing exactly what the reactionary classes want most. For now, when they start a revolt, they will have the people on their side from the beginning, because you have already made it clear that the same punishment is laid down both for the guilty and the innocent. In fact, however, even if they were guilty, you should pretend that they were not, in order to keep on your side the one element that is still not opposed to you. It is far more useful to us, I think, in preserving our empire, that we should voluntarily put up with injustice than that we should justly put to death the wrong people. As for Cleon's point—that in this act of vengeance both justice and self-interest are combined—this is not a case where such a combination is at all possible.

'I call upon you, therefore, to accept my proposal as the better one. Do not be swayed too much by pity or by ordinary decent feelings. I, no more than Cleon, wish you to be influenced by such emotions. It is simply on the basis of the argument which you have heard that I ask you to be guided by me, to try at your leisure the men whom Paches has considered guilty and sent to

Athens, and to allow the rest to live in their own city. In following this course you will be acting wisely for the future and will be doing something which will make your enemies fear you now. For those who make wise decisions are more formidable to their enemies than those who rush madly into strong action.'

This was the speech of Diodotus. And now, when these two motions, each so opposed to each, had been put forward, the Athenians, in spite of the recent change of feeling, still held conflicting opinions, and at the show of hands the votes were nearly equal. However, the motion of Diodotus was passed.

Immediately another trireme was sent out in all haste, since they feared that, unless it overtook the first trireme, they would find on their arrival that the city had been destroyed. The first trireme had a start of about twenty-four hours. The ambassadors from Mytilene provided wine and barley for the crew and promised great rewards if they arrived in time, and so the men made such speed on the voyage that they kept on rowing while they took their food (which was barley mixed with oil and wine) and rowed continually, taking it in turn to sleep. Luckily they had no wind against them, and as the first ship was not hurrying on its distasteful mission, while they were pressing on with such speed, what happened was that the first ship arrived so little ahead of them that Paches had just had time to read the decree and to prepare to put it into force, when the second ship put in to the harbour and prevented the massacre. So narrow had been the escape of Mytilene.

The other Mytilenians whom Paches had sent to Athens as being the ones chiefly responsible for the revolt were, on the motion of Cleon, put to death by the Athenians. There were rather more than 1,000 of them. The Athenians also destroyed the fortifications of Mytilene and took over their navy. Afterwards, instead of imposing a tribute on Lesbos, they divided all the land, except that belonging to the Methymnians, into 3,000 holdings, 300 of which were set apart as sacred for the gods, while the remainder was distributed by lot to Athenian shareholders, who were sent out to Lesbos. The Lesbians agreed with these shareholders to pay a yearly rent of two minae for each holding, and cultivated the land themselves. The Athenians also took over all the towns on the mainland that had been under the control of Mytilene. So for the future the Mytilenians became subjects of Athens. This completes the account of what took place in Lesbos.

Note

[1] This wording is echoed by Thucydides in VI, 35 when he introduces the Syracusan 'demagogue' Athenagoras.

from *History of the Peloponnesian War*

Thucydides

In 416 B.C., Athenian attempts at coercing Melos to join its alliance failed, so Athens sent an expedition to subjugate the island state. The expedition's generals argue with the Melian government that Melos should surrender rather than resist militarily.

The Melian Dialogue

Next summer Alcibiades sailed to Argos with twenty ships and seized 300 Argive citizens who were still suspected of being pro-Spartan. These were put by the Athenians into the nearby islands under Athenian control.

The Athenians also made an expedition against the island of Melos. They had thirty of their own ships, six from Chios, and two from Lesbos; 1,200 hoplites, 300 archers, and twenty mounted archers, all from Athens; and about 1,500 hoplites from the allies and the islanders.

The Melians are a colony from Sparta. They had refused to join the Athenian empire like the other islanders, and at first had remained neutral without helping either side; but afterwards, when the Athenians had brought force to bear on them by laying waste their land, they had become open enemies of Athens.

Now the generals Cleomedes, the son of Lycomedes, and Tisias, the son of Tisimachus, encamped with the above force in Melian territory and, before doing any harm to the land, first of all sent representatives to negotiate. The Melians did not invite these representatives to speak before the people, but asked them to make the statement for which they had come in front of the governing body and the few. The Athenian representatives then spoke as follows:

'So we are not to speak before the people, no doubt in case the mass of the people should hear once and for all and without interruption an argument from us which is both persuasive and incontrovertible, and should so be led astray. This, we realize, is your motive in bringing us here to speak before the few. Now suppose that you who sit here should make assurance doubly sure. Suppose that you, too, should refrain from dealing with every point in detail in a set speech, and should instead interrupt us whenever we say something controversial and deal with that before going on to the next point? Tell us first whether you approve of this suggestion of ours.'

The Council of the Melians replied as follows:

'No one can object to each of us putting forward our own views in a calm atmosphere. That is perfectly reasonable. What is scarcely consistent with such a proposal is the present threat, indeed the certainty, of your making war on us. We see that you have come prepared to judge the argument yourselves, and that the likely end of it all will be either war, if we prove that we are in the right, and so refuse to surrender, or else slavery.'

Athenians: If you are going to spend the time in enumerating your suspicions about the future, or if you have met here for any other reason except to look the facts in the face and on the basis of these facts to consider how you can save your city from destruction, there is no point in our going on with this discussion. If, however, you will do as we suggest, then we will speak on.

Melians: It is natural and understandable that people who are placed as we are should have recourse to all kinds of arguments and different points of view. However, you are right in saying that we are met together here to discuss the safety of our country and, if you will have it so, the discussion shall proceed on the lines that you have laid down.

Athenians: Then we on our side will use no fine phrases saying, for example, that we have a right to our empire because we defeated the Persians, or that we have come against you now because of the injuries you have done us—a great mass of words that nobody would believe. And we ask you on your side not to imagine that you will influence us by saying that you, though a colony of Sparta, have not joined Sparta in the war, or that you have never done us any harm. Instead we recommend that you should try to get what it is possible for you to get, taking into consideration what we both really do think; since you know as well as we do that, when these matters are discussed by practical people, the standard of justice depends on the equality of power to compel and that in fact the strong do what they have the power to do and the weak accept what they have to accept.

Melians: Then in our view (since you force us to leave justice out of account and to confine ourselves to self-interest)—in our view it is at any rate useful that you should not destroy a principle that is to the general good of all men—namely, that in the case of all who fall into danger there should be such a thing as fair play and just dealing, and that such people should be allowed to use and to profit by arguments that fall short of a mathematical accuracy. And this is a principle which affects you as much as anybody, since your own fall would be visited by the most terrible vengeance and would be an example to the world.

Athenians: As for us, even assuming that our empire does come to an end, we are not despondent about what would happen next. One is not so much frightened of being conquered by a power which rules over others, as Sparta does (not that we are concerned with Sparta now), as of what would happen if a ruling power is attacked and defeated by its own subjects. So far as this point is concerned, you can leave it to us to face the risks involved. What we shall do now is to show you that it is for the good of our own empire that we are here and that it is for the preservation of your city that we shall say what we are going to say. We do not want any trouble in bringing you into our empire, and we want you to be spared for the good both of yourselves and of ourselves.

Melians: And how could it be just as good for us to be the slaves as for you to be the masters?

Athenians: You, by giving in, would save yourselves from disaster; we, by not destroying you, would be able to profit from you.

Melians: So you would not agree to our being neutral, friends instead of enemies, but allies of neither side?

Athenians: No, because it is not so much your hostility that injures us; it is rather the case that, if we were on friendly terms with you, our subjects would regard that as a sign of weakness in us, whereas your hatred is evidence of our power.

Melians: Is that your subjects' idea of fair play—that no distinction should be made between people who are quite unconnected with you and people who are mostly your own colonists or else rebels whom you have conquered?

Athenians: So far as right and wrong are concerned they think that there is no difference between the two, that those who still preserve their independence do so because they are strong, and that if we fail to attack them it is because we are afraid. So that by conquering you we shall increase not only the size but the security of our empire. We rule the sea and you are islanders, and weaker islanders too than the others; it is therefore particularly important that you should not escape.

Melians: But do you think there is no security for you in what we suggest? For here again, since you will not let us mention justice, but tell us to give in to your interests, we, too, must tell you what our interests are and, if yours and ours happen to coincide, we must try to persuade you of the fact. Is it not certain that you will make enemies of all states who are at present neutral, when they see what is happening here and naturally conclude that in course of time you will attack them too? Does not this mean that you are strengthening the enemies you have already and are forcing others to become your enemies even against their intentions and their inclinations?

Athenians: As a matter of fact we are not so much frightened of states on the continent. They have their liberty, and this means that it will be a long time before they begin to take precautions against us. We are more concerned about islanders like yourselves, who are still unsubdued, or subjects who have already become embittered by the constraint which our empire imposes on them. These are the people who are most likely to act in a reckless manner and to bring themselves and us, too, into the most obvious danger.

Melians: Then surely, if such hazards are taken by you to keep your empire and by your subjects to escape from it, we who are still free would show ourselves great cowards and weaklings if we failed to face everything that comes rather than submit to slavery.

Athenians: No, not if you are sensible. This is no fair fight, with honour on one side and shame on the other. It is rather a question of saving your lives and not resisting those who are far too strong for you.

Melians: Yet we know that in war fortune sometimes makes the odds more level than could be expected from the difference in numbers of the two sides. And if we surrender, then all our hope is lost at once, whereas, so long as we remain in action, there is still a hope that we may yet stand upright.

Athenians: Hope, that comforter in danger! If one already has solid advantages to fall back upon, one can indulge in hope. It may do harm, but will not destroy one. But hope is by nature an expensive commodity, and those who are risking their all on one cast find out what it means only when they are already ruined; it never fails them in the period when such a knowledge would enable them to take precautions. Do not let this happen to you, you who are weak and whose fate depends on a single movement of the scale. And do not be like those people who, as so commonly happens, miss the chance of saving themselves in a human and practical way, and, when every clear and distinct hope has left them in their adversity, turn to what is blind and vague, to prophecies and oracles and such things which by encouraging hope lead men to ruin.

Melians: It is difficult, and you may be sure that we know it, for us to oppose your power and fortune, unless the terms be equal. Nevertheless we trust that the gods will give us fortune as good as yours, because we are standing for what is right against what is wrong; and as for what we lack in power, we trust that it will be made up for by our alliance with the Spartans, who are bound, if for no other reason, then for honour's sake, and because we are their kinsmen, to come to our help. Our confidence, therefore, is not so entirely irrational as you think.

Athenians: So far as the favour of the gods is concerned, we think we have as much right to that as you have. Our aims and our actions are perfectly consistent with the beliefs men hold about the gods and with the principles which govern their own conduct. Our opinion of the gods and our knowledge of men lead us to conclude that it is a general and necessary law of nature to rule whatever one can. This is not a law that we made ourselves, nor were we the first to act upon it when it was made. We found it already in existence, and we shall leave it to exist for ever among those who come after us. We are merely acting in accordance with it, and we know that you or anybody else with the same power as ours would be acting in precisely the same way. And therefore, so far as the gods are concerned, we see no good reason why we should fear to be at a disadvantage. But with regard to your views about Sparta and your confidence that she, out of a sense of honour, will come to your aid, we must say that we congratulate you on your simplicity but do not envy you your folly. In matters that concern themselves or their own constitution the Spartans are quite remarkably good; as for their relations with others, that is a long story, but it can be expressed shortly and clearly by saying that of all people we know the Spartans are most conspicuous for believing that what they like doing is honourable and what suits their interests is just. And this kind of attitude is not going to be of much help to you in your absurd quest for safety at the moment.

Melians: But this is the very point where we can feel most sure. Their own self-interest will make them refuse to betray their own colonists, the Melians, for that would mean losing the confidence of their friends among the Hellenes and doing good to their enemies.

Athenians: You seem to forget that if one follows one's self-interest one wants to be safe, whereas the path of justice and honour involves one in danger. And, where danger is concerned, the Spartans are not, as a rule, very venturesome.

Melians: But we think that they would even endanger themselves for our sake and count the risk more worth taking than in the case of others, because we are so close to the Peloponnese that they could operate more easily, and because they can depend on us more than on others, since we are of the same race and share the same feelings.

Athenians: Goodwill shown by the party that is asking for help does not mean security for the prospective ally. What is looked for is a positive preponderance of power in action. And the Spartans pay attention to this point even more than others do. Certainly they distrust their own native resources so much that when they attack a neighbour they bring a great army of allies with them. It is hardly likely therefore that, while we are in control of the sea, they will cross over to an island.

Melians: But they still might send others. The Cretan sea is a wide one, and it is harder for those who control it to intercept others than for those who want to slip through to do so safely. And even if they were to fail in this, they would turn against your own land and against those of your allies left unvisited by Brasidas. So, instead of troubling about a country which has nothing to do with you, you will find trouble nearer home, among your allies, and in your own country.

Athenians: It is a possibility, something that has in fact happened before. It may happen in your case, but you are well aware that the Athenians have never yet relinquished a single siege operation through fear of others. But we are somewhat shocked to find that, though you announced your intention of discussing how you could preserve yourselves, in all this talk you have said absolutely nothing which could justify a man in thinking that he could be preserved. Your chief points are concerned with what you hope may happen in the future, while your actual resources are too scanty to give you a chance of survival against the forces that are opposed to you at this moment. You will therefore be showing an extraordinary lack of common sense if, after you have asked us to retire from this meeting, you still fail to reach a conclusion wiser than anything you have mentioned so far. Do not be led astray by a false sense of honour—a thing which often brings men to ruin when they are faced with an obvious danger that somehow affects their pride. For in many cases men have still been able to see the dangers ahead of them, but this thing called dishonour, this word, by its own force of seduction, has drawn them into a state where they have surrendered to an idea, while in fact they have fallen voluntarily into irrevocable disaster, in dishonour that is all the more dishonourable because it has come to them from their own folly rather than their misfortune. You, if you take the right view, will be careful to avoid this. You will see that there is nothing disgraceful in giving way to the greatest city in Hellas when she is offering you such reasonable terms—alliance on a tribute-paying basis and liberty to enjoy your own property. And, when you are allowed to choose between war and safety, you will not be so insensitively arrogant as to make the wrong choice. This is the safe rule—to stand up to one's equals, to behave with deference towards one's superiors, and to treat one's inferiors with moderation. Think it over again, then, when we have withdrawn from the meeting, and let this be a point that constantly recurs to your minds—that you are discussing the fate of your country, that you have only one country, and that its future for good or ill depends on this one single decision which you are going to make.

The Athenians then withdrew from the discussion. The Melians, left to themselves, reached a conclusion which was much the same as they had indicated in their previous replies. Their answer was as follows:

'Our decision, Athenians, is just the same as it was at first. We are not prepared to give up in a short moment the liberty which our city has enjoyed from its foundation for 700 years. We put our trust in the fortune that the gods will send and which has saved us up to now, and in the help of men—that is, of the Spartans; and so we shall try to save ourselves. But we invite you to allow us to be friends of yours and enemies to neither side, to make a treaty which shall be agreeable to both you and us, and so to leave our country.'

The Melians made this reply, and the Athenians, just as they were breaking off the discussion, said:

'Well, at any rate, judging from this decision of yours, you seem to us quite unique in your ability to consider the future as something more certain than what is before your eyes, and to see uncertainties as realities, simply because you would like them to be so. As you have staked most on and trusted most in Spartans, luck, and hopes, so in all these you will find yourselves most completely deluded.'

The Athenian representatives then went back to the army, and the Athenian generals, finding that the Melians would not submit, immediately commenced hostilities and built a wall completely round the city of Melos, dividing the work out among the various states. Later they left behind a garrison of some of their own and some allied troops to blockade the place by land and sea, and with the greater part of their army returned home. The force left behind stayed on and continued with the siege.

About the same time the Argives invaded Phliasia and were ambushed by the Phliasians and the exiles from Argos, losing about eighty men.

Then, too, the Athenians at Pylos captured a great quantity of plunder from Spartan territory. Not even after this did the Spartans renounce the treaty and make war, but they issued a proclamation saying that any of their people who wished to do so were free to make raids on the Athenians. The Corinthians also made some attacks on the Athenians because of private quarrels of their own, but the rest of the Pelponnesians stayed quiet.

Meanwhile the Melians made a night attack and captured the part of the Athenian lines opposite the market-place. They killed some of the troops, and then, after bringing in corn and everything else useful that they could lay their hands on, retired again and made no further move, while the Athenians took measures to make their blockade more efficient in future. So the summer came to an end.

In the following winter the Spartans planned to invade the territory of Argos, but when the sacrifices for crossing the frontier turned out unfavourably, they gave up the expedition. The fact that they had intended to invade made the Argives suspect certain people in their city, some of whom they arrested, though others succeeded in escaping.

About this same time the Melians again captured another part of the Athenian lines where there were only a few of the garrison on guard. As a result of this, another force came out afterwards from Athens under the command of Philocrates, the son of Demeas. Siege operations were now carried on vigorously and, as there was also some treachery from inside, the Melians surrendered unconditionally to the Athenians, who put to death all the men of military age whom they took, and sold the women and children as slaves. Melos itself they took over for themselves, sending out later a colony of 500 men.[1]

Note

[1] That there were Melian survivors, who were restored by Lysander at the end of the war, is stated by Xenophon (*Hellenica*, II, 2, 9).

from *On the Nature of the Universe*

Lucretius
Translated by R. E. Latham

Book One—Matter and Space

Mother of Aeneas and his race, delight of men and gods, life-giving Venus, it is your doing that under the wheeling constellations of the sky all nature teems with life, both the sea that buoys up our ships and the earth that yields our food. Through you all living creatures are conceived and come forth to look upon the sunlight. Before you the winds flee, and at your coming the clouds forsake the sky. For you the inventive earth flings up sweet flowers. For you the ocean levels laugh, the sky is calmed and glows with diffused radiance. When first the day puts on the aspect of spring, when in all its force the fertilizing breath of Zephyr is unleashed, then, great goddess, the birds of air give the first intimation of your entry; for yours is the power that has pierced them to the heart. Next the wild beasts and farm animals alike run wild, frisk through the lush pastures and swim the swift-flowing streams. Spellbound by your charm, they follow your lead with fierce desire. So throughout seas and uplands, rushing torrents, verdurous meadows and the leafy shelters of the birds, into the breasts of one and all you instil alluring love, so that with passionate longing they reproduce their several breeds.

Since you alone are the guiding power of the universe and without you nothing emerges into the shining sunlit world to grow in joy and loveliness, yours is the partnership I seek in striving to compose these lines *On the Nature of the Universe* for my noble Memmius. For him, great goddess, you have willed outstanding excellence in every field and everlasting fame. For his sake, therefore, endow my verse with everlasting charm.

Meanwhile, grant that this brutal business of war by sea and land may everywhere be lulled to rest. For you alone have power to bestow on mortals the blessing of quiet peace. In your bosom Mars himself, supreme commander in this business of brutality, flings himself down at times, laid low by the irremediable wound of love. Gazing upward, his neck a prostrate column, he fixes hungry eyes on you, great goddess, and gluts them with love. As he lies outstretched, his breath hangs upon your lips. Stoop, then, goddess most glorious, and enfold him at rest in your hallowed bosom and whisper with those lips sweet words of prayer, beseeching for the people of Rome untroubled peace. In this evil hour of my country's history, I cannot pursue my task with a mind at ease, as an illustrious scion of the house of Memmius cannot at such a crisis withhold his service from the common weal. ⟨I beg you for peace⟩ since it is essential to the very nature of deity that it should enjoy immortal existence in utter tranquillity, aloof and detached from our affairs. It is free from all pain and peril, strong in its own resources, exempt from any need of us, indifferent to our merits and immune from anger.

For what is to follow, my Memmius, lay aside your cares and lend undistracted ears and an attentive mind to true reason. Do not scornfully reject, before you have understood them, the gifts I have marshalled for you with zealous devotion. I will set out to discourse to you on the ultimate realities of heaven and the gods. I will reveal those *atoms* from which nature creates all things and increases and feeds them and into which, when they perish, nature again resolves them. To these in my discourse I commonly give such names as the 'raw material', or 'generative bodies', or 'seeds' of things. Or I may call them 'primary particles', because they come first and everything else is composed of them.

When human life lay grovelling in all men's sight, crushed to the earth under the dead weight of superstition whose grim features loured menacingly upon mortals from the four quarters of the sky, a man of Greece was first to raise mortal eyes in defiance, first to stand erect and brave the challenge. Fables of the gods did not crush him, nor the lightning flash and the growling menace of the sky. Rather, they quickened the keen courage of his heart, so that he, first of all men, longed to smash the constraining locks of nature's doors. The vital vigour of his mind prevailed. He ventured far out beyond the flaming ramparts of the world and voyaged in mind throughout infinity. Returning victorious, he proclaimed to us what can be and what cannot: how the power of each thing is limited, and its boundary-stone sticks buried deep. Therefore superstition in its turn lies crushed beneath his feet, and we by his triumph are lifted level with the skies.

One thing that worries me is the fear that you may fancy yourself embarking on an impious course of philosophy, setting your feet on the path of sin. Far from it. More often it is this very superstition that is the mother of sinful and impious deeds. Remember how at Aulis the altar of the virgin goddess was foully stained with the blood of Iphigeneia by the leaders of the Greeks, the patterns of chivalry. The headband was bound about her virgin tresses and hung down evenly over both her cheeks. Suddenly she caught sight of her father standing sadly in front of the altar, the attendants beside him hiding the knife and her people bursting into tears when they saw her. Struck dumb with terror, she sank on her knees to the ground. Poor girl, at such a moment it did not help her that she had been first to give the name of father to a king. Raised by the hands of men, she was led trembling to the altar. Not for her the sacrament of marriage and the loud chant of Hymen. It was her fate in the very hour of marriage to fall a sinless victim to a sinful rite, slaughtered to her greater grief by a father's hand, so that a fleet might sail under happy auspices. Such are the heights of wickedness to which men have been driven by superstition.

You yourself, if you surrender your judgement at any time to the bloodcurdling declamations of the prophets, will want to desert our ranks. Only think what phantoms they can conjure up to overturn the tenor of your life and wreck your happiness with fear. And not without cause. For, if men saw that a term was set to their troubles, they would find strength in some way to withstand the hocus-pocus and intimidations of the prophets. As it is, they have no power of resistance, because they are haunted by the fear of eternal punishment after death. They know nothing of the nature of the spirit. Is it born, or is it implanted in us at birth? Does it perish with us, dissolved by death, or does it visit the murky depths and dreary sloughs of the Underworld? Or is it transplanted by divine power into other creatures, as described in the poems of our own Ennius, who first gathered on the delectable slopes of Helicon an evergreen garland destined to win renown among the nations of Italy? Ennius indeed in his immortal verses proclaims that there is also a Hell, which is peopled not by our actual spirits or bodies but only by shadowy images, ghastly pale. It is from this realm that he pictures the ghost of Homer, of unfading memory, as appearing to him, shedding salt tears and revealing the nature of the universe.

I must therefore give an account of celestial phenomena, explaining the movements of sun and moon and also the forces that determine events on earth. Next, and no less important, we must look with keen insight into the make-up of spirit and mind: we must consider those alarming phantasms that strike upon our minds when they are awake but disordered by sickness, or when they are buried in slumber, so that we seem to see and hear before us men whose dead bones lie in the embraces of earth.

I am well aware that it is not easy to elucidate in Latin verse the obscure discoveries of the Greeks. The poverty of our language and the novelty of the theme often compel me to coin new words for the purpose. But your merit and the joy I hope to derive from our delightful friendship encourage me to face any task however hard. This it is that leads me to stay awake through the quiet of the night, studying how by choice of words and the poet's art I can display before your mind a clear light by which you can gaze into the heart of hidden things.

This dread and darkness of the mind cannot be dispelled by the sunbeams, the shining shafts of day, but only by an understanding of the outward form and inner workings of nature. In tackling this theme, our starting-point will be this principle: *Nothing is ever created by divine power out of nothing.* The reason why all mortals are so gripped by fear is that they see all sorts of things happening on the earth and in the sky with no discernible cause, and these they attribute to the will of a god. Accordingly, when we have seen that nothing can be created out of nothing, we shall then have a clearer picture of the path ahead, the problem of how things are created and occasioned without the aid of gods.

First then, if things were made out of nothing, any species could spring from any source and nothing would require seed. Men could arise from the sea and scaly fish from the earth, and birds could be hatched out of the sky. Cattle and other farm animals and every kind of wild beast, multiplying indiscriminately, would occupy cultivated and waste lands alike. The same fruits would not grow constantly on the same trees, but they would keep changing: any tree might bear any fruit. If each species were not composed of its own generative bodies, why should each be born always of the same kind of mother? Actually, since each is formed out of specific seeds, it is born and emerges into the sunlit world only from a place where there exists the right material, the right kind of atoms. This is why everything cannot be born of everything, but a specific power of generation inheres in specific objects.

Again, why do we see roses appear in spring, grain in summer's heat, grapes under the spell of autumn? Surely, because it is only after specific seeds have drifted together at their own proper time that every created thing stands revealed, when the season is favourable and the life-giving earth can safely deliver delicate growths into the sunlit world. If they were made out of nothing, they would spring up suddenly after varying lapses of time and at abnormal seasons, since there would of course be no primary bodies that could be prevented by the harshness of the season from entering into generative unions. Similarly, there would be no need of any lapse of time for the accumulation of seed in order that things might grow. Tiny tots would turn suddenly into young men, and trees would shoot up spontaneously out of the earth. But it is obvious that none of these things happens since, as is natural, everything grows gradually from a specific seed and retains its specific character. It is a fair inference that each is increased and nourished by its own raw material.

Here is a further point. Without seasonable showers the earth cannot send up gladdening growths. Lacking food, animals cannot reproduce their kind or sustain life. This points to the conclusion that many elements are common to many things, as letters are to words, rather than to the theory that anything can come into existence without atoms.

Or again, why has not nature been able to produce men on such a scale that they could ford the ocean on foot or tear down high mountains with their hands or prolong their lives over many generations? Surely because each thing requires for its birth a particular material that determines what can be produced. It must therefore be admitted that nothing can be made out of nothing, because everything must be generated from a seed before it can emerge into the unresisting air.

Lastly, we see that tilled plots are superior to untilled, and their fruits are improved by cultivation. This is because the earth contains certain atoms that we rouse to productivity by turning the fruitful clods with the ploughshare and stirring up the soil. But for these, you would see great improvements arising spontaneously without any aid from our labours.

The second great principle is this: *nature resolves everything into its component atoms and never reduces anything to nothing.* If anything were perishable in all its parts, anything might perish all of a sudden and vanish from sight. There would be no need of any force to separate its parts and loosen their links. In actual fact, since everything is composed of indestructible seeds, nature obviously does not allow anything to perish till it has encountered a force that shatters it with a blow or creeps into chinks and unknits it.

If the things that are banished from the scene by age are annihilated through the exhaustion of their material, from what source does Venus bring back the several races of animals into the light of life? And, when they are brought back, where does the inventive earth find for each the special food required for its sustenance and growth? From what fount is the sea replenished by its native springs and the streams that flow into it from afar? From where does the ether draw nutriment for the stars? For everything consisting of a mortal body must have been exhausted by the long day of time, the illimitable past. If throughout this bygone eternity there have persisted bodies from which the universe has been perpetually renewed, they must certainly be possessed of immortality. Therefore things cannot be reduced to nothing.

Again, all objects would regularly be destroyed by the same force and the same cause were it not that they are sustained by imperishable matter more or less tightly fastened together. Why, a mere touch would be enough to bring about destruction supposing there were no imperishable bodies whose union could be dissolved only by the appropriate force. Actually, because the fastenings of the atoms are of various kinds while their matter is imperishable, compound objects remain intact until one of them encounters a force that proves strong enough to break up its particular constitution. Therefore nothing returns to nothing, but everything is resolved into its constituent bodies.

Lastly, showers perish when father ether has flung them down into the lap of mother earth. But the crops spring up fresh; the branches on the trees burst into leaf; the trees themselves grow and are weighed down with fruit. Hence in turn man and beast draw nourishment. Hence we see flourishing cities blest with children and every leafy thicket loud with new broods of songsters. Hence in lush pastures cattle wearied by their bulk fling down their bodies, and the white milky juice oozes from their swollen udders. Hence a new generation frolic friskily on wobbly legs through the fresh grass, their young minds tipsy with undiluted milk. Visible objects therefore do not perish utterly, since nature repairs one thing from another and allows nothing to be born without the aid of another's death.

Well, Memmius, I have taught you that things cannot be created out of nothing nor, once born, be summoned back to nothing. Perhaps, however, you are becoming mistrustful of my words, because these atoms of mine are not visible to the eye. Consider, therefore, this further evidence of *bodies whose existence you must acknowledge though they cannot be seen*. First, wind, when its force is roused, whips up waves, founders tall ships and scatters clouds. Sometimes scouring plains with hurricane force it strews them with huge trees and batters mountain peaks with blasts that hew down forests. Such is wind in its fury, when it whoops aloud with a mad menace in its shouting. Without question, therefore, there must be invisible particles of wind that sweep sea, that sweep land, that sweep the clouds in the sky, swooping upon them and whirling them along in a headlong hurricane. In the way they flow and the havoc they spread they are no different from a torrential flood of water when it rushes down in a sudden spate from the mountain heights, swollen by heavy rains, and heaps together wreckage from the forest and entire trees. Soft though it is by nature, the sudden shock of oncoming water is more than even stout bridges can withstand, so furious is the force with which the turbid, storm-flushed torrent surges against their piers. With a mighty roar it lays them low, rolling huge rocks under its waves and brushing aside every obstacle from its course. Such, therefore, must be the movement of blasts of wind also. When they have come surging along some course like a rushing river, they push obstacles before them and buffet them with repeated blows; and sometimes, eddying round and round, they snatch them up and carry them along in a swiftly circling vortex. Here then is proof upon proof that winds have invisible bodies, since in their actions and behaviour they are found to rival great rivers, whose bodies are plain to see.

Then again, we smell the various scents of things though we never see them approaching our nostrils. Similarly, we do not look upon scorching heat nor can we grasp cold in our eyes and we do not see sounds. Yet all these must be composed of physical bodies, since they are able to impinge upon our senses. For nothing can touch or be touched except bodies.

Again, clothes hung out on a surf-beaten shore grow moist. Spread in the sun they grow dry. But we do not see how the moisture has soaked into them, nor again how it has been dispelled by the heat. It follows that the moisture is split up into minute parts which the eye cannot possibly see.

Again, in the course of many annual revolutions of the sun a ring is worn thin next to the finger with continual rubbing. Dripping water hollows a stone. A curved ploughshare, iron though it is, dwindles imperceptibly in the furrow. We see the cobblestones of the highway worn by the feet of many wayfarers. The bronze statues by the city gates show their right hands worn thin by the touch of travellers who have greeted them in passing. We see that all these are being diminished, since they are worn away. But to perceive what particles drop off at any particular time is a power grudged to us by our ungenerous sense of sight.

To sum up, whatever is added to things gradually by nature and the passage of days, causing a cumulative increase, eludes the most attentive scrutiny of our eyes. Conversely, you cannot see what objects lose by the wastage of age—sheer sea cliffs, for instance, exposed to prolonged erosion by the mordant brine—or at what time the loss occurs. It follows that nature works through the agency of invisible bodies.

On the other hand, things are not hemmed in by the pressure of solid bodies in a tight mass. This is because *there is vacuity in things*. A grasp of this fact will be helpful to you in many respects and will save you from much bewildered doubting and questioning about the universe and from mistrust of my teaching. Well then, by vacuity I mean intangible and empty space. If it did not exist, things could not move at all. For the distinctive action of matter, which is counteraction and obstruction, would be in force always and everywhere. Nothing could move forward, because nothing would give it a starting-point by receding. As it is, we see with our eyes at sea and on land and high up in the sky that all sorts of things in all sorts of ways are on the move. If there were no empty space, these things would be denied the power of restless movement—or rather, they could not possibly have come into existence, embedded as they would have been in motionless matter.

Besides, there are clear indications that things that pass for solid are in fact porous. Even in rocky caves a trickle of water seeps through, and every surface weeps with brimming drops. Food percolates to every part of an animal's body. Trees grow and pour forth their fruit in season, because their food is distributed throughout their length from the tips of the roots through the trunk and along every branch. Noises pass through walls and fly into closed buildings. Freezing cold penetrates to the bones. If there were no vacancies through which the various bodies could make their way, none of these phenomena would be possible.

Again, why do we find some things outweigh others of equal volume? If there is as much matter in a ball of wool as in one of lead, it is natural that it should weigh as heavily, since it is the function of matter to press everything downwards, while it is the function of space on the other hand to remain weightless. Accordingly, when one thing is not less bulky than another but obviously lighter, it plainly declares that there is more vacuum in it, while the heavier object proclaims that there is more matter in it and much less empty space. We have therefore reached the goal of our diligent enquiry: there is in things an admixture of what we call vacuity.

In case you should be misled on this question by the idle imagining of certain theorists, I must anticipate their argument. They maintain that water yields and opens up liquid ways to the scaly bodies of fish that push against it, because they leave spaces behind them into which the yielding water can flow together. In the same way, they suppose, other things can move by mutually changing places, although every place remains filled. This theory has been adopted utterly without warrant. For how can the fish advance till the water has given way? And how can the water retire when the fish cannot move? There are thus only two alternatives: either all bodies are devoid of movement, or you must admit that things contain an admixture of vacuity whereby each is enabled to make the first move.

Lastly, if two broad bodies suddenly spring apart from contact, all the intervening space must be void until it is occupied by air. However quickly the air rushes in all round, the entire space cannot be filled instantaneously. The air must occupy one spot after another until it has taken possession of the whole space. If anyone supposes that this consequence of such springing apart is made possible by the condensation of air, he is mistaken. For condensation implies that something that was full becomes empty, or vice versa. And I contend that air could not condense so as to produce this effect; or, at any rate, if there were no vacuum, it could not thus shrink into itself and draw its parts together.

However many pleas you may advance to prolong the argument, you must end by admitting that there is vacuity in things. There are many other proofs that I could scrape together into the pile in order to strengthen conviction; but for an acute intelligence these small clues should suffice to discover the rest for yourself. As hounds often smell out the lairs of a mountain-ranging quarry screened in thickets, when once they have got on to the right trail, so in such questions one thing will lead on to another, till you can succeed by yourself in tracking down the truth to its lurking places and dragging it forth. If you grow weary and relax from the chase, there is one thing, Memmius, that I can safely promise you: my honeyed tongue will pour from the treasury of my breast such generous draughts, drawn from inexhaustible springs, that I am afraid slow plodding age may creep through my limbs and unbolt the bars of my life before the full flood of my arguments on any single point has flowed in verse through your ears.

To pick up the thread of my discourse, all nature as it is in itself consists of two things—bodies and the vacant space in which the bodies are situated and through which they move in different directions. The existence of bodies is vouched for by the agreement of the senses. If a belief resting directly on this foundation is not valid, there will be no standard to which we can refer any doubt on obscure questions for rational confirmation. If there were no place and space, which we call vacuity, these bodies could not be situated anywhere or move in any direction whatever. This I have just demonstrated. It remains to show that *nothing exists that is distinct both from body and from vacuity* and could be ranked with the others as a third substance. For whatever *is* must also be something. If it offers resistance to touch, however light and slight, it will increase the mass of body by such amount, great or small, as it may amount to, and will rank with it. If, on the other hand, it is intangible, so that it offers no resistance whatever to anything passing through it, then it will be that empty space which we call vacuity. Besides, whatever it may be in itself, either it will act in some way, or react to other things acting upon it, or else it will be such that things can be and happen in it. But without body nothing can act or react; and nothing can afford a place except emptiness and vacancy.

Therefore, besides matter and vacuity, we cannot include in the number of things any third substance that can either affect our senses at any time or be grasped by the reasoning of our minds.

You will find that anything that can be named is either a property or an accident of these two. A *property* is something that cannot be detached or separated from a thing without destroying it, as weight is a property of rocks, heat of fire, fluidity of water, tangibility of all bodies, intangibility of vacuum. On the other hand, servitude, poverty and riches, freedom, war, peace and all other things whose advent or departure leaves the essence of a thing intact, all these it is our practice to call by their appropriate name, *accidents*.

Similarly, time by itself does not exist; but from things themselves there results a sense of what has already taken place, what is now going on and what is to ensue. It must not be claimed that anyone can sense time by itself apart from the movement of things or their restful immobility.

Again, when men say it *is* a fact that Helen was ravished or the Trojans were conquered, we must not let anyone drive us to the admission that any such factual event *exists* independently of any object, on the ground that the generations of men of whom these events were accidents have been swept away by the irrevocable lapse of time. For we could put it that whatever has taken place is an accident of a particular tract of earth or of the space it occupied. If there had been no matter and no space or place in which things could happen, no spark of love kindled by the beauty of Tyndareus' daughter would ever have glowed inside the breast of Phrygian Paris to light that dazzling blaze of pitiless war; no Wooden Horse, unmarked by the sons of Troy, would have set the towers of Ilium aflame through the midnight issue of Greeks from its womb. So you may see that events cannot be said to *be* by themselves like matter or in the same sense as space. Rather, you should describe them as accidents of matter, or of the place in which things happen.

Material objects are of two kinds, atoms and compounds of atoms. The atoms themselves cannot be swamped by any force, for they are preserved indefinitely by their absolute solidity. Admittedly, it is hard to believe that anything can exist that is absolutely solid. The lightning stroke from the sky penetrates closed buildings, as do shouts and other noises. Iron glows white-hot in the fire, and rocks crack in savage scorching heat. Hard gold is softened and melted by heat; and the ice of bronze is liquefied by flame. Both heat and piercing cold seep through silver, since we feel both alike when a cooling shower of water is poured into a goblet that we hold ceremonially in our hands. All these facts point to the conclusion that nothing is really solid. But sound reasoning and nature itself drive us to the opposite conclusion. Pay attention, therefore, while I demonstrate in a few lines that there exist certain bodies that are absolutely solid and indestructible, namely those atoms which according to our teaching are the seeds of prime units of things from which the whole universe is built up.

In the first place, we have found that nature is twofold, consisting of two totally different things, matter and the space in which things happen. Hence each of these must exist by itself without admixture of the other. For, where there is empty space (what we call vacuity), there matter is not; where matter exists, there cannot be a vacuum. Therefore the prime units of matter are solid and free from vacuity.

Again, since composite things contain some vacuum, the surrounding matter must be solid. For you cannot reasonably maintain that anything can hide vacuity and hold it within its body unless you allow that the container itself is solid. And what contains the vacuum in things can only be an accumulation of matter. Hence matter, which possesses absolute solidity, can be everlasting when other things are decomposed.

Again, if there were no empty space, everything would be one solid mass; if there were no material objects with the property of filling the space they occupy, all existing space would be utterly void. It is clear, then, that there is an alternation of matter and vacuity, mutually distinct, since the whole is neither completely full nor completely empty. There are therefore solid bodies, causing the distinction between empty space and full. And these, as I have just shown, can be neither decomposed by blows from without nor invaded and unknit from within nor destroyed by any other form of assault. For it seems that a thing without vacuum can be neither knocked to bits nor snapped nor chopped in two by cutting; nor can it let in moisture or seeping cold or piercing fire, the universal agents of destruction. The more vacuum a thing contains within it, the more readily it yields to these assailants. Hence, if the units of matter are solid and without vacuity, as I have shown, they must be everlasting.

Yet again, if the matter in things had not been everlasting, everything by now would have gone back to nothing, and the things we see would be the product of rebirth out of nothing. But, since I have already shown that nothing can be created out of nothing nor any existing thing be summoned back to nothing, the atoms must be made of imperishable stuff into which everything can be resolved in the end, so that there may be a stock of matter for building the world anew. The atoms, therefore, are absolutely solid and unalloyed. In no other way could they have survived throughout infinite time to keep the world renewed.

Furthermore, if nature had set no limit to the breaking of things, the particles of matter in the course of ages would have been ground so small that nothing could be generated from them so as to attain from them in the fullness of time to the summit of its growth. For we see that anything can be more speedily disintegrated than put together again. Hence, what the long day of time, the bygone eternity, has already shaken and loosened to fragments could never in the residue of time be reconstructed. As it is, there is evidently a limit set to breaking, since we see that everything is renewed and each according to its kind has a fixed period in which to grow to its prime.

Here is a further argument. Granted that the particles of matter are absolutely solid, we can still explain the composition and behaviour of soft things—air, water, earth, fire—by their intermixture with empty space. On the other hand, supposing the atoms to be soft, we cannot account for the origin of hard flint and iron. For there would be no foundation for nature to build on. Therefore there must be bodies strong in their unalloyed solidity by whose closer clustering things can be knit together and display unyielding toughness.

If we suppose that there is no limit set to the breaking of matter, we must still admit that material objects consist of particles which throughout eternity have resisted the forces of destruction. To say that these are breakable does not square with the fact that they have survived throughout eternity under a perpetual bombardment of innumerable blows.

Again, there is laid down for each thing a specific limit to its growth and its tenure of life, and the laws of nature ordain what each can do and what it cannot. No species is ever changed, but each remains so much itself that every kind of bird displays on its body its own specific markings. This is a further proof that their bodies are made of changeless matter. For, if the atoms could yield in any way to change, there would be no certainty as to what could arise and what could not, at what point the power of everything was limited by an immovable frontier post; nor could successive generations so regularly repeat the nature, behaviour, habits and movements of their parents.

To proceed with our argument, there is an kultimate point in visible objects that represents the smallest thing that can be seen. So also there must be anl ultimate point in objects that lie below the limit of perception by our senses. This point is without parts and is the smallest thing that can exist. It never has been and never will be able to exist by itself, but only as one primary part of something else. It is with a mass of such parts, solidly jammed together in formation, that matter is filled up. Since they cannot exist by themselves, they must needs stick together in a mass from which they cannot by any means be prized loose. The atoms, therefore, are absolutely solid and unalloyed, consisting of a mass of least parts tightly packed together. They are not compounds formed by the coalescence of their parts, but bodies of absolute and everlasting solidity. To these nature allows no loss or diminution, but guards them as seeds for things. If there are no such least parts, even the smallest bodies consist of an infinite number of parts, since they can always be halved and their halves halved again without limit. On this showing, what difference will there be between the whole universe and the very least of things? None at all. For, however endlessly infinite the universe may be, yet the smallest things will equally consist of an infinite number of parts. Since true reason cries out against this and denies that the mind can believe it, you must needs give in and admit that there are least parts which themselves are partless. Granted that these parts exist, you must needs admit that the atoms they compose are also solid and everlasting. But, if all things were compelled by all-creating nature to be broken up into these least parts, nature would lack the power to rebuild anything out of them. For partless objects cannot have the essential properties of generative matter—those varieties of attachment, weight, impetus, impact and movement on which everything depends.

For all these reasons, *those who have imagined that the raw material of things is fire and the universe consists of fire alone have evidently wandered far from the truth.* Of these the first champion to plunge into the fray was Heraclitus, illustrious for the darkness of his speech, though rather among the lighter-witted of the Greeks than among those who are earnest seekers after truth. For fools are more impressed and intrigued by what they detect under a screen of riddling words, and accept as true what pleasantly tickles their ears and all that is dyed with a smart sound. I should like to know how things can be so manifold if they are created out of nothing but sheer fire. It would not help if hot fire were condensed or rarefied, so long as the particles of fire retained the same nature that fire posesses as a whole. Its heat would simply be fiercer as its parts were more concentrated, milder as they were dispersed and dissipated. There is no further effect that you could attribute to such causes—no possibility that the infinite variety of things could result from variations in the density or rarity of fire. Even these variations in density could not occur unless we allow in things an intermixture of vacuity. But, because these theorists see that many things run counter to their theories, they dodge the issue and decline to leave any pure vacuum in things. Shunning the steep, they lose the true path. They do not see that without vacuity everything would be condensed and would become one body, which could not throw off anything at high speed from itself as blazing fire throws off light and heat, so that you can see that its parts are not solidly compacted.

If, on the other hand, they think that there is some other way in which fires in combination can be quenched and change their substance, then obviously—if they do not shrink from any implication of this view—the fieriness must be completely annihilated and whatever emerges must be a new creation out of nothing. For, if ever anything is so transformed as to overstep its own limits, this means the immediate death of what was before. It follows that they must leave something intact, or you would find everything reduced to nothing and the stock of things reborn and reinvigorated from nothing. As it is, there are certain definite bodies that always keep the same nature, and it is by the withdrawal or advent of these and their reshuffling that things change their nature and material objects are transformed. And these primary bodies cannot be fiery. So long as they possessed and retained a fiery nature, it would make no odds if some of them were detached and withdrawn and others tacked on and some were reshuffled. Whatever they created would still be simply fire. The truth, as I maintain, is this: there are certain bodies whose impacts, movements, order, position and shapes produce fires. When their order is changed, they change their nature. In themselves they do not resemble fire or anything else that can bombard our senses with particles or impinge on our organs of touch.

To say, as Heraclitus does, that everything is fire, and nothing can be numbered among things as a reality except fire, seems utterly crazy. On the basis of the senses he attacks and unsettles the senses—the foundation of all belief and the only source of his knowledge of that which he calls fire. He believes that the senses clearly perceive fire, but not the other things that are in fact no less clear. This strikes me as not only pointless but mad. For what is to be our standard of reference? What can be a surer guide to the distinction of true from false than our own senses? What grounds have we for taking everything else and leaving fire, any more than for taking away everything else and leaving some other thing? Either procedure appears equally insane.

For this reason those who have thought that fire is the raw material of things and the universe can consist of fire and those who have made *air* the starting-point for the growth of things or have supposed that *water* by itself could form everything or that *earth* could create all things and be transformed into their natures—all these have evidently wandered far from the truth.

Not less mistaken are those who make the elements two-fold, coupling air with fire and earth with water, *and those who think that everything can grow from four elements*, fire and earth and air and rain. Conspicuous among these is Empedocles of Acragas, born in the three-cornered confines of that Isle round which surges the Ionian deep, rushing far into creeks and dashing up salt spray from its grey-green billows. The sea that parts it from Aeolian shores runs headlong through its narrow channel. Here is deadly Charybdis. Here the rumbling of Etna's flames is a warning that it is rallying its wrath that once again its force may spew out fires bursting in a torrent from its throat, to bring its flashing flames back up to the sky. This great country is acknowledged to have many claims to the admiration of mankind and the attention of sight-seekers. But, for all its surfeit of good things and its ample garrison of men, it has surely held nothing more glorious than this man, nothing holier, nothing more wonderful, nothing more precious. Indeed, the songs that took shape in his divine breast proclaim in ringing tones such glorious discoveries that he scarcely seems a scion of mortal stock. Empedocles and those lesser men of whom we have spoken above, who rank far and away below him, have certainly made many excellent and divine discoveries and uttered oracles from the inner sanctuary of their hearts with more sanctity and far surer reason than those the Delphic prophetess pronounces, drugged by the laurel fumes, from Apollo's tripod. Yet among the very foundations of things they have come to grief. Great as they were, great has been their fall.

Their first error is this: they postulate movement while banishing empty space from the universe, and they admit the existence of soft and flimsy things—air, sun, water, earth, animals, vegetables—without allowing their bodies an intermixture of vacuity.

Secondly, they acknowledge no limit to the splitting of things, no rest from crumbling, no smallest unit of matter, although we see that every object has an ultimate point that seems to our senses to be the smallest, from which you may infer that the things you cannot perceive have also an ultimate point which actually is the smallest. Besides, since they rank as elements soft things that we perceive to be neither birthless nor deathless, the universe ought by now to have returned to nothing and whatever exists ought to be a new creation and growth out of nothing, both of which suppositions you already know to be false. Furthermore, these supposed elements are in many ways hurtful and lethal to one another, so that they will either be destroyed on contact or will rush apart, as when a storm has gathered we see lightning flashes, rainclouds and winds rush apart.

Again, if everything is created from four things and resolved into them, why should we say that these are the elements of things rather than the reverse—that other things are the elements of these? For one gives birth to another continually, and they interchange their colours and their entire natures throughout the whole of time. If, on the other hand, you believe that particles of fire and earth, airy wind and watery moisture, combine without changing their natures in combination, then nothing can be created from them, either animate or (like a tree) with inanimate body. For each element in a composite assemblage will betray its own nature; air will appear mixed with earth, and fire will remain side by side with moisture. But in fact the elements, in giving birth to things, must contribute a nature that is hidden and viewless, so that nothing may show that conflicts with the thing created and prevents it from being distinctively itself.

These authors trace everything back to the sky and its fires. First they make fire transform itself into the winds of air; hence is born rain, and from rain is created earth. Then the process is reversed: first from earth is born moisture, then comes air, then fire. And things never cease to interchange, migrating from heaven to earth, from earth to the starry firmament. This is something elements ought never to do. For it is essential that something should remain immutable, or everything would be reduced to nothing. For, if ever anything is so transformed that it oversteps its own limits, this means the immediate death of what was before. Therefore, since the substances just mentioned enter into interchange, they must needs consist of other substances that cannot be altered, so that you may not find everything reduced to nothing. You ought rather to postulate bodies possessed of such a nature that, if they happen to have created fire, they only need a few subtractions and additions and some change of order and movement to make gusty air. In this way we can account for any change from one thing to another.

'But,' you say, 'observation clearly shows that all growing things do grow up into the gusty air out of the earth and it is from the earth that they draw their food. And, unless an auspicious season gives free play to the rain, so that trees reel beneath the dissolving clouds, and unless the sun in turn provides fostering warmth, there can be no growth of crops, trees, or animals.' Yes, and unless we ourselves were sustained by dry food and fluid juices, our bodies would waste away till every bit of life had escaped from all our sinews and bones. There can be no doubt that we are fed and sustained by certain specific things, other things by others, and so forth. Obviously, it is because there are in things many elements common to many commingled in many ways that various things draw their food from various sources. It often makes a big difference in what combinations and positions the selfsame elements occur, and what motions they mutually pass on or take over. For the same elements compose sky, sea and lands, rivers and sun, crops, trees and animals, but they are moving differently and in different combinations. Consider how in my verses, for instance, you see many letters common to many words; yet you must admit that different verses and words differ in substance and in audible sound. So much can be accomplished by letters through mere change of order. But the elements can bring more factors into play so as to create things in all their variety.

Now let us look into the theory of Anaxagoras, which the Greeks call *homoeomeria*: the poverty of our native language will not let me translate the word, but the thing itself can be expressed readily enough. Understand, then, that in speaking of the *homoeomeria* of things Anaxagoras means that bones are formed of minute miniature bones, flesh of minute miniature morsels of flesh, blood by the coalescence of many drops of blood; gold consists of grains of gold; earth is a conglomeration of little earths, fire of fires, moisture of moistures. And he pictures everything else as formed in the same way. At the same time he does not admit any vacuum in things, or any limit to the splitting of matter, on both of which counts he seems to me guilty of the same error as the others. Add to this that he makes the elements too frail, if indeed we can allow the name of 'elements' to bodies that have the same nature as the things themselves, that suffer and decay no less than they do and are not reined in by any force in their race to destruction. For which of these things will withstand violent assault, so as to escape extinction in the very jaws of death? Will fire or water or air? Which of these? Blood or bones? Nothing, I maintain, will escape, where everything is as perishable as those objects that we see vanishing from before our eyes under stress of some force or other. In proof of the impossibility of such annihilation and regrowth from nothing, I appeal to the evidence already adduced.

Again, since food builds up and nourishes our bodies, our veins and bones and blood kand sinews must be composed of matter unlike themselves.l

Alternatively, if it is alleged that all foods are of mixed substance and contain little morsels of sinews and bones and veins and drops of blood, it must be supposed that all food, whether solid or fluid, consists of unlike matter, namely of a mixture of bones and sinews, pus and blood. Similarly, if the material of all the things that grow out of the earth occurs in the earth, earth must consist of unlike matter that rises out of it. Turn to other phenomena, and the same words will hold good. If flame, smoke and ashes lurk unseen in wood, then wood must consist of unlike matter that rises out of it. Furthermore, all the material atoms that the earth feeds and makes to grow kmust consist of things unlike themselves—and they in their turn must also contain things unlike themselves.l

Here there is left some scanty cover for escaping detection, and Anaxagoras avails himself of it. He asserts that there is in everything a mixture of everything, but all the ingredients escape detection except the one whose particles are most numerous and conspicuous and stand in the front line. This is far removed from the truth. Otherwise it would naturally happen that corn, when it is crushed by the dire force of the grindstone, would often show some trace of blood, and that blood would exude when we crush between stones any of those things that derive material from our bodies. Similarly, grass and water ought often to emit sweet drops of the same flavour as the milk in the udders of fleecy ewes. When clods of soil are crumbled, finely divided particles of different plants and grains and leaves ought to become visible, lurking among the soil. When sticks are snapped, ashes and smoke ought to be revealed, and tiny hidden fires. But observation plainly shows that none of these things happens. It is clear therefore that one sort of thing is not intermingled with another in this way, but there must be in things a mixture of invisible seeds that are common to many sorts.

'But,' you may object, 'it often happens in mountainous country that nearby tops of tall trees are rubbed together by the force of strong south winds till suddenly they blossom out into a blaze of flame.' Agreed. And yet there is no fire embedded in the wood. What it does contain is a multitude of seeds of heat, which start a conflagration in the forest only when they have been concentrated by rubbing. If there were ready-made flame concealed in the wood, the fires could not be hidden for any length of time; they would spread havoc through the woodland and burn the trees to ashes. Now do you see the point of my previous remark, that it makes a great difference in what combinations and positions the same elements occur and what motions they mutually pass on and take over, so that with a little reshuffling the same ones may produce forests and fires? This is just how the words themselves are formed, by a little reshuffling of the letters, when we pronounce 'forests' and 'fires' as two distinct utterances.

If you cannot account for what you see happen without inventing particles of matter with the same sort of nature as the whole objects, there is an end of your elements altogether; you will have to postulate particles that shake their sides with uproarious guffaws and bedew their cheeks with salt tears.

And now pay special attention to what follows and listen more intently. I am well aware how full it is of obscurity. But high hope of fame has struck my heart with its holy staff and in so doing has implanted in my breast the sweet love of the Muses. That is the spur that lends my spirit strength to pioneer through pathless tracts of their Pierian realm where no foot has ever trod before. What joy it is to light upon virgin springs and drink their waters. What joy to pluck new flowers and gather for my brow a glorious garland from fields whose blossoms were never yet wreathed by the Muses round any head. This is my reward for teaching on these lofty topics, for struggling to loose men's minds from the tight knots of superstition and shedding on dark material the bright beams of my song that irradiate everything with the sparkle of the Muses. My art is not without a purpose. Physicians, when they wish to treat children with a nasty dose of wormwood, first smear the rim of the cup with the sweet yellow fluid of honey. The children, too young as yet for foresight, are lured by the sweetness at their lips into swallowing the bitter draught. So they are tricked but not trapped, for the treatment restores them to health. In the same way our doctrine often seems unpalatable to those who have not handled it, and the masses shrink from it. That is why I have tried to administer my philosophy to you in the dulcet strains of poesy, to touch it with the sweet honey of the Muses. My object has been to engage your mind with my verses while you gain insight into the nature of the universe and the pattern of its architecture.

Well then, since I have shown that there are completely solid indestructible particles of matter flying about through all eternity, let us unroll whether or not there is any limit to their number. Similarly, as we have found that there is a vacuum, the place or space in which things happen, let us see whether its whole extent is limited or whether it stretches far and wide into immeasurable depths.

Learn, therefore, that *the universe is not bounded in any direction.* If it were, it would necessarily have a limit somewhere. But clearly a thing cannot have a limit unless there is something outside to limit it, so that the eye can follow it up to a certain point but not beyond. Since you must admit that there is nothing outside the universe, it can have no limit and is accordingly without end or measure. It makes no odds in which part of it you may take your stand: whatever spot anyone may occupy, the universe stretches away from him just the same in all directions without limit. Suppose for a moment that the whole of space were bounded and that someone made his way to its uttermost boundary and threw a flying dart. Do you choose to suppose that the missile, hurled with might and main, would speed along the course on which it was aimed? Or do you think something would block the way and stop it? You must assume one alternative or the other. But neither of them leaves you a loophole. Both force you to admit that the universe continues without end. Whether there is some obstacle lying on the boundary line that prevents the dart from going farther on its course or whether it flies on beyond, it cannot in fact have started from the boundary. With this argument I will pursue you. Wherever you may place the ultimate limit of things, I will ask you: 'Well then, what does happen to the dart?' The upshot is that the boundary cannot stand firm anywhere, and final escape from this conclusion is precluded by the limitless possibility of running away from it.

Further, if all the space in the universe were shut in and confined on every side by definite boundaries, the supply of matter would already have accumulated by its own weight at the bottom, and nothing could happen under the dome of the sky—indeed, there would be no sky and no sunlight, since all the available matter would have settled down and would be lying in a heap throughout eternity. As it is, no rest is given to the atoms, because there is no bottom where they can accumulate and take up their abode. Things go on happening all the time through ceaseless movement in every direction; and atoms of matter bouncing up from below are supplied out of the infinite. Lastly it is a matter of observation that one thing is limited by another. The hills are demarcated by air, and air by the hills. Land sets bounds to sea, and sea to every land. But the universe has nothing outside to limit it. There is therefore a limitless abyss of space, such that even the dazzling flashes of the lightning cannot traverse it in their course, racing through an interminable tract of time, nor can they even shorten the distance still to be covered. So vast is the scope that lies open to things far and wide without limit in any dimension.

The universe is restrained from setting any limit to itself by nature, which compels body to be bounded by vacuum and vacuum by body. Thus nature either makes them both infinite in alternation, or else one of them, if it is not bounded by the other, must extend in a pure state without limit. kSpace, however, being infinite, so must matter be. Otherwisel neither sea nor land nor the bright zones of the sky nor mortal beings nor the holy bodies of the gods could endure for one brief hour of time. The supply of matter would be shaken loose from combination and swept through the vastness of the void in isolated particles; or rather, it would never have coalesced to form anything, since its scattered particles could never have been driven into union.

Certainly the atoms did not post themselves purposefully in due order by an act of intelligence, nor did they stipulate what movements each should perform. As they have been rushing everlastingly throughout all space in their myriads, undergoing a myriad changes under the disturbing impact of collisions, they have experienced every variety of movement and conjunction till they have fallen into the particular pattern by which this world of ours is constituted. This world has persisted many a long year, having once been set going in the appropriate motions. From these everything else follows. The rivers replenish the thirsty sea with profuse streams of water. Incubated by the sun's heat, the earth renews its fruits, and the brood of animals that springs from it grows lustily. The gliding fires of ether sustain their life. None of these results would be possible if there were not an ample supply of matter to bounce up out of infinite space in replacement of all that is lost. Just as animals deprived of food waste away through loss of body, so everything must decay as soon as its supply of matter goes astray and is cut off.

Whatever world the atoms have combined to form, impacts from without cannot preserve it at every point. By continual battering they can hold back part of it till others come along to make good the deficiency. But they are compelled now and then to bounce back and in so doing to leave ample space and time for the atoms to break free from combination. It is thus essential that there should be great numbers of atoms coming up. Indeed, the impacts themselves could not be maintained without an unlimited supply of matter from all quarters.

There is one belief, Memmius, that you must beware of entertaining—*the theory that everything tends towards what they call 'the centre of the universe'.* On this theory, the world stands fast without any impacts from without, and top and bottom cannot be parted in any direction, because everything has been tending towards the centre—if you can believe that anything rests upon itself. Whatever heavy bodies there may be under the earth must then tend upwards and rest against the surface upside down, like the images of things which we now see reflected in water. In the same way they would have it that animals walk about topsy-turvy and cannot fall off the earth into the nether quarters of the sky any more than our bodies can soar up spontaneously into the heavenly regions. When they are looking at the sun, we see the stars of night; so they share the hours with us alternately and experience nights corresponding to our days. But this is an idle fancy of fools who have got hold of the wrong end of the stick. There can be no centre in infinity. And, even if there were, nothing could stand fast there rather than flee from it. For all place or space, at the centre no less than elsewhere, must give way to heavy bodies, no matter in what direction they are moving. There is no place to which bodies can come where they lose the property of weight and stand still in the void. And vacuum cannot support anything but rather must allow it free passage, as its own nature demands. Therefore things cannot be held in combination by this means through surrender to a craving for the centre.

Besides, they do not claim that all bodies have this tendency towards the centre, but only those of moisture and earth—the waters of the deep and the floods that pour down from the hills and in general whatever is composed of a more or less earthy body. But according to their teaching the light breaths of air and hot fires are simultaneously wafted outwards away from the centre. The reason why the encircling ether twinkles with stars and the sun feeds its flames in the blue pastures of the sky is supposed to be that fire all congregates there in its flight from the centre. Similarly, the topmost branches of trees could not break into leaf unless their food had this same upward urge. kBut, if you allow matter to escape from the world in this way,l you are leaving the ramparts of the world at liberty to crumble of a sudden and take flight with the speed of flame into the boundless void. The rest will follow. The thunder-breeding quarters of the sky will rush down from aloft. The ground will fall away from our feet, its particles dissolved amid the mingled wreckage of heaven and earth. The whole world will vanish into the abyss, and in the twinkling of an eye no remnant will be left but empty space and invisible atoms. At whatever point you first allow matter to fall short, this will be the gateway to perdition. Through this gate the whole concourse of matter will come streaming out.

If you take a little trouble, you will attain to a thorough understanding of these truths. For one thing will be illumined by another, and eyeless night will not rob you of your road till you have looked into the heart of nature's darkest mysteries. So surely will facts throw light upon facts.

Book Two—Movements and Shapes of Atoms

What joy it is, when out at sea the stormwinds are lashing the waters, to gaze from the shore at the heavy stress some other man is enduring! Not that anyone's afflictions are in themselves a source of delight; but to realize from what troubles you yourself are free is joy indeed. What joy, again, to watch opposing hosts marshalled on the field of battle when you have yourself no part in their peril! But this is the greatest joy of all: to possess a quiet sanctuary, stoutly fortified by the teaching of the wise, and to gaze down from that elevation on others wandering aimlessly in search of a way of life, pitting their wits one against another, disputing for precedence, struggling night and day with unstinted effort to scale the pinnacles of wealth and power. O joyless hearts of men! O minds without vision! How dark and dangerous the life in which this tiny span is lived away! Do you not see that nature is barking for two things only, a body free from pain, a mind released from worry and fear for the enjoyment of pleasurable sensations?

So we find that the requirements of our bodily nature are few indeed, no more than is necessary to banish pain, and also to spread out many pleasures for ourselves. Nature does not periodically seek anything more gratifying than this, not complaining if there are no golden images of youths about the house, holding flaming torches in their right hands to illumine banquets prolonged into the night. What matter if the hall does not sparkle with silver and gleam with gold, and no carved and gilded rafters ring to the music of the lute? Nature does not miss these luxuries when men recline in company on the soft grass by a running stream under the branches of a tall tree and refresh their bodies pleasurably at small expense. Better still if the weather smiles upon them, and the season of the year stipples the green herbage with flowers. Burning fevers flee no swifter from your body if you toss under figured counterpanes and coverlets of crimson than if you must lie in rude homespun.

If our bodies are not profited by treasures or titles or the majesty of kingship, we must go on to admit that neither are our minds. Or tell me, Memmius, when you see your legions thronging the Campus Martius in the ardour of mimic warfare, supported by ample auxiliaries and a force of cavalry, magnificently armed and fired by a common purpose, does that sight scare the terrors of superstition from your mind? Does the fear of death retire from your breast and leave it carefree? Or do we not find such resources absurdly ineffective? The fears and anxieties that dog the human breast do not shrink from the clash of arms or the fierce rain of missiles. They stalk unabashed among princes and potentates. They are not awestruck by the gleam of gold or the bright sheen of purple robes.

Can you doubt then that this power rests with reason alone? All life is a struggle in the dark. As children in blank darkness tremble and start at everything, so we in broad daylight are oppressed at times by fears as baseless as those horrors which children imagine coming upon them in the dark. This dread and darkness of the mind cannot be dispelled by the sunbeams, the shining shafts of day, but only by an understanding of the outward form and inner workings of nature.

And now to business. I will explain *the motion by which the generative bodies of matter give birth to various things*, and, after they are born, dissolve them once more; the force that compels them to do this; and the power of movement through the boundless void with which they are endowed. It is for you to devote yourself attentively to my words.

Be sure that matter does not stick together in a solid mass. For we see that everything grows less and seems to melt away with the lapse of time and withdraw its old age from our eyes. And yet we see no diminution in the sum of things. This is because the bodies that are shed lessen the thing they leave but enlarge the thing they join; here they bring decay, there full bloom, but they do not settle. So the sum of things is perpetually renewed. Mortals live by mutual interchange. One race increases by another's decrease. The generations of living things pass in swift succession and like runners hand on the torch of life.

If you think that the atoms can stop and by their stopping generate new motions in things, you are wandering far from the path of truth. Since the atoms are moving freely through the void, they must all be kept in motion either by their own weight or on occasion by the impact of another atom. For it must often happen that two of them in their course knock together and immediately bounce apart in opposite directions, a natural consequence of their hardness and solidity and the absence of anything behind to stop them.

As a further indication that all particles of matter are on the move, remember that the universe is bottomless: there is no place where the atoms could come to rest. As I have already shown by various arguments and proved conclusively, space is without end or limit and spreads out immeasurably in all directions alike.

It clearly follows that no rest is given to the atoms in their course through the depths of space. Driven along in an incessant but variable movement, some of them bounce far apart after a collision while others recoil only a short distance from the impact. From those that do not recoil far, being driven into a closer union and held there by the entanglement of their interlocking shapes, are composed firmly rooted rock, the stubborn strength of steel and the like. Those others that move freely through larger tracts of space—few and far between, springing far apart and carried far by the rebound—these provide for us thin air and blazing sunlight. Besides these, there are many other atoms at large in empty space that have been thrown out of compound bodies and have nowhere even been granted admittance so as to bring their motions into harmony.

This process, as I might point out, is illustrated by an image of it that is continually taking place before our very eyes. Observe what happens when sunbeams are admitted into a building and shed light on its shadowy places. You will see a multitude of tiny particles mingling in a multitude of ways in the empty space within the actual light of the beam, as though contending in everlasting conflict, rushing into battle rank upon rank with never a moment's pause in a rapid sequence of unions and disunions. From this you may picture what it is for the atoms to be perpetually tossed about in the illimitable void. To some extent a small thing may afford an illustration and an imperfect image of great things. Besides, there is a further reason why you should give your mind to these particles that are seen dancing in a sunbeam: their dancing is an actual indication of underlying movements of matter that are hidden from sight. There you will see many particles under the impact of invisible blows changing their course and driven back upon their tracks, this way and that, in all directions. You must understand that they all derive this restlessness from the atoms. It originates with the atoms, which move of themselves. Then those small compound bodies that are least removed from the impetus of the atoms are set in motion by the impact of their invisible blows and in turn cannon against slightly larger blows. So the movement mounts up from the atoms and gradually emerges to the level of our senses, so that those bodies are in motion that we see in sunbeams, moved by blows that remain invisible.

And now, Memmius, as to the rate at which the atoms move, you may gauge this readily from these few indications. First, when dawn sprays the earth with new-born light and the birds, flitting through pathless thickets, fill the neighbourhood according to their kind with liquid notes that glide through the thin air, it is plain and palpable for all to see how suddenly the sun at the moment of his rising drenches and clothes the world with his radiance. But the heat and the bright light that the sun emits do not travel through empty space. Therefore they are forced to move more slowly, cleaving their way as it were through waves of air. And the atoms that compose this radiance do not travel as isolated individuals but linked and massed together. Thus their pace is retarded by one dragging back another as well as by external obstacles. But, when separate atoms are travelling in solitary solidity through empty space, they encounter no obstruction from without and move as single units, being composed of their own parts, on the course on which they have embarked. Obviously therefore they must far outstrip the sunlight in speed of movement and traverse an extent of space many times as great in the time it takes for the sun's rays to flash across the sky . . . kNo wonder that menl cannot follow the individual atoms, so as to discern the agency by which everything is brought about.

In the face of these truths, some people who know nothing of matter believe that nature without the guidance of the gods could not bring round the changing seasons in such perfect conformity to human needs, creating the crops and those other blessings that mortals are led to enjoy by the guide of life, divine pleasure, which coaxes them through the arts of Venus to reproduce their kind, lest the human race should perish. Obviously, in imagining that the gods established everything for the sake of men, they have stumbled in all respects far from the path of truth. Even if I knew nothing of the atoms, I would venture to assert on the evidence of the celestial phenomena themselves, supported by many other arguments, that the universe was certainly not created for us by divine power: it is so full of imperfections. All this, Memmius, I will elucidate for you at a later stage. Now let me complete my account of atomic movements.

Now, I should judge, is the place to insert a demonstration that *no material thing can be uplifted or travel upwards by its own power.* Do not be misled by the particles that compose flame. The fact that all weights taken by themselves tend downwards does not prevent lusty crops and trees from being born with an upward thrust and from growing and increasing upwards. Similarly, when fires leap up to the housetops and lick beams and rafters with rapid flame, it must not be supposed that they do this of their own accord with no force to fling them up. Their behavior is like that of blood released from our body when it spouts forth and springs aloft in a gory fountain. Observe also with what force beams and rafters are heaved up by water. The more we have shoved them down into the depths, many of us struggling strenuously together to push them under, the more eagerly the water spews and ejects them back again, so that more than half their bulk shoots up above the surface. And yet, I should judge, we have no doubt that all these, taken by themselves, would move downwards through empty space. It must be just the same with flames: under pressure they can shoot up through the gusty air, although their weight, taken by itself, strives to tug them down. Do you observe how the nocturnal torches of the sky in their lofty flight draw in their wake long trails of flame in whatever direction nature has set their course? Do you see how stars and meteors fall upon the earth? The sun from the summit of the sky scatters heat in all directions and sows the fields with light. The sun's radiance therefore tends also towards the earth. Note again how the lightning flies through the rain-storms aslant. The fires that break out of the clouds rush together, now this way, now that; often enough the fiery force falls upon the earth.

In this connection there is another fact that I want you to grasp. *When the atoms are travelling straight down through empty space by their own weight, at quite indeterminate times and places they swerve ever so little from their course*, just so much that you can call it a change of direction. If it were not for this swerve, everything would fall downwards like raindrops through the abyss of space. No collision would take place and no impact of atom upon atom would be created. Thus nature would never have created anything.

If anyone supposes that heavier atoms on a straight course through empty space could outstrip lighter ones and fall on them from above, thus causing impacts that might give rise to generative motions, he is going far astray from the path of truth. The reason why objects falling through water or thin air must accelerate their fall in proportion to their weight is simply that the matter composing water or air cannot obstruct all objects equally, but is forced to give way more speedily to heavier ones. But empty space can offer no resistance to any object in any quarter at any time, so as not to yield free passage as its own nature demands. Therefore, through undisturbed vacuum all bodies must travel at equal speed though impelled by unequal weights. The heavier will never be able to fall on the lighter from above or generate of themselves impacts leading to that variety of motions out of which nature can produce things. We are thus forced back to the conclusion that the atoms swerve a little—but only by a minimum, or we shall be caught imagining slantwise movements, and the facts will prove us wrong. For we see plainly and indisputably that weights, when they come tumbling down, have no power of their own to move aslant, so far as meets the eye. But who can possibly perceive that they do not diverge in the very least from a vertical course?

Again, if all movement is always interconnected, the new arising from the old in a determinate order—if the atoms never swerve so as to originate some new movement that will snap the bonds of fate, the everlasting sequence of cause and effect—what is the source of the free will possessed by living things throughout the earth? What, I repeat, is the source of that willpower snatched from the fates, whereby we follow the path along which we are severally led by pleasure, swerving from our course at no set time or place but at the bidding of our own hearts? There is no doubt that on these occasions the will of the individual originates the movements that trickle through his limbs. Observe, when the starting-barriers are flung back, how the racehorses in the eagerness of their strength cannot break away as suddenly as their hearts desire. For the whole supply of matter must first be mobilized throughout every member of the body: only then, when it is mustered in a continuous array, can it respond to the prompting of the heart. So you may see that the beginning of movement is generated by the heart; starting from the voluntary action of the mind, it is then transmitted throughout the body and the limbs. Quite different is our experience when we are shoved along by a blow inflicted with compulsive force by someone else. In that case it is obvious that all the matter of our body is set going and pushed along against our will, till a check is imposed through the limbs by the will. Do you see the difference? Although many men are driven by an external force and often constrained involuntarily to advance or to rush headlong, yet there is within the human breast something that can fight against this force and resist it. At its command the supply of matter is forced at times to take a new course through our limbs and joints or is checked in its course and brought once more to a halt. So also in the atoms you must recognize the same possibility: besides weight and impact there must be a third cause of movement, the source of this inborn power of ours, since we see that nothing can come out of nothing. For the weight of an atom prevents its movements from being completely determined by the impact of other atoms. But the fact that the mind itself has no internal necessity to determine its every act and compel it to suffer in helpless passivity—this is due to the slight swerve of the atoms at no determinate time or place.

The supply of matter in the universe was never more tightly packed than it is now, or more widely spaced out. For nothing is ever added to it or subtracted from it. It follows that the movement of atoms today is no different from what it was in bygone ages and always will be. So the things that have regularly come into being will continue to come into being in the same manner; they will be and grow and flourish so far as each is allowed by the laws of nature. The sum of things cannot be changed by any force. For there is no place into which any kind of matter might escape out of the universe or out of which some newly risen force could break into the universe and transform the whole nature of things and reverse their movements.

In this connection there is one fact that need occasion no surprise. *Although all the atoms are in motion, their totality appears to stand totally motionless,* except for such movements as particular objects may make with their own bodies. This is because the atoms all lie far below the range of our senses. Since they are themselves invisible, their movements must also elude observation. Indeed, even visible objects, when set at a distance, often disguise their movements. Often on a hillside fleecy sheep, as they crop their lush pasture, creep slowly onward, lured this way or that by grass that sparkles with fresh dew, while the full-fed lambs gaily frisk and butt. And yet, when we gaze from a distance, we see only a blur—a white patch stationary on the green hillside. Take another example. Mighty legions, waging mimic war, are thronging the plain with their manoeuvres. The dazzling sheen flashes to the sky and all around the earth is ablaze with bronze. Down below there sounds the tramp of mighty marching men's feet. A noise of shouting strikes upon the hills and reverberates to the celestial vault. Wheeling horsemen gallop hotfoot across the midst of the plain, till it quakes under the fury of their charge. And yet there is a vantage-ground high among the hills from which all these appear immobile—a blaze of light stationary upon the plain. . . .

Give your mind now to the true reasoning I have to unfold. A new fact is battling strenuously for access to your ears. A new aspect of the universe is striving to reveal itself. But no fact is so simple that it is not harder to believe than to doubt at the first presentation. Equally, there is nothing so mighty or so marvellous that the wonder it evokes does not tend to diminish in time. Take first the pure and undimmed lustre of the sky and all that it enshrines: the stars that roam across its surface, the moon and the surpassing splendour of the sunlight. If all these sights were now displayed to mortal view for the first time by a swift unforeseen revelation, what miracle could be recounted greater than this? What would men before the revelation have been less prone to conceive as possible? Nothing, surely. So marvellous would have been that sight—a sight which no one now, you will admit, thinks worthy of an upward glance into the luminous regions of the sky. So has satiety blunted the appetite of our eyes. Desist, therefore, from thrusting out reasoning from your mind because of its disconcerting novelty. Weigh it, rather, with discerning judgement. Then, if it seems to you true, give in. If it is false, gird yourself to oppose it. For the mind wants to discover by reasoning what exists in the infinity of space that lies out there, beyond the ramparts of this world—that region into which the intellect longs to peer and into which the free projection of the mind does actually extend its flight.

Here, then, is my first point. In all directions alike, on this side or that, upward or downward through the universe, there is no end. This I have shown, and indeed the fact proclaims itself aloud and the nature of space makes it crystal clear. Granted, then, that empty space extends without limit in every direction and that seeds innumerable in number are rushing on countless courses through an unfathomable universe under the impulse of perpetual motion, *it is in the highest degree unlikely that this earth and sky is the only one to have been created* and that all those particles of matter outside are accomplishing nothing. This follows from the fact that our world has been made by nature through the spontaneous and casual collision and the multifarious, accidental, random and purposeless congregation and coalescence of atoms whose suddenly formed combinations could serve on each occasion as the starting-point of substantial fabrics—earth and sea and sky and the races of living creatures. On every ground, therefore, you must admit that there exist elsewhere other clusters of matter similar to this one which the ether clasps in ardent embrace.

When there is plenty of matter in readiness, when space is available and no cause or circumstance impedes, then surely things must be wrought and effected. You have a store of atoms that could not be counted out by the whole population of living creatures throughout history. You have the same natural force to congregate them in any place precisely as they have been congregated here. You are bound therefore to acknowledge that in other regions there are other earths and various tribes of men and breeds of beasts.

Add to this the fact that nothing in the universe is the only one of its kind, unique and solitary in its birth and growth; everything is a member of a species comprising many individuals. Turn your mind first to the animals. You will find the rule applies to the brutes that prowl the mountains, to the double-breed of men, the voiceless scaly fish and all the forms of flying things. So you must admit that sky, earth, sun, moon, sea and the rest are not solitary, but rather numberless. For a firmly established limit is set to their lives also and their bodies also are a product of birth, no less than that of any creature that flourishes here according to its kind.

Bear this well in mind, and you will immediately perceive that *nature is free and uncontrolled by proud masters* and runs the universe by herself without the aid of gods. For who—by the sacred hearts of the gods who pass their unruffled lives, their placid aeon, in calm and peace!—who can rule the sum total of the measureless? Who can hold in coercive hand the strong reins of the unfathomable? Who can spin all the firmaments alike and foment with the fires of ether all the fruitful earths? Who can be in all places at all times, ready to darken the clear sky with clouds and rock it with a thunderclap— to launch bolts that may often wreck his own temples, or retire and spend his fury letting fly at deserts with that missile which often passes by the guilty and slays the innocent and blameless?

After the natal season of the world, the birthday of sea and lands and the uprising of the sun, many atoms have been added from without, many seeds contributed on every side by bombardment from the universe at large. From these the sea and land could gather increase: the dome of heaven could gain more room and lift its rafters high above the earth, and the air could climb upwards. From every corner of the universe atoms are being chipped and circulated to each thing according to its own kind: water goes to water, earth swells with earthy matter; fire is forged by fires, ether by ether. At length everything is brought to its utmost limit of growth by nature, the creatress and perfectress. This is reached when what is poured into the veins of life is no more than what flows and drains away. Here the growing-time of everything must halt. Here nature checks the increase of her own strength. The things you see growing merrily in stature and climbing the stairs of maturity step by step— these are gaining more atoms than they lose. The food is easily introduced into all their veins; and they themselves are not so widely expanded as to shed much matter and squander more than their age absorbs as nourishment. It must, of course, be conceded that many particles ebb and drain away from things. But more particles must accrue, until they have touched the topmost peak of growth. Thereafter the strength and vigour of maturity is gradually broken, and age slides down the path of decay. Obviously the bulkier anything is and the more expanded when it begins to wane, the more particles it sheds and gives off from every surface. The food is not easily distributed through all its veins, or supplied in sufficient quantities to make good the copious effluences it exudes. It is natural, therefore, that everything should perish when it is thinned out by the ebbing out of matter and succumbs to blows from without. The food supply is no longer adequate for its aged frame, and the deadly bombardment of particles from without never pauses in the work of dissolution and subdual.

In this way the ramparts of the great world also will be breached and collapse in crumbling ruin about us. For everything must be restored and renewed by food, and by food buttressed and sustained. And the process is doomed to failure, because the veins do not admit enough and nature does not supply all that is needed. Already the life-force is broken. The earth, which generated every living species and once brought forth from its womb the bodies of huge beasts, has now scarcely strength to generate tiny creatures. For I assume that the races of mortal creatures were not let down into the fields from heaven by a golden cord, nor generated from the sea or the rock-beating surf, but born of the same earth that now provides their nurture. The same earth in her prime spontaneously generated for mortals smiling crops and lusty vines, sweet fruits and gladsome pastures, which now can scarcely be made to grow by our toil. We wear down the oxen and wear out the strength of farmers, we wear out the ploughshare and find ourselves scarcely supplied by the fields that grudge their fruits and multiply our toil. Already the ploughman of ripe years shakes his head with many a sigh that his heavy labours have gone for nothing: and, when he compares the present with the past, he often applauds his father's luck. In the same despondent vein, the cultivator of old and wilted vines decries the trend of the times and rails at heaven. He grumbles that past generations, when men were old-fashioned and god-fearing, supported life easily enough on their small farms, though one man's holding was then far less than now. He does not realize that everything is gradually decaying and going aground onto the rocks, worn out by old age.

from *Elements*

Definitions, Postulates, Common Notions, and Propositions 1–3 from Book I

Euclid

Based on the Translation by Sir Thomas L. Heath

Book I

Definitions

1. A point is that which has no part.
2. A line is breadthless length.
3. The extremities of a line are points.
4. A straight line is a line which lies evenly with the points on itself.
5. A surface is that which has length and breadth only.
6. The extremities of a surface are lines.
7. A plane surface is a surface which lies evenly with the straight lines on itself.
8. A plane angle is the inclination to one another of two lines in a plane which meet one another and do not lie in a straight line.
9. And when the lines containing the angle are straight, the angle is called rectilineal.
10. When a straight line set up on a straight line makes the adjacent angles equal to one another, each of the equal angles is right, and the straight line standing on the other is called a perpendicular to that on which it stands.
11. An obtuse angle is an angle greater than a right angle.
12. An acute angle is an angle less than a right angle.
13. A boundary is that which is an extremity of anything.
14. A figure is that which is contained by any boundary or boundaries.

15. A circle is a plane figure contained by one line such that all the straight lines falling upon it from one point among those lying within the figure are equal to one another;
16. And the point is called the center of the circle.
17. A diameter of the circle is any straight line drawn through the center and terminated in both directions by the circumference of the circle, and such a straight line also bisects the circle.
18. A semicircle is the figure contained by the diameter and the circumference cut off by it. And the center of the semicircle is the same as that of the circle.
19. Rectilineal figures are those which are contained by straight lines, trilateral figures being those contained by three, quadrilateral those contained by four, and multilateral those contained by more than four straight lines.
20. Of trilateral figures, an equilateral triangle is that which has its three sides equal, an isosceles triangle that which has two of its sides alone equal, and a scalene triangle is that which has its sides unequal.
21. Further, of trilateral figures, a right-angled triangle is that which has a right angle, an obtuse-angled triangle that which has an obtuse angle, and an acute-angled triangle that which has its three angles acute.
22. Of quadrilateral figures, a square is that which is both equilateral and right-angled; an oblong that which is right-angled but not equilateral; a rhombus that which is equilateral but not right-angled; and a rhomboid that which has its opposite sides and angles equal to one another but is neither equilateral nor right-angled. And let quadrilaterals other than these be called trapezia.
23. Parallel straight lines are straight lines which, being in the same plane and being produced indefinitely in both directions, do not meet one another in either direction.

Postulates

Let the following be postulated:

1. To draw a straight line from any point to any point.
2. To produce a finite straight line continuously in a straight line.
3. To describe a circle with any center and distance.

4. That all right angles are equal to one another.
5. That, if a straight line falling on two straight lines makes the interior angles on the same side less than two right angles, the two straight lines, if produced indefinitely, meet on that side on which are the angles less than the two right angles.

Common Notions

1. Things which are equal to the same thing are also equal to one another.
2. If equals be added to equals, the wholes are equal.
3. If equals be subtracted from equals, the remainders are equal.
4. Things which coincide with one another are equal to one another.
5. The whole is greater than the part.

Propositions

Proposition 1

On a given finite straight line to construct an equilateral triangle.

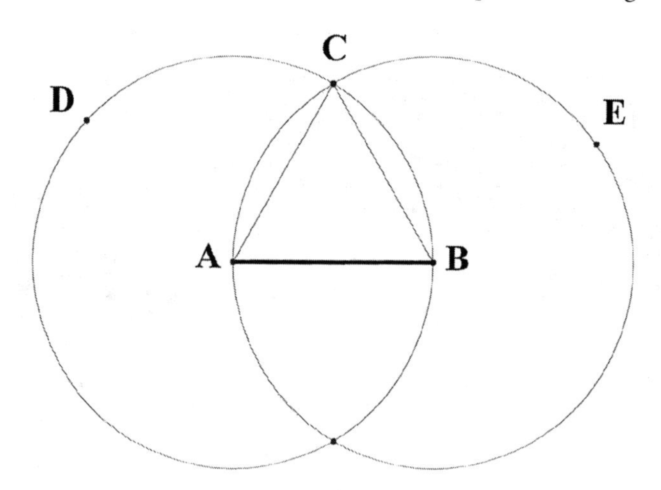

Let AB be the given finite straight line.

Thus it is required to construct an equilateral triangle on the straight line AB.

With center A and distance AB let the circle BCD be described; again, with center B and distance BA let the circle ACE be described; and from the point C, in which the circles cut one another, to the points A, B let the straight lines CA, CB be joined.

Now, since the point A is the center of the circle CDB,

AC is equal to AB.

Again, since the point B is the center of the circle CAE,

BC is equal to BA.

But CA was also proved equal to AB; therefore each of the straight lines CA, CB is equal to AB.

And things which are equal to the same thing are also equal to one another;

therefore CA is also equal to CB.

Therefore the three straight lines CA, AB, BC are equal to one another.

Therefore the triangle ABC is equilateral; and it has been constructed on the given finite straight line AB, (being) what it was required to do.

Proposition 2

To place at a given point (as an extremity) a straight line equal to a given straight line.

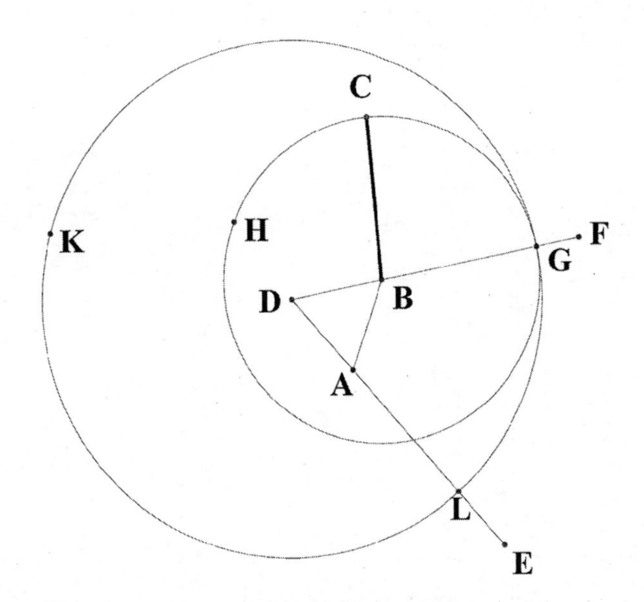

Let A be the given point, and BC the given straight line.

Thus it is required to place at the point A (as an extremity) a straight line equal to the given straight line BC.

From the point A to the point B let the straight line AB be joined; and on it let the equilateral triangle DAB be constructed.

Let the straight lines AE, BF be produced in a straight line with DA, DB; with center B and distance BC let the circle CGH be described; and again, with center D and distance DG let the circle GKL be described.

Then, since the point B is the center of the circle CGH,

BC is equal to BG.

Again, since the point D is the center of the circle GKL,

DL is equal to DG.

And in these DA is equal to DB;

therefore the remainder AL is equal to the remainder BG.

But BC was also proved equal to BG;

therefore each of the straight lines AL, BC is equal to BG.

And things which are equal to the same thing are also equal to one another;

therefore AL is also equal to BC.

Therefore at the given point A the straight line AL is placed equal to the given straight line BC, (being) what it was required to do.

Proposition 3

Given two unequal straight lines, to cut off from the greater a straight line equal to the less.

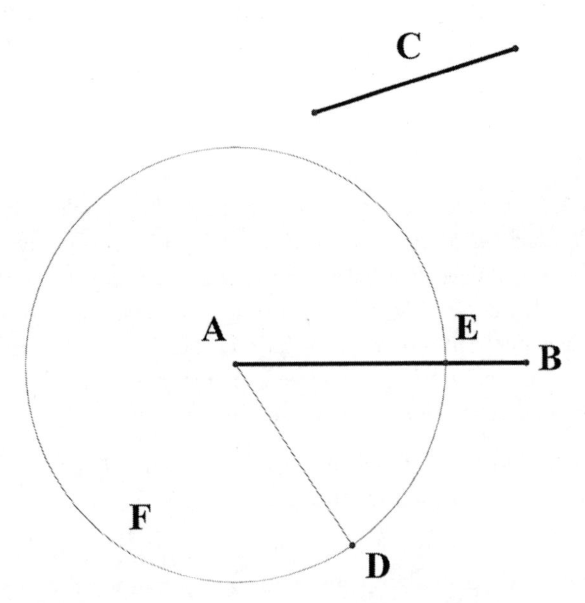

Let AB, C be the two given unequal straight lines and let AB be the greater of them.

Thus it is required to cut off from AB the greater a straight line equal to C the less.

At the point A let AD be placed equal to the straight line C; and with center A and distance AD let the circle DEF be described.

Now, since the point A is the center of the circle DEF,

AE is equal to AD.

But C is also equal to AD.

Therefore each of the straight lines AE, C is equal to AD;

so that AE is also equal to C.

Therefore, given the two straight lines AB, C, from AB the greater AE has been cut off equal to C the less, (being) what it was required to do.

from *Meditations*

Marcus Aurelius

Book 4

Wherever it is in agreement with nature, the ruling power within us takes a flexible approach to circumstances, always adapting itself easily to both practicality and the given event. It has no favoured material for its work, but sets out on its objects in a conditional way, turning any obstacle into material for its own use. It is like a fire mastering whatever falls into it. A small flame would be extinguished, but a bright fire rapidly claims as its own all that is heaped on it, devours it all, and leaps up yet higher in consequence.

No action should be undertaken without aim, or other than in conformity with a principle affirming the art of life.

Men seek retreats for themselves—in the country, by the sea, in the hills—and you yourself are particularly prone to this yearning. But all this is quite unphilosophic, when it is open to you, at any time you want, to retreat into yourself. No retreat offers someone more quiet and relaxation than that into his own mind, especially if he can dip into thoughts there which put him at immediate and complete ease: and by ease I simply mean a well-ordered life. So constantly give yourself this retreat, and renew yourself. The doctrines you will visit there should be few and fundamental, sufficient at one meeting to wash away all your pain and send you back free of resentment at what you must rejoin.

And what is it you will resent? Human wickedness? Recall the conclusion that rational creatures are born for each other's sake, that tolerance is a part of justice, that wrongdoing is not deliberate. Consider the number of people who spent their lives in enmity, suspicion, hatred, outright war, and were then laid out for burial or reduced to ashes. Stop, then. Or will you fret at your allocation from the Whole? Revisit the alternatives—providence or atoms—and the many indications that the universe is a kind of community. But will matters of the flesh still have their hold on you? Consider that the mind, once it has abstracted itself and come to know its own defining power, has no contact with the movement of the bodily spirit, be that smooth or troubled: and finally remember all that you have heard and agreed about pain and pleasure.

Well then, will a little fame distract you? Look at the speed of universal oblivion, the gulf of immeasurable time both before and after, the vacuity of applause, the indiscriminate fickleness of your apparent supporters, the tiny room in which all this is confined. The whole earth is a mere point in space: what a minute cranny within this is your own habitation, and how many and what sort will sing your praises here!

Finally, then, remember this retreat into your own little territory within yourself. Above all, no agonies, no tensions. Be your own master, and look at things as a man, as a human being, as a citizen, as a mortal creature. And here are two of the most immediately useful thoughts you will dip into. First that *things* cannot touch the mind: they are external and inert; anxieties can only come from your internal judgement. Second, that all these things you see will change almost as you look at them, and then will be no more. Constantly bring to mind all that you yourself have already seen changed. The universe is change: life is judgement.

If mind is common to us all, then we have reason also in common—that which makes us rational beings. If so, then common too is the reason which dictates what we should or should not do. If so, then law too is common to us all. If so, then we are citizens. If so, we share in a constitution. If so, the universe is a kind of community. In what else could one say that the whole human race shares a common constitution?

From there, then, this common city, we take our very mind, our reason, our law—from where else? Just as the earthy part of me has been derived from some earth, the watery from the next element, the air of my breath from some other source, the hot and fiery from its own origin (for nothing comes from nothing, nor returns to nothing)—so the mind also has its source.

Death, just like birth, is a mystery of nature: first a combination, then a dissolution, of the same elements. Certainly no cause for shame: because nothing out of the order for an intelligent being or contrary to the principle of his constitution.

With such people such an outcome is both natural and inevitable—if you wish it otherwise you are hoping that figs will no longer produce their rennet. In any case remember that in a very brief time both you and he will be dead, and shortly after not even your names will be left.

Remove the judgement, and you have removed the thought 'I am hurt': remove the thought 'I am hurt', and the hurt itself is removed.

What does not make a human being worse in himself cannot make his life worse either: it cannot harm him from outside or inside.

The nature of the beneficial was bound to act thus.

'All's right that happens in the world.' Examine this saying carefully, and you will find it true. I do not mean 'right' simply in the context of cause and effect, but in the sense of 'just'—as if some adjudicator were assigning dues. So keep on observing this, as you have started, and in all that you do combine doing it with being a good man, in the specific conception of 'good man'. Preserve this in every sphere of action.

When someone does you wrong, do not judge things as he interprets them or would like *you* to interpret them. Just see them as they are, in plain truth.

Always have these two principles in readiness. First, to do only what the reason inherent in kingly and judicial power prescribes for the benefit of mankind. Second, to change your ground, if in fact there is someone to correct and guide you away from some notion. But this transference must always spring from a conviction of justice or the common good: and your preferred course must be likewise, not simply for apparent pleasure or popularity.

'Do you possess reason?' 'I do.' 'Why not use it then? With reason doing its job, what else do you want?'

You have subsisted as a part of the Whole. You will vanish into that which gave you birth: or rather you will be changed, taken up into the generative principle of the universe.

Many grains of incense on the same altar. One falls to ash first, another later: no difference.

Within ten days you will be regarded as a god by those very people who now see you as beast or baboon—if you return to your principles and the worship of Reason.

No, you do not have thousands of years to live. Urgency is on you. While you live, while you can, become good.

What ease of mind, you gain from not looking at what your neighbour has said or done or thought, but only at your own actions, to make them just, reverential, imbued with good! So do not glance at the black characters either side, but run right on to the line: straight, not straggly.

One who is all in a flutter over his subsequent fame fails to imagine that all those who remember him will very soon be dead—and he too. Then the same will be true of all successors, until the whole memory of him will be extinguished in a sequence of lamps lit and snuffed out. But suppose immortality in those who will remember you, and everlasting memory. Even so, what is that to you? And I do not simply mean that this is nothing to the dead, but to the living also what is the point of praise, other than for some practical aspect of management?

As it is, you are losing the opportunity of that gift of nature which does not depend on another's word. So . . .

Everything in any way beautiful has its beauty of itself, inherent and self-sufficient: praise is no part of it. At any rate, praise does not make anything better or worse. This applies even to the popular conception of beauty, as in material things or works or art. So does the truly beautiful need anything beyond itself? No more than law, no more than truth, no more than kindness or integrity. Which of these things derives its beauty from praise, or withers under criticism? Does an emerald lose its quality if it is not praised? And what of gold, ivory, purple, a lyre, a dagger, a flower, a bush?

You may ask how, if souls live on, the air can accommodate them all from the beginning of time. Well, how does the earth accommodate all those bodies buried in it over the same eternity? Just as here on earth, once bodies have kept their residence for whatever time, their change and decomposition makes room for other bodies, so it is with souls migrated to the air. They continue for a time, then change, dissolve, and take fire as they are assumed into the generative principle of the Whole: in this way they make room for successive residents. Such would be one's answer on the assumption that souls do live on.

We should consider, though, not only the multitude of bodies thus buried, but also the number of animals eaten every day by us and other creatures—a huge quantity consumed and in a sense buried in the bodies of those who feed on them. And yet there is room for them, because they are reduced to blood and changed into the elements of air and fire.

How to investigate the truth of this? By distinguishing the material and the causal.

No wandering. In every impulse, give what is right: in every thought, stick to what is certain.

Universe, your harmony is my harmony: nothing in your good time is too early or too late for me. Nature, all that your seasons bring is fruit to me: all comes from you, exists in you, returns to you. The poet says, 'Dear city of Cecrops': will you not say, 'Dear city of Zeus'?

'If you want to be happy', says Democritus, 'do little.' May it not be better to do what is necessary, what the reason of a naturally social being demands, and the way reason demands it done? This brings the happiness both of right action and of little action. Most of what we say and do is unnecessary: remove the superfluity, and you will have more time and less bother. So in every case one should prompt oneself: 'Is this, or is it not, something necessary?' And the removal of the unnecessary should apply not only to actions but to thoughts also: then no redundant actions either will follow.

Try out too how the life of the good man goes for you—the man content with his dispensation from the Whole, and satisfied in his own just action and kind disposition.

You have seen that: now look at this. Do not trouble yourself, keep yourself simple. Someone does wrong? He does wrong to himself. Has something happened to you? Fine. All that happens has been fated by the Whole from the beginning and spun for your own destiny. In sum, life is short: make your gain from the present moment with right reason and justice. Keep sober and relaxed.

Either an ordered universe, or a stew of mixed ingredients, yet still coherent order. Otherwise how could a sort of private order subsist within you, if there is disorder in the Whole? Especially given that all things, distinct as they are, nevertheless permeate and respond to each other.

A black character, an effeminate, unbending character, the character of a brute or dumb animal: infantile, stupid, fraudulent, coarse, mercenary, despotic.

If one who does not recognize the contents of the universe is a stranger in it, no less a stranger is the one who fails to recognize what happens in it. He is a fugitive if he runs away from social principle; blind, if he shuts the eye of the mind; a beggar, if he depends on others and does not possess within him all he needs for life; a tumour on the universe, if he stands aside and separates himself from the principle of our common nature in disaffection with his lot (for it is nature which brings this about, just as it brought you about too); a social splinter, if he splits his own soul away from the soul of all rational beings, which is a unity.

One philosopher has no shirt, one has no book. Here is another half-naked: 'I have no bread', he says, 'but I am faithful to Reason.' But I for my part have all the food of learning, and yet I am not faithful.

Love the art which you have learnt, and take comfort in it. Go through the remainder of your life in sincere commitment of all your being to the gods, and never making yourself tyrant or slave to any man.

Consider, for example, the time of Vespasian. You will see everything the same. People marrying, having children, falling ill, dying, fighting, feasting, trading, farming, flattering, pushing, suspecting, plotting, praying for the death of others, grumbling at their lot, falling in love, storing up wealth, longing for consulships and kingships. And now that life of theirs is gone, vanished.

Pass on again to the time of Trajan. Again, everything the same. That life too is dead.

Similarly, look at the histories of other eras and indeed whole nations, and see how many lives of striving met with a quick fall and resolution into the elements. Above all, review in your mind those you have seen yourself in empty struggles, refusing to act in accord with their own natural constitution, to hold tight to it and find it sufficient. And in this context you must remember that there is proportionate value in our attention to each action—so you will not lose heart if you devote no more time than they warrant to matters of less importance.

"Words in common use long ago are obsolete now. So too the names of those once famed are in a sense obsolete—Camillus, Caeso, Volesus, Dentatus; a little later Scipio and Cato, then Augustus too, then Hadrian and Antoninus. All things fade and quickly turn to myth: quickly too utter oblivion drowns them. And I am talking of those who shone with some wonderful brilliance: the rest, once they have breathed their last, are immediately 'beyond sight, beyond knowledge'. But what in any case is everlasting memory? Utter emptiness.

So where should a man direct his endeavour? Here only—a right mind, action for the common good, speech incapable of lies, a disposition to welcome all that happens as necessary, intelligible, flowing from an equally intelligible spring of origin.

Gladly surrender yourself to Clotho: let her spin your thread into whatever web she wills.

All is ephemeral, both memory and the object of memory.

Constantly observe all that comes about through change, and habituate yourself to the thought that the nature of the Whole loves nothing so much as to change one form of existence into another, similar but new. All that exists is in a sense the seed of its successor: but your concept of 'seed' is simply what is put into the earth or the womb—that is very unphilosophic thinking.

Your death will soon be on you: and you are not yet clear-minded, or untroubled, or free from the fear of external harm; or kindly to all people, or convinced that justice of action is the only wisdom.

Look into their directing minds: observe what even the wise will avoid or pursue.

Harm to you cannot subsist in another's directing mind, nor indeed in any turn or change of circumstance. Where, then? In that part of you which judges harm. So no such judgement, and all is well. Even if what is closest to it, your own body, is subjected to knife or cautery, or left to suppurate or mortify, even so that faculty in you which judges these things should stay untroubled. That is, it should assess nothing either bad or good which can happen equally to the bad man or the good: because what can happen to a man irrespective of his life's conformity to nature is not of itself either in accordance with nature or contrary to it.

Think always of the universe as one living creature, comprising one substance and one soul: how all is absorbed into this one consciousness; how a single impulse governs all its actions; how all things collaborate in all that happens; the very web and mesh of it all.

You are a soul carrying a corpse, as Epictetus used to say.

Change: nothing inherently bad in the process, nothing inherently good in the result.

There is a river of creation, and time is a violent stream. As soon as one thing comes into sight, it is swept past and another is carried down: it too will be taken on its way.

All that happens is as habitual and familiar as roses in spring and fruit in the summer. True too of disease, death, defamation, and conspiracy—and all that delights or gives pain to fools.

What comes after is always in affinity to what went before. Not some simple enumeration of disparate things and a merely necessary sequence, but a rational connection: and just as existing things are harmoniously interconnected, so the processes of becoming exhibit no mere succession, but a wonderfully inherent affinity.

Always remember Heraclitus: 'The death of earth is the birth of water; the death of water is the birth of air; the death of air is fire, and back again.' Remember too his image of the man who forgets his way home; his saying that men are at odds with their most constant companion, the Reason which governs all things; that their everyday experience takes them by surprise; that we must not act or speak as if asleep, and sleep brings the illusion of speech and action; and that we should not be like children with their parents, simply accepting what we are told.

Just as if a god told you that you would die tomorrow or at least the day after tomorrow, you would attach no importance to the difference of one day, unless you are a complete coward (such is the tiny gap of time): so you should think there no great difference between life to the umpteenth year and life to tomorrow.

Think constantly how many doctors have died, after knitting their brows over their own patients; how many astrologers, after predicting the deaths of others, as if death were something important; how many philosophers, after endless deliberation on death or immortality; how many heroes, after the many others they killed; how many tyrants, after using their power over men's lives with monstrous insolence, as if they themselves were immortal. Think too how many whole cities have 'died'—Helice, Pompeii, Herculaneum, innumerable others. Go over now all those you have known yourself, one after the other: one man follows a friend's funeral and is then laid out himself, then another follows him—and all in a brief space of time. The conclusion of this? You should always look on human life as short and cheap. Yesterday sperm: tomorrow a mummy or ashes.

So one should pass through this tiny fragment of time in tune with nature, and leave it gladly, as an olive might fall when ripe, blessing the earth which bore it and grateful to the tree which gave it growth.

Be like the rocky headland on which the waves constantly break. It stands firm, and round it the seething waters are laid to rest.

'It is my bad luck that this has happened to me.' No, you should rather say: 'It is my good luck that, although this has happened to me, I can bear it without pain, neither crushed by the present nor fearful of the future.' Because such a thing could have happened to any man, but not every man could have borne it without pain. So why see more misfortune in the event than good fortune in your ability to bear it? Or in general would you call anything a misfortune for a man which is not a deviation from man's nature? Or anything a deviation from man's nature which is not contrary to the purpose of his nature? Well, then. You have learnt what that purpose is. Can there be anything, then, in this happening which prevents you being just, high-minded, self-controlled, intelligent, judicious, truthful, honourable and free—or any other of those attributes whose combination is the fulfilment of man's proper nature? So in all future events which might induce sadness remember to call on this principle: 'this is no misfortune, but to bear it true to yourself is good fortune.'

An unphilosophic but nonetheless effective help to putting death in its place is to run over the list of those who have clung long to life. What did they gain over the untimely dead? At any rate they are all in their graves by now—Caedicianus, Fabius, Julianus, Lepidus, and all others like them who took part in many funerals and then their own. In truth, the distance we have to travel is small: and we drag it out with such labour, in such poor company, in such a feeble body. No great thing, then. Look behind you at the huge gulf of time, and another infinity ahead. In this perspective what is the difference between an infant of three days and a Nestor of three generations?

Always run on the short road: and nature's road is short. Go then for the healthiest in all you say and do. Such a purpose releases a man from the labours of service, from all need to manage or impress.

Book 5

At break of day, when you are reluctant to get up, have this thought ready to mind: 'I am getting up for a man's work. Do I still then resent it, if I am going out to do what I was born for, the purpose for which I was brought into the world? Or was I created to wrap myself in blankets and keep warm?' 'But this is more pleasant.' Were you then born for pleasure—all for feeling, not for action? Can you not see plants, birds, ants, spiders, bees all doing their own work, each helping in their own way to order the world? And then you do not want to do the work of a human being—you do not hurry to the demands of your own nature. 'But one needs rest too.' One does indeed: I agree. But nature has set limits to this too, just as it has to eating and drinking, and yet you go beyond these limits, beyond what you need. Not in your actions, though, not any longer: here you stay below your capability.

The point is that you do not love yourself—otherwise you would love both your own nature and her purpose for you. Other men love their own pursuit and absorb themselves in its performance to the exclusion of bath and food: but you have less regard for your own nature than the smith has for his metal-work, the dancer for his dancing, the money-grubber for his money, the exhibitionist for his little moment of fame. Yet these people, when impassioned, give up food and sleep for the promotion of their pursuits: and you think social action less important, less worthy of effort?

How easy it is to drive away or obliterate from one's mind every impression which is troublesome or alien, and then to be immediately in perfect calm.

Judge yourself entitled to any word or action which is in accord with nature, and do not let any subsequent criticism or persuasion from anyone talk you out of it. No, if it was a good thing to do or say, do not revoke your entitlement. Those others are guided by their own minds and pursue their own impulses. Do not be distracted by any of this, but continue straight ahead, following your own nature and universal nature: these two have one and the same path.

I travel on by nature's path until I fall and find rest, breathing my last into that air from which I draw my daily breath, and falling on that earth which gave my father his seed, my mother her blood, my nurse her milk; the earth which for so many years has fed and watered me day by day; the earth which bears my tread and all the ways in which I abuse her.

They cannot admire you for intellect. Granted—but there are many other qualities of which you cannot say, 'but that is not the way I am made'. So display those virtues which are wholly in your own power—integrity, dignity, hard work, self-denial, contentment, frugality, kindness, independence, simplicity, discretion, magnanimity. Do you not see how many virtues you can already display without any excuse of lack of talent or aptitude? And yet you are still content to lag behind. Or does the fact that you have no inborn talent oblige you to grumble, to scrimp, to toady, to blame your poor body, to suck up, to brag, to have your mind in such turmoil? No, by heaven, it does not! You could have got rid of all this long ago, and only be charged—if charge there is—with being rather slow and dull of comprehension. And yet even this can be worked on—unless you ignore or welcome your stupidity.

One sort of person, when he has done a kindness to another, is quick also to chalk up the return due to him. A second is not so quick in that way, but even so he privately thinks of the other as his debtor, and is well aware of what he has done. A third sort is in a way not even conscious of his action, but is like the vine which has produced grapes and looks for nothing else once it has borne its own fruit. A horse that has raced, a dog that has tracked, a bee that has made honey, and a man that has done good—none of these knows what they have done, but they pass on to the next action, just as the vine passes on to bear grapes again in due season. So you ought to be one of those who, in a sense, are unconscious of the good they do. 'Yes', he says, 'but this is precisely what one should be conscious of: because it defines the social being to be aware of his social action, and indeed to want his fellow to be aware of it also.' 'True, but you misunderstand the point I am now making: and for that reason you will fall into one of the first categories I mentioned. They too are misled by some sort of plausible logic. But if you want to follow my meaning, don't fear that this will lead you to any deficiency of social action.'

A prayer of the Athenian people:

> Rain, rain, dear Zeus:
> rain on the cornfields
> and the plains of Athens.

Prayer should be thus simple and open, or not at all.

Just as it is commonly said that Asclepius has prescribed someone horse-riding, or cold baths, or walking barefoot, so we could say that the nature of the Whole has prescribed him disease, disablement, loss, or any other such affliction. In the first case 'prescribed' means something like this: 'ordered this course for this person as conducive to his health'. In the second the meaning is that what happens to each individual is somehow arranged to conduce to his destiny. We speak of the fitness of these happenings as masons speak of the 'fit' of squared stones in walls or pyramids, when they join each other in a defined relation.

In the whole of things there is one harmony: and just as all material bodies combine to make the world one body, a harmonious whole, so all causes combine to make Destiny one harmonious cause. Even quite unsophisticated people intuit what I mean. They say: 'Fate brought this on him.' Now if 'brought', also 'prescribed'. So let us accept these prescriptions just as we accept those of Asclepius—many of them too are harsh, but we welcome them in the hope of health.

You should take the same view of the process and completion of the design of universal nature as you do of your own health: and so welcome all that happens to you, even if it seems rather cruel, because its purpose leads to the health of the universe and the prosperity and success of Zeus. He would not bring this on anyone, if it did not also bring advantage to the Whole: no more than any given natural principle brings anything inappropriate to what it governs.

So there are two reasons why you should be content with your experience. One is that this has happened to you, was prescribed for you, and is related to you, a thread of destiny spun for you from the first by the most ancient causes. The second is that what comes to each individual is a determining part of the welfare, the perfection, and indeed the very coherence of that which governs the Whole. Because the complete Whole is maimed if you sever even the tiniest fraction of its connection and continuity: this is true of its constituent parts, and true likewise of its causes. And you do sever something, to the extent that you can, whenever you fret at your lot: this is, in a sense, a destruction.

Do not give up in disgust or impatience if you do not find action on the right principles consolidated into a habit in all that you do. No: if you have taken a fall, come bade again, and be glad if most of your actions are on the right side of humanity. And love what you return to. Do not come back to philosophy as schoolboy to tutor, but rather as a man with ophthalmia returns to his sponge and salve, or another to his poultice or lotion. In this way you will prove that obedience to reason is no great burden, but a source of relief. Remember too that philosophy wants only what your nature wants: whereas you were wanting something unnatural to you. Now what could be more agreeable than the needs of your own nature? This is the same way that pleasure trips us: but look and see whether there is not something more agreeable in magnanimity, generosity, simplicity, consideration, piety. And what is more agreeable than wisdom itself, when you reflect on the sure and constant flow of our faculty for application and understanding?

Realities are wrapped in such a veil (as it were) that several philosophers of distinction have thought them altogether beyond comprehension, while even the Stoics think them hard to comprehend. And every assent we may give to our perceptions is fallible: the infallible man does not exist. Pass, then, to the very objects of our experience—how short-lived they are, how shoddy: a catamite, a whore, a thief could own them. Go on now to the characters of your fellows: it is hard to tolerate even the best of them, not to speak of one's difficulty in enduring even oneself.

In all this murk and dirt, in all this flux of being, time, movement, things moved, I cannot begin to see what on earth there is to value or even to aim for. Rather the opposite: one should console oneself with the anticipation of natural release, not impatient of its delay, but taking comfort in just these two thoughts. One, that nothing will happen to me which is not in accordance with the nature of the Whole: the other, that it is in my control to do nothing contrary to my god and the divinity within me—no one can force me to this offence.

To what use, then, am I now putting my soul? Ask yourself this question on every occasion. Examine yourself. 'What do I now have in this part of me called the directing mind? What sort of soul do I have after all? Is it that of a child? A boy? A woman? A despot? A beast of the field? A wild animal?'

Here is a way to understand what sort of things the majority take to be 'goods'. If you think of the true goods there are—wisdom, for example, self-control, justice, courage—with these in your mind you could not give any credence to the popular saying of 'too many goods to make room', because it will not apply. But bearing in mind what the majority see as goods you will hear and readily accept what the comic poet says as a fair comment. Even the majority can intuit this difference. Otherwise this saying would not both cause offence and rejection, while at the same time we take it as a telling and witty comment on wealth and the privileges of luxury and fame. Go on, then, and ask whether we should value and judge as goods those things which, when we have thought of them, would properly apply to their owner the saying, 'He is so rich, he has no room to shit.'

I am made up of the causal and the material. Neither of these will disappear into nothing, just as neither came to be out of nothing. So every part of me will be assigned its changed place in some part of the universe, and that will change again into another part of the universe, and so on to infinity. A similar sequence of change brought me into existence, and my parents before me, and so back in another infinity of regression. Nothing forbids this assertion, even if the universe is subject to the completion of cycles.

Reason and the art of reasoning are faculties self-determined by their own nature and their own products. They start from the relevant premise and follow the path to the proposed end. That is why acts of reason are called 'right' acts, signifying the rightness of the path thus followed.

One should pay no attention to any of those things which do not belong to man's portion incumbent on him as a human being. They are not demanded of a man; man's nature does not proclaim them; they are not consummations of that nature. Therefore they do not constitute man's end either, nor yet any means to that end—that is, good. Further, if any of these things were incumbent on a man, then it would not have been incumbent on him to disdain or resist them; we would not commend the man who shows himself free from need of them; if these things were truly 'goods', a man who fails to press for his full share of any of them could not be a good man. But in fact the more a man deprives himself of these or suchlike, or tolerates others depriving him, the better a man he is.

Your mind will take on the character of your most frequent thoughts: souls are dyed by thoughts. So dye your own with a succession of thoughts like these. For example: where life can be lived, so can a good life; but life can be lived in a palace; therefore a good life can be lived in a palace. Again: each creature is made in the interest of another; its course is directed to that for which it was made; its end lies in that to which its course is directed; and where its end is, there also for each is its benefit and its good. It follows that the good of a rational creature is community. It has long been shown that we are born for community—or was it riot clear that inferior creatures are made in the interest of the superior, and the superior in the interest of each other? But animate is superior to inanimate, and rational to the merely animate.

To pursue the impossible is madness: and it is impossible for bad men not to act in character.

Nothing happens to any creature beyond its own natural endurance. Another has the same experience as you: either through failure to recognize what has happened to him, or in a display of courage, he remains calm and untroubled. Strange, then, that ignorance and pretension should be stronger than wisdom.

Things of themselves cannot touch the soul at all. They have no entry to the soul, and cannot turn or move it. The soul alone turns and moves itself, making all externals presented to it cohere with the judgements it thinks worthy of itself.

In one respect man is something with the closest affinity to us, in that it is our duty to do good to men and tolerate them. But in so far as some are obstacles to my proper work, man joins the category of things indifferent to me—no less than the sun, the wind, a wild animal. These can impede some activity, yes, but they form no impediments to my impulse or my disposition, because here there is conditional commitment and the power of adaptation. The mind adapts and turns round any obstacle to action to serve its objective: a hindrance to a given work is turned to its furtherance, an obstacle in a given path becomes an advance.

Revere the ultimate power in the universe: this is what makes use of all things and directs all things. But similarly revere the ultimate power in yourself: this is akin to that other power. In you too this is what makes use of all else, and your life is governed by it.

What is not harmful to the city does not harm the citizen either. Whenever you imagine you have been harmed, apply this criterion: if the city is not harmed by this, then I have not been harmed either. If on the other hand harm is done to the city, you should not be angry, but demonstrate to the doer of this harm what he has failed to see himself.

Reflect often on the speed with which all things in being, or coming into being, are carried past and swept away. Existence is like a river in ceaseless flow, its actions a constant succession of change, its causes innumerable in their variety: scarcely anything stands still, even what is most immediate. Reflect too on the yawning gulf of past and future time, in which all things vanish. So in all this it must be folly for anyone to be puffed with ambition, racked in struggle, or indignant at his lot—as if this was anything lasting or likely to trouble him for long.

Think of the whole of existence, of which you are the tiniest part; think of the whole of time, in which you have been assigned a brief and fleeting moment; think of destiny—what fraction of that are you?

Another does wrong. What is that to me? Let him see to it: he has his own disposition, his own action. I have now what universal nature wishes me to have now, and do what my own nature wishes me to do now.

The directing and sovereign part of your soul must stay immune to any current in the flesh, either smooth or troubled, and keep its independence: it must define its own sphere and confine those affections to the parts they affect. When, though, as must happen in a composite unity, these affections are transmitted to the mind along the reverse route of sympathy, then you must not try to deny the perception of them: but your directing mind must not of itself add any judgement of good or bad.

'Live with the gods.' He lives with the gods who consistently shows them his soul content with its lot, and performing the wishes of that divinity, that fragment of himself which Zeus has given each person to guard and guide him. In each of us this divinity is our mind and reason.

Are you angry with the man who smells like a goat, or the one with foul breath? What will you have him do? That's the way his mouth is, that's the way his armpits are, so it is inevitable that they should give out odours to match. 'But the man is endowed with reason', you say, 'and if he puts his mind to it he can work out why he causes offence.' Well, good for you! So you too are no less endowed with reason: bring your rationality, then, to bear on his rationality—show him, tell him. If he listens, you will cure him, and no need for anger.

Neither hypocrite nor whore.

You can live here in this world just as you intend to live when you have left it. But if this is not allowed you, then you should depart life itself—but not as if this were some misfortune. 'The fire smokes and I leave the house.' Why think this any big matter? But as long as no such thing drives me out, I remain a free man and no one will prevent me doing what I wish to do: and my wish is to follow the nature of a rational and social being.

The intelligence of the Whole is a social intelligence. Certainly it has made the lower for the sake of the higher, and set the higher in harmony with each other. You can see how it has subordinated some creatures, coordinated others, given each its proper place, and brought together the superior beings in unity of mind.

How have you behaved up to now towards gods, parents, brother, wife, children, teachers, tutors, friends, relations, servants? Has your principle up to now with all of these been 'say no evil, do no evil'? Remind yourself what you have been through and had the strength to endure; that the story of your life is fully told and your service completed; how often you have seen beauty, disregarded pleasure and pain, forgone glory, and been land to the unkind.

Why do unskilled and ignorant minds confound the skilful and the wise? Well, what is the mind of true skill and wisdom? It is the mind which knows the beginning and the end, and knows the Reason which informs all of existence and governs the Whole in appointed cycles through all eternity.

In no time at all ashes or bare bones, a mere name or not even a name: and if a name, only sound and echo. The 'prizes' of life empty, rotten, puny: puppies snapping at each other, children squabbling, laughter turning straight to tears. And. Faith, Honour, Justice and Truth 'fled up to Olympus from the wide-wayed earth'.

So what is there left to keep us here, if the objects of sense are ever changeable and unstable, if our senses themselves are blurred and easily smudged like wax, if our very soul is a mere exhalation of blood, if success in such a world is vacuous? What, then? A calm wait for whatever it is, either extinction or translation. And until the time for that comes, what do we need? Only to worship and praise the gods, and to do good to men—to bear and forbear. And to remember that all that lies within the limits of our poor carcass and our little breath is neither yours nor in your power.

You can always ensure the right current to your life if you can first follow the right path—if, that is, your judgements and actions follow the path of reason. There are two things common to the souls of all rational creatures, god or man: they are immune to any external impediment, and the good they seek resides in a just disposition and just action, with this the limit of their desire.

If this is no wrongdoing of mine, nor the result of any wrong done to me, and if the community is not harmed, then why do I let it trouble me? And what is the harm that can be done to the community?

Don't let the impression of other people's grief carry you away indiscriminately. Help them, yes, as best you can and as the case deserves, even if their grief is for the loss of something indifferent: but do not imagine their loss as any real harm—that is the wrong way of thinking. Rather, you should be like the old man in the play who reclaimed at the end his foster-child's favourite toy, never forgetting that it was only a toy. So there you are, broadcasting your pity on the hustings—have you forgotten, man, what these things are worth? 'Yes, but they are important to these folk.' Is that any reason for you to join their folly?

'There was a time when I met luck at every turn.' But luck is the good fortune you determine for yourself: and good fortune consists in good inclinations of the soul, good impulses, good actions.

Luke 15:11–32

New American Bible

The Prodigal Son

11 15 Then he said, "A man had two sons,

12 and the younger son said to his father, 'Father, give me the share of your estate that should come to me.' So the father divided the property between them.

13 After a few days, the younger son collected all his belongings and set off to a distant country where he squandered his inheritance on a life of dissipation.

14 When he had freely spent everything, a severe famine struck that country, and he found himself in dire need.

15 So he hired himself out to one of the local citizens who sent him to his farm to tend the swine.

16 And he longed to eat his fill of the pods on which the swine fed, but nobody gave him any.

17 Coming to his senses he thought, 'How many of my father's hired workers have more than enough food to eat, but here am I, dying from hunger.

18 I shall get up and go to my father and I shall say to him, "Father, I have sinned against heaven and against you.

19 I no longer deserve to be called your son; treat me as you would treat one of your hired workers."'

20 So he got up and went back to his father. While he was still a long way off, his father caught sight of him, and was filled with compassion. He ran to his son, embraced him and kissed him.

21 His son said to him, 'Father, I have sinned against heaven and against you; I no longer deserve to be called your son.'

22 But his father ordered his servants, 'Quickly bring the finest robe and put it on him; put a ring on his finger and sandals on his feet.

23 Take the fattened calf and slaughter it. Then let us celebrate with a feast,

24 because this son of mine was dead, and has come to life again; he was lost, and has been found.' Then the celebration began.

25 Now the older son had been out in the field and, on his way back, as he neared the house, he heard the sound of music and dancing.

26 He called one of the servants and asked what this might mean.

27 The servant said to him, 'Your brother has returned and your father has slaughtered the fattened calf because he has him back safe and sound.'

28 He became angry, and when he refused to enter the house, his father came out and pleaded with him.

29 He said to his father in reply, 'Look, all these years I served you and not once did I disobey your orders; yet you never gave me even a young goat to feast on with my friends.

30 But when your son returns who swallowed up your property with prostitutes, for him you slaughter the fattened calf.'

31 He said to him, 'My son, you are here with me always; everything I have is yours.

32 But now we must celebrate and rejoice, because your brother was dead and has come to life again; he was lost and has been found.'"

Luke 10:25–37

New American Bible

The Good Samaritan

25 10 There was a scholar of the law who stood up to test him and said, "Teacher, what must I do to inherit eternal life?"

26 Jesus said to him, "What is written in the law? How do you read it?"

27 He said in reply, "You shall love the Lord, your God, with all your heart, with all your being, with all your strength, and with all your mind, and your neighbor as yourself."

28 He replied to him, "You have answered correctly; do this and you will live."

29 But because he wished to justify himself, he said to Jesus, "And who is my neighbor?"

30 Jesus replied, "A man fell victim to robbers as he went down from Jerusalem to Jericho. They stripped and beat him and went off leaving him half-dead.

31 A priest happened to be going down that road, but when he saw him, he passed by on the opposite side.

32 Likewise a Levite came to the place, and when he saw him, he passed by on the opposite side.

33 But a Samaritan traveler who came upon him was moved with compassion at the sight.

34 He approached the victim, poured oil and wine over his wounds and bandaged them. Then he lifted him up on his own animal, took him to an inn and cared for him.

35 The next day he took out two silver coins and gave them to the innkeeper with the instruction, 'Take care of him. If you spend more than what I have given you, I shall repay you on my way back.'

36 Which of these three, in your opinion, was neighbor to the robbers' victim?"

37 He answered, "The one who treated him with mercy." Jesus said to him, "Go and do likewise."

Matthew 20:1–15

New American Bible

Workers in the Vineyard ("Day Laborers")

1 20 "The kingdom of heaven is like a landowner who went out at dawn to hire laborers for his vineyard.

2 After agreeing with them for the usual daily wage, he sent them into his vineyard.

3 Going out about nine o'clock, he saw others standing idle in the marketplace,

4 and he said to them, 'You too go into my vineyard, and I will give you what is just.'

5 So they went off. (And) he went out again around noon, and around three o'clock, and did likewise.

6 Going out about five o'clock, he found others standing around, and said to them, 'Why do you stand here idle all day?'

7 They answered, 'Because no one has hired us.' He said to them, 'You too go into my vineyard.'

8 When it was evening the owner of the vineyard said to his foreman, 'Summon the laborers and give them their pay, beginning with the last and ending with the first.'

9 When those who had started about five o'clock came, each received the usual daily wage.

10 So when the first came, they thought that they would receive more, but each of them also got the usual wage.

11 And on receiving it they grumbled against the landowner,

12 saying, 'These last ones worked only one hour, and you have made them equal to us, who bore the day's burden and the heat.'

13 He said to one of them in reply, 'My friend, I am not cheating you. Did you not agree with me for the usual daily wage?

14 Take what is yours and go. What if I wish to give this last one the same as you?

15 (Or) am I not free to do as I wish with my own money? Are you envious because I am generous?'

from *The Lais of Marie de France*

Marie de France

Prologue

Whoever has received knowledge
and eloquence in speech from God
should not be silent or secretive
but demonstrate it willingly.
When a great good is widely heard of, 5
then, and only then, does it bloom,
and when that good is praised by many,
it has spread its blossoms.
The custom among the ancients—
as Priscian testifies— 10
was to speak quite obscurely
in the books they wrote,
so that those who were to come after
and study them
might gloss the letter 15
and supply its significance from their own wisdom.
Philosophers knew this,
they understood among themselves
that the more time they spent,
the more subtle their minds would become 20
and the better they would know how to keep themselves
from whatever was to be avoided.
He who would guard himself from vice
should study and understand
and begin a weighty work 25
by which he might keep vice at a distance,
and free himself from great sorrow.
That's why I began to think
about composing some good stories
and translating from Latin to Romance; 30

but that was not to bring me fame:
too many others have done it.
Then I thought of the *lais* I'd heard.
I did not doubt, indeed I knew well,
that those who first began them 35
and sent them forth
composed them in order to preserve
adventures they had heard.
I have heard many told;
and I don't want to neglect or forget them. 40
To put them into word and rhyme
I've often stayed awake.

In your honor, noble King,
who are so brave and courteous,
repository of all joys 45
in whose heart all goodness takes root,
I undertook to assemble these *lais*
to compose and recount them in rhyme.
In my heart I thought and determined,
sire, that I would present them to you. 50
If it pleases you to receive them,
you will give me great joy;
I shall be happy forever.
Do not think me presumptuous
if I dare present them to you. 55
Now hear how they begin.

Guigemar

Whoever deals with good material
feels pain if it's treated improperly.
Listen, my lords, to the words of Marie,
who does not forget her responsibilities when her turn comes.

People should praise anyone 5
who wins admiring comments for herself.
But anywhere there is

a man or a woman of great worth,
people who envy their good fortune
often say evil things about them; 10
they want to ruin their reputations.
Thus they act like
vicious, cowardly dogs
who bite people treacherously.
I don't propose to give up because of that; 15
if spiteful critics or slanderers
wish to turn my accomplishments against me,
they have a right to their evil talk.

The tales—and I know they're true—
from which the Bretons made their *lais* 20
I'll now recount for you briefly;
and at the very beginning of this enterprise,
just the way it was written down,
I'll relate an adventure
that took place in Brittany, 25
in the old days.

At that time, Hoel ruled Brittany,
sometimes peacefully, sometimes at war.
The king had a vassal
who was lord of Leonnais; 30
his name was Oridial
and he was on very intimate terms with his lord.
A worthy and valiant knight,
he had, by his wife, two children,
a son and a beautiful daughter. 35
The girl's name was Noguent;
they called the boy Guigemar.
There wasn't a more handsome youngster in the kingdom.
His mother had a wonderful love for him,
and his father a great devotion; 40
when he could bring himself to part with the boy,
his father sent him to serve the king.
The boy was intelligent and brave,
and made himself loved by all.
When his time of probation was at an end, 45
and he was mature in body and mind,

the king dubbed him knight,
giving him luxurious armor, which was exactly what he desired.
Guigemar left the court,
but not before dispensing many rich gifts. 50
He journeyed to Flanders to seek his fame;
there was always a war, or a battle raging there.
Neither in Lorraine nor in Burgundy,
in Anjou nor in Gascony,
could one find, in those days, 55
Guigemar's equal as a fine knight.
But in forming him nature had so badly erred
that he never gave any thought to love.
There wasn't a lady or a maid on earth,
no matter how noble, or how beautiful, 60
who wouldn't have willingly granted him her love,
had he asked her for it.
Many maids asked him,
but he wasn't interested in such things;
no one could discover in him 65
the slightest desire to love.
Therefore both friends and strangers
gave him up for lost.
At the height of his fame,
this baron, Guigemar, returned to his own land 70
to visit his father and his lord,
his good mother and his sister,
all of whom were most eager to see him.
Guigemar stayed with them,
I believe, an entire month. 75
Then he was seized by a desire to hunt;
that night he summoned his companions in arms,
his huntsmen, and his beaters;
next morning he set out for the woods
to indulge in the sport that gave him much pleasure. 80
They gathered in pursuit of a great stag;
the dogs were unleashed.
The hunters ran ahead
while the young man lingered behind;
a squire carried his bow, 85

his hunting knife, and his quiver.
He wanted to fire some arrows, if he had the opportunity,
before he left the spot.
In the thickest part of a great bush
Guigemar saw a hind with a fawn; 90
a completely white beast,
with deer's antlers on her head.
Spurred by the barking of the dogs, she sprang into the open.
Guigemar took his bow and shot at her,
striking her in the breastbone. 95
She fell at once,
but the arrow rebounded,
gave Guigemar such a wound—
it went through his thigh right into the horse's flank—
that he had to dismount. 100
He collapsed on the thick grass
beside the hind he'd struck.
The hind, wounded as she was,
suffered pain and groaned.
Then she spoke, in this fashion: 105
"Alas! I'm dying!
And you, vassal, who wounded me,
this be your destiny:
may you never get medicine for your wound!
Neither herb nor root, 110
neither physician nor potion,
will cure you
of that wound in your thigh,
until a woman heals you,
one who will suffer, out of love for you, 115
pain and grief
such as no woman ever suffered before.
And out of love for her, you'll suffer as much;
the affair will be a marvel
to lovers, past and present, 120
and to all those yet to come.
Now go away, leave me in peace!"
Guigemar was badly wounded;
what he had heard dismayed him.

He began to consider carefully 125
what land he might set out for
to have his wound healed.
He didn't want to remain there and die.
He knew, he reminded himself,
that he'd never seen a woman 130
to whom he wanted to offer his love,
nor one who could cure his pain.
He called his squire to him;
"Friend," he said, "go quickly!
Bring my companions back here; 135
I want to talk to them."
The squire rode off and Guigemar remained;
he complained bitterly to himself.
Making his shirt into a bandage,
he bound his wound tightly; 140
Then he mounted his horse and left that spot.
He was anxious to get far away;
he didn't want any of his men to come along,
who might interfere, or try to detain him.
Through the woods he followed 145
a grassy path, which led him
out into open country; there, at the edge of the plain,
he saw a cliff and a steep bank
overlooking a body of water below:
a bay that formed a harbor. 150
There was a solitary ship in the harbor;
Guigemar saw its sail.
It was fit and ready to go,
calked outside and in—
no one could discover a seam in its hull. 155
Every deck rail and peg
was solid ebony;
no gold under the sun could be worth more.
The sail was pure silk;
it would look beautiful when unfurled. 160
    The knight was troubled;
he had never heard it said
anywhere in that region

that ships could land there.
He went down to the harbor 165
and, in great pain, boarded the ship.
He expected to discover men inside,
guarding the vessel,
but he saw no one, no one at all.
Amidships he found a bed 170
whose posts and frame
were wrought in the fashion of Solomon,
of cypress and ivory,
with designs in inlaid gold.
The quilt on the bed was made 175
of silken cloth, woven with gold.
I don't know how to estimate the value of the other bedclothes,
but I'll tell you this much about the pillow:
whoever rested his head on it
would never have white hair. 180
The sable bedspread
was lined with Alexandrian silk.
Two candelabra of fine gold—
the lesser of the two worth a fortune—
were placed at the head of the cabin, 185
lighted tapers placed in them.
Guigemar, astonished by all this,
reclined on the bed
and rested; his wound hurt.
Then he rose and tried to leave the ship, 190
but he couldn't return to land.
The vessel was already on the high seas,
carrying him swiftly with it.
A good, gentle wind was blowing,
so turning back now was out of the question. 195
Guigemar was very upset; he didn't know what to do.
It's no wonder he was frightened,
especially as his wound was paining him a great deal.
Still, he had to see the adventure through.
He prayed to God to watch over him, 200
to use his power to bring him back to land,
and to protect him from death.

He lay down on the bed, and fell asleep.
That day he'd survived the worst;
before sundown he would arrive 205
at the place where he'd be cured—
near an ancient city,
the capital of its realm.
The lord who ruled over that city
was a very aged man who had a wife, 210
a woman of high lineage,
noble, courteous, beautiful, intelligent;
he was extremely jealous,
which accorded with his nature.
(All old folk are jealous; 215
every one of them hates the thought of being cuckolded,
such is the perversity of age.)
The watch he kept over her was no joke.
The grove beneath the tower
was enclosed all around 220
with walls of green marble,
very high and thick.
There was only one entrance,
and it was guarded day and night.
On the other side, the sea enclosed it; 225
no one could enter, no one leave,
except by means of a boat,
as the castle might require it.
Inside the castle walls,
the lord had built a chamber— 230
none more beautiful anywhere—to keep his wife under guard—
And its entrance was a chapel.
The room was painted with images all around;
Venus the goddess of love
was skillfully depicted in the painting, 235
her nature and her traits were illustrated,
whereby men might learn how to behave in love,
and to serve love loyally.
Ovid's book, the one in which he instructs
lovers how to control their love, 240
was being thrown by Venus into a fire,

and she was excommunicating all those
who ever perused this book
or followed its teachings.
That's where the wife was locked up. 245
Her husband had given her
a girl to serve her,
one who was noble and well educated—
she was his niece, the daughter of his sister.
There was great affection between the two women. 250
She stayed with her mistress when he went off,
remaining with her until he returned.
No one else came there, man or woman,
nor could the wife leave the walls of the enclosure.
An old priest, hoary with age, 255
kept the gate key;
he'd lost his nether member
or he wouldn't have been trusted.
He said mass for her
and served her her food. 260
That same day, as soon as she rose from a nap,
the wife went into the grove;
she had slept after dinner,
and now she set out to amuse herself,
taking her maid with her. 265
Looking out to sea,
they saw the ship on the rising tide
come sailing into the harbor.
They could see nothing guiding it.
The lady started to flee— 270
it's not surprising if she was afraid;
her face grew red from fear.
But the girl, who was wise
and more courageous,
comforted and reassured her, 275
and they went toward the water, fast as they could.
The damsel removed her cloak,
and boarded the beautiful ship.
She found no living thing
except the sleeping knight. 280

She saw how pale he was and thought him dead;
she stopped and looked at him.
Then she went back
quickly, and called her mistress,
told her what she'd found, 285
and lamented the dead man she'd seen.
The lady answered, "Let's go see him!
If he's dead, we'll bury him;
the priest will help us.
If I find that he's alive, he'll tell us all about this." 290

Without tarrying any longer, they returned together,
the lady first, then the girl.
When the lady entered the ship,
she stopped in front of the bed.
She examined the knight, 295
lamenting his beauty and fine body;
she was full of sorrow on his account,
and said it was a shame he'd died so young.
She put her hand on his breast,
and felt that it was warm, and his heart healthy, 300
beating beneath his ribs.
The knight, who was only asleep,
now woke up and saw her;
he was delighted, and greeted her—
he realized he'd come to land. 305
The lady, upset and weeping,
answered him politely
and asked him how
he got there, what country he came from,
if he'd been exiled because of war. 310
"My lady," he said, "not at all.
But if you'd like me to tell you
the truth, I'll do so;
I'll hide nothing from you.

I come from Brittany. 315
Today I went out hunting in the woods,
and shot a white hind;
the arrow rebounded,
giving me such a wound in the thigh

that I've given up hope of being cured. 320
The hind complained and spoke to me,
cursed me, swore
that I'd never be healed
except by a girl;
I don't know where she might be found. 325
When I heard my destiny,
I quickly left the woods:
I found this boat in a harbor,
and made a big mistake: I went on board.
The boat raced off to sea with me on it; 330
I don't know where I've arrived,
or what this city's called.
Beautiful one, I beg you, for God's sake,
please advise me!
I don't know where to go 335
and I can't even steer this ship!"
She answered him, "My dear lord,
I'll be happy to advise you;
this is my husband's city,
and so is the region around it. 340
He is a rich man of high lineage,
but extremely old;
he's also terribly jealous.
On my word of honor,
he has locked me up in this stronghold. 345
There's only one entrance,
and an old priest guards the gate:
may God let him burn in hell!
I'm shut in here night and day.
I'd never dare 350
to leave except at his command,
when my lord asks for me.
Here I have my room and my chapel,
and this girl lives with me.
If it pleases you to stay here 355
until you're better able to travel,
we'll be happy to put you up,
we'll serve you willingly."

When he hears this,
Guigemar thanks the lady warmly, 360
and says he'll stay with her.
He rose from the bed;
with some difficulty they supported him,
and the lady brought him to her chamber.
The young man lay down 365
on the girl's bed,
behind a drape that was hung
across her room like a curtain.
They brought him water in a golden basin,
washed his thigh, 370
and with a fine, white silk cloth
they wiped the blood from his wound.
Then they bound it tightly.
They treated him very kindly.
When their evening meal came, 375
the girl left enough of hers
for the knight to have some;
he ate and drank quite well.
But now love struck him to the quick;
great strife was in his heart 380
because the lady had wounded him so badly
that he forgot his homeland.
His other wound no longer bothered him,
but he sighed with new anguish.
He begged the girl, who was assigned to take care of him, 385
to let him sleep.
She left him and went away,
since he had requested it,
returning to her mistress,
who was also feeling somewhat scorched 390
by the same fire Guigemar felt
igniting and consuming his heart.
The knight was alone now,
preoccupied and in distress.
He didn't yet know what was wrong, 395
but this much he could tell:
if the lady didn't cure him,

he was sure to die.
"Alas!" he said, "what shall I do?
I'll go to her and tell her 400
that she should have mercy and pity
on a poor, disconsolate wretch like me.
If she refuses my plea,
shows herself so proud and scornful,
then I'll have to die of grief, 405
languishing forever in this pain."
He sighed; but a little later
formed a new resolution,
and said to himself he'd have to keep suffering;
you have to endure what you can't change. 410
He lay awake all night,
sighing in distress.
He turned over in his mind
her words and appearance,
the bright eyes, the fair mouth 415
whose sweetness had touched his heart.
Under his breath he cried for mercy;
he almost called her his beloved.
If he only knew what she was feeling—
how love was torturing her— 420
I think he would have been very happy;
that little bit of consolation
would have diminished the pain
that drained him of his color.
If he was suffering from love of her, 425
she had nothing to gloat about, either.
Next morning, before dawn,
the lady arose.
She'd been awake all night, that was her complaint.
It was the fault of love, pressing her hard. 430
The damsel, who was with her,
noticed from the appearance of her lady
that she was in love
with the knight who was staying
in her chamber until he was healed; 435
but her mistress didn't know whether or not he loved her.

The lady went off to church
and the girl went off to the knight.
    She sat down by the bed;
he spoke to her, saying, 440
"My dear friend, where has my lady gone?
Why did she rise so early?"
He paused, and sighed.
The girl spoke frankly:
"My lord," she said, "you're in love; 445
take care not to hide it too well!
The love you offer
may in fact be well received.
Anyone whom my lady chooses to love
certainly ought to think well of her. 450
This love would be suitable
if both of you were constant:
you're handsome and she's beautiful."
He answered the girl,
"I'm so in love with her 455
that if I don't get relief soon
I'll be in a very bad way.
Advise me, dear friend!
What should I do about my passion?"
The girl very sweetly 460
comforted the knight,
promised to help him
in every way she could;
she was very good-hearted and well bred.
    When the lady had heard mass 465
she returned; she was anything but neglectful:
she wanted to know whether the man
whom she couldn't help loving
was awake or asleep.
The girl called her 470
and brought her to the knight;
now she'll have all the time she needs
to tell him what she's feeling,
for better or for worse.
He greeted her and she him; 475

they were both very scared now.
He didn't dare ask anything from her,
for he was a foreigner
and was afraid, if he told her what he felt,
she'd hate him for it, send him away. 480
But he who hides his sickness
can hardly be brought back to health;
love is a wound in the body,
and yet nothing appears on the outside.
It's a sickness that lasts a long time, 485
because it comes from nature.
Many people treat it lightly,
like these false courtiers
who have affairs everywhere they go,
then boast about their conquests; 490
that's not love but folly,
evil and lechery.
If you can find a loyal love,
you should love and serve it faithfully,
be at its command. 495
Guigemar was deeply in love;
he must either get help quickly
or live in misery.
So love inspires bravery in him:
he reveals his desires to the lady. 500
"Lady," he said, "I'm dying because of you;
my heart is full of anguish.
if you won't cure me,
I'll have to perish sooner or later.
I beg you to love me— 505
fair one, don't deny me!"
When she had heard him out,
she gave a fitting answer.
She laughed, and said, "My love,
I'd be ill advised to act too quickly 510
in granting your prayer.
I'm not accustomed to such a request."
"My lady," he replied, "for God's sake, have mercy!
Don't be annoyed if I speak like this to you.

It's appropriate for an inconstant woman 515
to make some one plead with her a long time
to enhance her worth; that way he won't think
she's used to such sport.
But a woman of good character,
sensible as well as virtuous, 520
if she finds a man to her liking,
oughtn't to treat him too disdainfully.
Rather she should love and enjoy him;
this way, before anyone knows or hears of it,
they'll have done a lot that's to their advantage. 525
Now, dear lady, let's end this discussion."
The lady realized he was telling the truth,
and immediately granted him
her love; then he kissed her.
From now on, Guigemar is at ease. 530
They lie down together and converse,
kissing and embracing often.
I hope they also enjoy whatever else
others do on such occasions.
It appears to me that Guigemar 535
stayed with her a year and a half.
Their life was full of pleasure.
But fortune, who never forgets her duty,
turns her wheel suddenly,
raising one person up while casting another down; 540
and so it happened with the lovers,
because suddenly they were discovered.
One summer morning,
the lady was lying beside her young lover;
she kissed his mouth and eyes, 545
and said to him, "Dear, sweet love,
my heart tells me I'm going to lose you.
We're going to be found out.
If you die, I want to die, too,
but if you can escape, 550
you'll go find another love
while I stay here in misery."
"Lady," he said, "don't say such a thing!

I would never have any joy or peace
if I turned to another woman. 555
You needn't be afraid of that!"
"Beloved, I need your promise.
Give me your shirt;
I'll make a knot in the tail.
You have my leave to love the woman, 560
whoever she may be,
who will be able to undo it."
He gave her the shirt, and his promise;
she made the knot in such a way
that no woman could untie it 565
except with scissors or knife.
She gave him back the shirt,
and he took it on condition
that she should make a similar pledge to him,
by means of a belt 570
that she would wear next to her bare flesh,
tightened about her flanks.
Whoever could open the buckle
without breaking it or severing it from the belt,
would be the one he would urge her to love. 575
He kissed her, and left it at that.
That day they were discovered—
spied upon and found out
by an evil, cunning chamberlain,
sent by the husband. 580
He wanted to speak with the lady,
and couldn't get into her chamber;
he looked in a window and saw the lovers,
he went and told his lord.
When he heard about it, 585
the lord was sorrier than he'd ever been before.
He called for three of his henchmen
and straightaway went to the wife's chamber;
he had the door broken down.
Inside he found the knight. 590
He was so furious
that he gave orders to kill the stranger.

Guigemar got up,
not at all afraid.
He grabbed a wooden rod 595
on which clothes were usually hung,
and waited for his assailants.
Guigemar will make some of them suffer for this;
before they get close to him,
he'll have maimed them all. 600

The lord stared at him for a long time,
and finally asked him
who he was, where he came from,
how he'd gotten in there.
Guigemar told him how he'd come there 605
and how the lady had received him;
he told him all about the adventure
of the wounded hind,
about his wound and the ship;
now he is entirely in the other's power. 610
The lord replied that he didn't believe him,
but if it really was the way he had told it
and if he could find the ship,
he'd send Guigemar back out to sea.
If he survived, that would be a shame; 615
he'd be happier if Guigemar drowned.

When he had made this pledge,
they went together to the harbor,
and found the ship; they put Guigemar on it—
it will take him back to his own land. 620
The ship got under way without waiting.
The knight sighed and cried,
often lamenting his lady
and praying to almighty God
to grant him a quick death, 625
and never let him come to port
if he couldn't regain his mistress,
whom he desired more than his own life.
He persisted in his grief
until the ship came to the port 630
where he'd first found it;

he was now very near his native land.
He left the ship as quickly as he could.
A boy whom Guigemar had raised
came by, following a knight, 635
and leading a war-horse.
Guigemar recognized him and called to him;
the squire looked at him,
recognized his lord, dismounted,
and presented the charger to him. 640
Guigemar went off with him; all his friends
rejoiced that they had found him again.
He was highly honored in his land,
but through it all he was sad and distracted.
His friends wanted him to take a wife, 645
but he refused them altogether;
he'll never have to do with a woman,
for love or money,
if she can't untie
his knotted shirt without tearing it. 650
The news traveled throughout Brittany;
all the women and girls
came to try their luck,
but none could untie the knot.
Now I want to tell you about the lady 655
whom Guigemar loved so dearly.
On the advice of one of his barons,
her husband had her imprisoned
in a dark marble tower.
There she passed bad days, worse nights. 660
No one in the world could describe
the pain, the suffering,
the anguish and the grief,
that she endured in that tower.
She remained there two years and more, I believe, 665
without ever having a moment of pleasure.
Often, she mourned for her lover:
"Guigemar, my lord, why did I ever lay eyes on you?
I'd rather die quickly
than suffer this lingering torture. 670

My love, if I could escape,
I'd go to where you put out to sea
and drown myself." Then she got up;
in astonishment she went to the door
and found it unlocked; 675
by good fortune, she got outside—
no one bothered her.
She came to the harbor, and found the boat.
It was tied to the rock
where she had intended to drown herself. 680
When she saw it there, she went aboard;
she could think of only one thing—
that this was where her lover had perished.
Suddenly, she couldn't stand up.
If she could have gotten back up on deck, 685
she would have thrown herself overboard,
so great was her suffering.
The boat set out, taking her with it.
It came to port in Brittany,
beneath a strong, well-built castle. 690
The lord of the castle
was named Meriaduc.
He was fighting a war with a neighbor,
and had risen early that morning
because he wanted to dispatch his troops 695
to attack his enemy.
Standing at a window,
he saw the ship arrive.
He went downstairs
and called his chamberlain; 700
quickly they went to the ship,
climbed up its ladder;
inside they found the woman
who had a fairylike beauty.
He took her by the cloak 705
and brought her with him to his castle.
He was delighted with his discovery,
for she was incredibly beautiful;
whoever had put her on the boat,

he could tell she came from high lineage. 710
He felt for her a love
as great as he'd ever had for a woman.
He had a young sister,
a beautiful maiden, in his care;
he commended the lady to her attention. 715
So she was waited on and made much of;
the damsel dressed her richly.
But she remained constantly sad and preoccupied.
The lord often came to speak with her,
since he wanted to love her with all his heart. 720
He pleaded for her love; she didn't want it,
instead she showed him her belt:
she would never love any man
except the one who could open the belt
without breaking it. When he heard that, 725
Meriaduc replied angrily,
"There's another one like you in this land,
a very worthy knight,
who avoids, in a similar manner, taking a wife
by means of a shirt 730
the right tail of which is knotted;
it can't be untied
except by using scissors or a knife.
I think you must have made that knot!"
When the lady heard this, she sighed, 735
and almost fainted.
He took her in his arms,
cut the laces of her tunic,
and tried to open the belt.
But he didn't succeed. 740
There wasn't a knight in the region
whom he didn't summon to try his luck.
Things went on like this for quite a while,
up to the time of a tournament
that Meriaduc had proclaimed 745
against the lord he was fighting.
He sent for knights and enlisted them in his service,
knowing very well that Guigemar would come.

He asked him as a special favor,
as his friend and companion, 750
not to let him down in this hour of need,
but to come help him.
So Guigemar set out, richly supplied,
leading more than one hundred knights.
Meriaduc entertained him 755
as an honored guest in his stronghold.
He then sent two knights to his sister,
and commanded her
to prepare herself and come to him,
bringing with her the woman he so much loved. 760
The girl obeyed his order.
Lavishly outfitted,
they came hand in hand into the great hall.
The lady was pale and upset;
she heard Guigemar's name 765
and couldn't stand up.
If the damsel hadn't supported her,
she'd have fallen to the ground.
Guigemar arose when the women entered;
he looked at the lady and noticed 770
her appearance and behavior;
involuntarily, he shrank back a bit.
"Is this," he said, "my dear love,
my hope, my heart, and my life—
my beautiful lady who loved me? 775
Where did she come from? Who brought her here?
Now, that was a foolish thought!
I know it can't be she;
women often look alike—
I got all excited for no reason. 780
But because she looks like the one
for whom my heart aches and sighs,
I'll gladly speak to her."
Then the knight came forward,
he kissed her and sat her down beside him; 785
he didn't say another word,
except that he asked her to sit down.

Meriaduc looked at them closely,
upset by the sight of them together.
He called Guigemar cheerfully: 790
"My lord," he said, "please
let this girl try
to untie your shirt,
to see if she can manage to do it."
Guigemar answered, "Certainly." 795
He summoned a chamberlain
who was in charge of the shirt
and commanded him to bring it.
It was given to the girl,
but she couldn't untie it at all. 800
The lady knew the knot very well;
her heart is greatly agitated,
for she would love to try to untie it,
if she dared and could.
Meriaduc saw this clearly; 805
he was as sorry as he could be.
"My lady," he said, "now try
to untie it, if you can."
When she heard his order,
she took the shirttail 810
and easily untied the knot.
Guigemar was thunderstruck;
he knew her very well, and yet
he couldn't bring himself to believe firmly it was she.
So he spoke to her in this way: 815
"Beloved, sweet creature,
is that you? Tell me truly!
Let me see your body,
and the belt I put on you."
He put his hands on her hips, 820
and found the belt.
"My beautiful one," he said, "what a lucky adventure
that I've found you like this!
Who brought you here?"
She told him about the grief, 825
the great pains, the monotony

of the prison where she was held captive,
and everything that had happened to her—
how she escaped,
how she wished to drown, but found the ship instead, 830
and how she entered it and was brought to this port;
and how the lord of the castle kept her in custody,
guarding her in luxury
but constantly asking for her love.
Now her joy has returned: 835
"My love, take back your beloved!"
Guigemar got up.
"My lords," he said, "listen to me!
Here I have the mistress
I thought I had lost forever. 840
Now I ask and implore Meriaduc
to give her back to me out of kindness.
I will become his vassal,
serve him two or three years,
with one hundred knights, or more!" 845
Meriaduc answered,
"Guigemar," he said, "my handsome friend,
I'm not so harried
or so afflicted by any war
that you can bargain with me about this. 850
I found this woman and I propose to take care of her
and defend her against you."
When Guigemar heard that, he quickly
commanded his men to mount.
He galloped away, defying Meriaduc. 855
It upset him to leave his beloved behind.
Guigemar took with him
every knight who had come
to the town for the tournament.
Each declared his loyalty to Guigemar; 860
they'll accompany him wherever he goes.
Whoever fails him now will truly be dishonored!
That night they came to the castle
of Meriaduc's opponent.
The lord of the castle put them up; 865

he was joyful and delighted
that Guigemar came over to his side, bringing help with him.
Now he's sure the war's as good as over.
The next morning they arose,
and equipped themselves at their lodgings. 870
They departed from the village, noisily;
Guigemar came first, leading them.
Arriving at Meriaduc's castle, they assaulted it;
but it was very strong and they failed to take it.
Guigemar besieged the town; 875
he won't leave until it has fallen.
His friends and other troops increased so greatly
that he was able to starve everyone inside.
He captured and destroyed the castle,
killed its lord. 880
Guigemar led away his mistress with great rejoicing;
all his pain was now at an end.
From this story that you have heard
the *lai* of Guigemar was composed,
which is now recited to the harp and rote; 885
the music is a pleasure to hear.

from *Summa Theologica*
First Part: On the Existence of God

Thomas Aquinas
Translated by Fathers of the English Dominican Province

Because the chief aim of sacred doctrine is to teach the knowledge of God, not only as He is in Himself, but also as He is the beginning of things and their last end, and especially of rational creatures, as is clear from what has been already said, therefore, in our endeavor to expound this science, we shall treat: (1) Of God; (2) Of the rational creature's advance towards God; (3) Of Christ, Who as man, is our way to God.

In treating of God there will be a threefold division, for we shall consider: (1) Whatever concerns the Divine Essence; (2) Whatever concerns the distinctions of Persons; (3) Whatever concerns the procession of creatures from Him.

Concerning the Divine Essence, we must consider: (1) Whether God exists? (2) The manner of His existence, or, rather, what is NOT the manner of His existence; (3) Whatever concerns His operations—namely, His knowledge, will, power.

Concerning the first, there are three points of inquiry:

(1) Whether the proposition "God exists" is self-evident?
(2) Whether it is demonstrable?
(3) Whether God exists?

Whether the existence of God is self-evident?

Objection 1: It seems that the existence of God is self-evident. Now those things are said to be self-evident to us the knowledge of which is naturally implanted in us, as we can see in regard to first principles. But as Damascene says (De Fide Oth. i, 1,3), "the knowledge of God is naturally implanted in all." Therefore the existence of God is self-evident.

Objection 2: Further, those things are said to be self-evident which are known as soon as the terms are known, which the Philosopher (1 Poster. iii) says is true of the first principles of demonstration. Thus, when the nature of a whole and of a part is known, it is at once recognized that every whole is greater than its part. But as soon as the signification of the word "God" is understood, it is at once seen that God exists. For by this word is signified that thing than which nothing greater can be conceived. But that which exists actually and mentally is greater than that which exists only mentally. Therefore, since as soon as the word "God" is understood it exists mentally, it also follows that it exists actually. Therefore the proposition "God exists" is self-evident.

Objection 3: Further, the existence of truth is self-evident. For whoever denies the existence of truth grants that truth does not exist: and, if truth does not exist, then the proposition "Truth does not exist" is true: and if there is anything true, there must be truth. But God is truth itself: "I am the way, the truth, and the life" (Jn. 14:6) Therefore "God exists" is self-evident.

On the contrary, No one can mentally admit the opposite of what is self-evident; as the Philosopher (Metaph. iv, lect. vi) states concerning the first principles of demonstration. But the opposite of the proposition "God is" can be mentally admitted: "The fool said in his heart, There is no God" (Ps. 52:1). Therefore, that God exists is not self-evident.

I answer that, A thing can be self-evident in either of two ways: on the one hand, self-evident in itself, though not to us; on the other, self-evident in itself, and to us. A proposition is self-evident because the predicate is included in the essence of the subject, as "Man is an animal," for animal is contained in the essence of man. If, therefore the essence of the predicate and subject be known to all, the proposition will be self-evident to all; as is clear with regard to the first principles of demonstration, the terms of which are common things that no one is ignorant of, such as being and non-being, whole and part, and such like. If, however, there are some to whom the essence of the predicate and subject is unknown, the proposition will be self-evident in itself, but not to those who do not know the meaning of the predicate and subject of the proposition. Therefore, it happens, as Boethius says (Hebdom., the title of which is: "Whether all that is, is good"), "that there are some mental concepts self-evident only to the learned, as that incorporeal substances are not in space." Therefore I say that this proposition, "God exists," of itself is self-evident, for the predicate is the same as the subject, because God is His own existence as will be hereafter shown (Question [3], Article [4]). Now because we do not know the essence of God, the proposition is not self-evident to us; but needs to be demonstrated by things that are more known to us, though less known in their nature—namely, by effects.

Reply to Objection 1: To know that God exists in a general and confused way is implanted in us by nature, inasmuch as God is man's beatitude. For man naturally desires happiness, and what is naturally desired by man must be naturally known to him. This, however, is not to know absolutely that God exists; just as to know that someone is approaching is not the same as to know that Peter is approaching, even though it is Peter who is approaching; for many there are who imagine that man's perfect good which is happiness, consists in riches, and others in pleasures, and others in something else.

Reply to Objection 2: Perhaps not everyone who hears this word "God" understands it to signify something than which nothing greater can be thought, seeing that some have believed God to be a body. Yet, granted that everyone understands that by this word "God" is signified something than which nothing greater can be thought, nevertheless, it does not therefore follow that he understands that what the word signifies exists actually, but only that it exists mentally. Nor can it be argued that it actually exists, unless it be admitted that there actually exists something than which nothing greater can be thought; and this precisely is not admitted by those who hold that God does not exist.

Reply to Objection 3: The existence of truth in general is self-evident but the existence of a Primal Truth is not self-evident to us.

Whether it can be demonstrated that God exists?

Objection 1: It seems that the existence of God cannot be demonstrated. For it is an article of faith that God exists. But what is of faith cannot be demonstrated, because a demonstration produces scientific knowledge; whereas faith is of the unseen (Heb 11:1). Therefore it cannot be demonstrated that God exists.

Objection 2: Further, the essence is the middle term of demonstration. But we cannot know in what God's essence consists, but solely in what it does not consist; as Damascene says De Fide Orth. i, 4). Therefore we cannot demonstrate that God exists.

Objection 3: Further, if the existence of God were demonstrated, this could only be from His effects. But His effects are not proportionate to Him, since He is infinite and His effects are finite; and between the finite and infinite there is no proportion. Therefore, since a cause cannot be demonstrated by an effect not proportionate to it, it seems that the existence of God cannot be demonstrated.

On the contrary, The Apostle says: "The invisible things of Him are clearly seen, being understood by the things that are made" (Rm. 1:20). But this would not be unless the existence of God could be demonstrated through the things that are made; for the first thing we must know of anything is whether it exists.

I answer that, Demonstration can be made in two ways: One is through the cause, and is called "a priori," and this is to argue from what is prior absolutely. The other is through the effect, and is called a demonstration "a posteriori"; this is to argue from what is prior relatively only to us. When an effect is better known to us than its cause, from the effect we proceed to the knowledge of the cause. And from every effect the existence of its proper cause can be demonstrated, so long as its effects are better known to us; because since every effect depends upon its cause, if the effect exists, the cause must pre-exist. Hence the existence of God, in so far as it is not self-evident to us, can be demonstrated from those of His effects which are known to us.

Reply to Objection 1: The existence of God and other like truths about God, which can be known by natural reason, are not articles of faith, but are preambles to the articles; for faith presupposes natural knowledge, even as grace presupposes nature, and perfection supposes something that can be perfected. Nevertheless, there is nothing to prevent a man, who cannot grasp a proof, accepting, as a matter of faith, something which in itself is capable of being scientifically known and demonstrated.

Reply to Objection 2: When the existence of a cause is demonstrated from an effect, this effect takes the place of the definition of the cause in proof of the cause's existence. This is especially the case in regard to God, because, in order to prove the existence of anything, it is necessary to accept as a middle term the meaning of the word, and not its essence, for the question of its essence follows on the question of its existence. Now the names given to God are derived from His effects; consequently, in demonstrating the existence of God from His effects, we may take for the middle term the meaning of the word "God".

Reply to Objection 3: From effects not proportionate to the cause no perfect knowledge of that cause can be obtained. Yet from every effect the existence of the cause can be clearly demonstrated, and so we can demonstrate the existence of God from His effects; though from them we cannot perfectly know God as He is in His essence.

Whether God exists?

Objection 1: It seems that God does not exist; because if one of two contraries be infinite, the other would be altogether destroyed. But the word "God" means that He is infinite goodness. If, therefore, God existed, there would be no evil discoverable; but there is evil in the world. Therefore God does not exist.

Objection 2: Further, it is superfluous to suppose that what can be accounted for by a few principles has been produced by many. But it seems that everything we see in the world can be accounted for by other principles, supposing God did not exist. For all natural things can be reduced to one principle which is nature; and all voluntary things can be reduced to one principle which is human reason, or will. Therefore there is no need to suppose God's existence.

On the contrary, It is said in the person of God: "I am Who am." (Ex. 3:14)

I answer that, The existence of God can be proved in five ways.

The first and more manifest way is the argument from motion. It is certain, and evident to our senses, that in the world some things are in motion. Now whatever is in motion is put in motion by another, for nothing can be in motion except it is in potentiality to that towards which it is in motion; whereas a thing moves inasmuch as it is in act. For motion is nothing else than the reduction of something from potentiality to actuality. But nothing can be reduced from potentiality to actuality, except by something in a state of actuality. Thus that which is actually hot, as fire, makes wood, which is potentially hot, to be actually hot and thereby moves and changes it. Now it is not possible that the same thing should be at once in actuality and potentiality in the same respect, but only in different respects. For what is actually hot cannot simultaneously be potentially hot; but it is simultaneously potentially cold. It is therefore impossible that in the same respect and in the same way a thing should be both mover and moved, i.e. that it should move itself. Therefore, whatever is in motion must be put in motion by another. If that by which it is put in motion be itself put in motion, then this also must needs be put in motion by another, and that by another again. But this cannot go on to infinity, because then there would be no first mover, and, consequently, no other mover; seeing that subsequent movers move only inasmuch as they are put in motion by the first mover; as the staff moves only because it is put in motion by the hand. Therefore it is necessary to arrive at a first mover, put in motion by no other; and this everyone understands to be God.

The second way is from the nature of the efficient cause. In the world of sense we find there is an order of efficient causes. There is no case known (neither is it, indeed, possible) in which a thing is found to be the efficient cause of itself; for so it would be prior to itself, which is impossible. Now in efficient causes it is not possible to go on to infinity, because in all efficient causes following in order, the first is the cause of the intermediate cause, and the intermediate is the cause of the ultimate cause, whether the intermediate cause be several, or only one. Now to take away the cause is to take away the effect.

Therefore, if there be no first cause among efficient causes, there will be no ultimate, nor any intermediate cause. But if in efficient causes it is possible to go on to infinity, there will be no first efficient cause, neither will there be an ultimate effect, nor any intermediate efficient causes; all of which is plainly false. Therefore it is necessary to admit a first efficient cause, to which everyone gives the name of God.

The third way is taken from possibility and necessity, and runs thus. We find in nature things that are possible to be and not to be, since they are found to be generated, and to corrupt, and consequently, they are possible to be and not to be. But it is impossible for these always to exist, for that which is possible not to be at some time is not. Therefore, if everything is possible not to be, then at one time there could have been nothing in existence. Now if this were true, even now there would be nothing in existence, because that which does not exist only begins to exist by something already existing. Therefore, if at one time nothing was in existence, it would have been impossible for anything to have begun to exist; and thus even now nothing would be in existence—which is absurd. Therefore, not all beings are merely possible, but there must exist something the existence of which is necessary. But every necessary thing either has its necessity caused by another, or not. Now it is impossible to go on to infinity in necessary things which have their necessity caused by another, as has been already proved in regard to efficient causes. Therefore we cannot but postulate the existence of some being having of itself its own necessity, and not receiving it from another, but rather causing in others their necessity. This all men speak of as God.

The fourth way is taken from the gradation to be found in things. Among beings there are some more and some less good, true, noble and the like. But "more" and "less" are predicated of different things, according as they resemble in their different ways something which is the maximum, as a thing is said to be hotter according as it more nearly resembles that which is hottest; so that there is something which is truest, something best, something noblest and, consequently, something which is uttermost being; for those things that are greatest in truth are greatest in being, as it is written in Metaph. ii. Now the maximum in any genus is the cause of all in that genus; as fire, which is the maximum heat, is the cause of all hot things. Therefore there must also be something which is to all beings the cause of their being, goodness, and every other perfection; and this we call God.

The fifth way is taken from the governance of the world. We see that things which lack intelligence, such as natural bodies, act for an end, and this is evident from their acting always, or nearly always, in the same way, so as to obtain the best result. Hence it is plain that not fortuitously, but designedly, do they achieve their end. Now whatever lacks intelligence cannot move towards an end, unless it be directed by some being endowed with knowledge and intelligence; as the arrow is shot to its mark by the archer. Therefore some intelligent being exists by whom all natural things are directed to their end; and this being we call God.

Reply to Objection 1: As Augustine says (Enchiridion xi): "Since God is the highest good, He would not allow any evil to exist in His works, unless His omnipotence and goodness were such as to bring good even out of evil." This is part of the infmite goodness of God, that He should allow evil to exist, and out of it produce good.

Reply to Objection 2: Since nature works for a determinate end under the direction of a higher agent, whatever is done by nature must needs be traced back to God, as to its first cause. So also whatever is done voluntarily must also be traced back to some higher cause other than human reason or will, since these can change or fail; for all things that are changeable and capable of defect must be traced back to an immovable and self-necessary first principle, as was shown in the body of the Article.

from *Inferno*

Dante Alighieri
Translated by Allen Mandelbaum

CANTO I

Nel mezzo del cammin di nostra vita
mi ritrovai per una selva oscura,
ché la diritta via era smarrita.
Ahi quanto a dir qual era è cosa dura 4
esta selva selvaggia e aspra e forte
che nel pensier rinova la paura!
Tant' è amara che poco è più morte; 7
ma per trattar del ben ch'i' vi trovai,
dirò de l'altre cose ch'i' v'ho scorte.
Io non so ben ridir com' i' v'intrai, 10
tant' era pien di sonno a quel punto
che la verace via abbandonai.
Ma poi ch'i' fui al piè d'un colle giunto, 13
là dove terminava quella valle
che m'avea di paura il cor compunto,
guardai in alto e vidi le sue spalle 16
vestite già de' raggi del pianeta
che mena dritto altrui per ogne calle.
Allor fu la paura un poco queta, 19
che nel lago del cor m'era durata
la notte ch'i' passai con tanta pieta.
E come quei che con lena affannata, 22
uscito fuor del pelago a la riva,
si volge a l'acqua perigliosa e guata,
così l'animo mio, ch'ancor fuggiva, 25
si volse a retro a rimirar lo passo
che non lasciò già mai persona viva.
Poi ch'èi posato un poco il corpo lasso, 28
ripresi via per la piaggia diserta,
sì che 'l piè fermo sempre era 'l più basso.

The voyager-narrator astray by night in a dark forest. Morning and the sunlit hill. Three beasts that impede his ascent. The encounter with Virgil, who offers his guidance and an alternative path through two of the three realms the voyager must visit.

When I had journeyed half of our life's way,
I found myself within a shadowed forest,
for I had lost the path that does not stray.
Ah, it is hard to speak of what it was, 4
that savage forest, dense and difficult,
which even in recall renews my fear:
so bitter—death is hardly more severe! 7
But to retell the good discovered there,
I'll also tell the other things I saw.
I cannot clearly say how I had entered 10
the wood; I was so full of sleep just at
the point where I abandoned the true path.
But when I'd reached the bottom of a hill— 13
it rose along the boundary of the valley
that had harassed my heart with so much fear—
I looked on high and saw its shoulders clothed 16
already by the rays of that same planet
which serves to lead men straight along all roads.
At this my fear was somewhat quieted; 19
for through the night of sorrow I had spent,
the lake within my heart felt terror present.
And just as he who, with exhausted breath, 22
having escaped from sea to shore, turns back
to watch the dangerous waters he has quit,
so did my spirit, still a fugitive, 25
turn back to look intently at the pass
that never has let any man survive.
I let my tired body rest awhile. 28
Moving again, I tried the lonely slope—
my firm foot always was the one below.

Ed ecco, quasi al cominciar de l'erta, 31
una lonza leggiera e presta molto,
che di pel macolato era coverta;
e non mi si partia dinanzi al volto, 34
anzi 'mpediva tanto il mio cammino,
ch'i' fui per ritornar più volte vòlto.
Temp' era dal principio del mattino, 37
e 'l sol montava 'n sù con quelle stelle
ch'eran con lui quando l'amor divino
mosse di prima quelle cose belle; 40
sì ch'a bene sperar m'era cagione
di quella fiera a la gaetta pelle
l'ora del tempo e la dolce stagione; 43
ma non sì che paura non mi desse
la vista che m'apparve d'un leone.
Questi parea che contra me venisse 46
con la test' alta e con rabbiosa fame,
sì che parea che l'aere ne tremesse.
Ed una lupa, che di tutte brame 49
sembiava carca ne la sua magrezza,
e molte genti fé già viver grame,
questa mi porse tanto di gravezza 52
con la paura ch'uscia di sua vista,
ch'io perdei la speranza de l'altezza.
E qual è quei che volontieri acquista, 55
e giugne 'l tempo che perder lo face,
che 'n tutti suoi pensier piange e s'attrista;
tal mi fece la bestia sanza pace, 58
che, venendomi 'ncontro, a poco a poco
mi ripigneva là dove 'l sol tace.
Mentre ch'i' rovinava in basso loco, 61
dinanzi a li occhi mi si fu offerto
chi per lungo silenzio parea fioco.
Quando vidi costui nel gran diserto, 64
"*Miserere* di me," gridai a lui,
"qual che tu sii, od ombra od omo certo!"
Rispuosemi: "Non omo, omo già fui, 67
e li parenti miei furon lombardi,
mantoani per patrïa ambedui.

And almost where the hillside starts to rise— 31
look there!—a leopard, very quick and lithe,
a leopard covered with a spotted hide.
He did not disappear from sight, but stayed; 34
indeed, he so impeded my ascent
that I had often to turn back again.
The time was the beginning of the morning; 37
the sun was rising now in fellowship
with the same stars that had escorted it
when Divine Love first moved those things of beauty; 40
so that the hour and the gentle season
gave me good cause for hopefulness on seeing
that beast before me with his speckled skin; 43
but hope was hardly able to prevent
the fear I felt when I beheld a lion.
His head held high and ravenous with hunger— 46
even the air around him seemed to shudder—
this lion seemed to make his way against me.
And then a she-wolf showed herself; she seemed 49
to carry every craving in her leanness;
she had already brought despair to many.
The very sight of her so weighted me 52
with fearfulness that I abandoned hope
of ever climbing up that mountain slope.
Even as he who glories while he gains 55
will, when the time has come to tally loss,
lament with every thought and turn despondent,
so was I when I faced that restless beast, 58
which, even as she stalked me, step by step
had thrust me back to where the sun is speechless.
While I retreated down to lower ground, 61
before my eyes there suddenly appeared
one who seemed faint because of the long silence.
When I saw him in that vast wilderness, 64
"Have pity on me," were the words I cried,
"whatever you may be—a shade, a man."
He answered me: "Not man; I once was man. 67
Both of my parents came from Lombardy,
and both claimed Mantua as native city.

Nacqui *sub Iulio,* ancor che fosse tardi, 70
e vissi a Roma sotto 'l buono Augusto
nel tempo de li dèi falsi e bugiardi.
Poeta fui, e cantai di quel giusto 73
figliuol d'Anchise che venne di Troia,
poi che 'l superbo Ilïón fu combusto.
Ma tu perché ritorni a tanta noia? 76
perché non sali il dilettoso monte
ch'è principio e cagion di tutta gioia?"
"Or se' tu quel Virgilio e quella fonte 79
che spandi di parlar sì largo fiume?"
rispuos' io lui con vergognosa fronte.
"O de li altri poeti onore e lume, 82
vagliami 'l lungo studio e 'l grande amore
che m'ha fatto cercar lo tuo volume.
Tu se' lo mio maestro e 'l mio autore, 85
tu se' solo colui da cu' io tolsi
lo bello stilo che m'ha fatto onore.
Vedi la bestia per cu' io mi volsi; 88
aiutami da lei, famoso saggio,
ch'ella mi fa tremar le vene e i polsi."
"A te convien tenere altro vïaggio," 91
rispuose, poi che lagrimar mi vide,
"se vuo' campar d'esto loco selvaggio;
ché questa bestia, per la qual tu gride, 94
non lascia altrui passar per la sua via,
ma tanto lo 'mpedisce che l'uccide;
e ha natura sì malvagia e ria, 97
che mai non empie la bramosa voglia,
e dopo 'l pasto ha più fame che pria.
Molti son li animali a cui s'ammoglia, 100
e più saranno ancora, infin che 'l veltro
verrà, che la farà morir con doglia.
Questi non ciberà terra né peltro, 103
ma sapïenza, amore e virtute,
e sua nazion sarà tra feltro e feltro.
Di quella umile Italia fia salute 106
per cui morì la vergine Cammilla,
Eurialo e Turno e Niso di ferute.

And I was born, though late, *sub Julio,* 70
and lived in Rome under the good Augustus—
the season of the false and lying gods.
I was a poet, and I sang the righteous 73
son of Anchises who had come from Troy
when flames destroyed the pride of Ilium.
But why do you return to wretchedness? 76
Why not climb up the mountain of delight,
the origin and cause of every joy?"
"And are you then that Virgil, you the fountain 79
that freely pours so rich a stream of speech?"
I answered him with shame upon my brow.
"O light and honor of all other poets, 82
may my long study and the intense love
that made me search your volume serve me now.
You are my master and my author, you— 85
the only one from whom my writing drew
the noble style for which I have been honored.
You see the beast that made me turn aside; 88
help me, o famous sage, to stand against her,
for she has made my blood and pulses shudder."
"It is another path that you must take," 91
he answered when he saw my tearfulness,
"if you would leave this savage wilderness;
the beast that is the cause of your outcry 94
allows no man to pass along her track,
but blocks him even to the point of death;
her nature is so squalid, so malicious 97
that she can never sate her greedy will;
when she has fed, she's hungrier than ever.
She mates with many living souls and shall 100
yet mate with many more, until the Greyhound
arrives, inflicting painful death on her.
That Hound will never feed on land or pewter, 103
but find his fare in wisdom, love, and virtue;
his place of birth shall be between two felts.
He will restore low-lying Italy 106
for which the maid Camilla died of wounds,
and Nisus, Turnus, and Euryalus.

Questi la caccerà per ogne villa, 109
fin che l'avrà rimessa ne lo 'nferno,
là onde 'nvidia prima dipartilla.
Ond' io per lo tuo me' penso e discerno 112
che tu mi segui, e io sarò tua guida,
e trarrotti di qui per loco etterno,
ove udirai le disperate strida, 115
vedrai li antichi spiriti dolenti,
ch'a la seconda morte ciascun grida;
e vederai color che son contenti 118
nel foco, perché speran di venire
quando che sia a le beate genti.
A le quai poi se tu vorrai salire, 121
anima fia a ciò più di me degna:
con lei ti lascerò nel mio partire;
ché quello imperador che là sù regna, 124
perch' i' fu' ribellante a la sua legge,
non vuol che 'n sua città per me si vegna.
In tutte parti impera e quivi regge; 127
quivi è la sua città e l'alto seggio:
oh felice colui cu' ivi elegge!"
E io a lui: "Poeta, io ti richeggio 130
per quello Dio che tu non conoscesti,
a ciò ch'io fugga questo male e peggio,
che tu mi meni là dov' or dicesti, 133
sì ch'io veggia la porta di san Pietro
e color cui tu fai cotanto mesti."
Allor si mosse, e io li tenni dietro. 136

And he will hunt that beast through every city 109
until he thrusts her back again to Hell,
from which she was first sent above by envy.
Therefore, I think and judge it best for you 112
to follow me, and I shall guide you, taking
you from this place through an eternal place,
where you shall hear the howls of desperation 115
and see the ancient spirits in their pain,
as each of them laments his second death;
and you shall see those souls who are content 118
within the fire, for they hope to reach—
whenever that may be—the blessed people.
If you would then ascend as high as these, 121
a soul more worthy than I am will guide you;
I'll leave you in her care when I depart,
because that Emperor who reigns above, 124
since I have been rebellious to His law,
will not allow me entry to His city.
He governs everywhere, but rules from there; 127
there is His city, His high capital:
o happy those He chooses to be there!"
And I replied: "O poet—by that God 130
whom you had never come to know—I beg you,
that I may flee this evil and worse evils,
to lead me to the place of which you spoke, 133
that I may see the gateway of Saint Peter
and those whom you describe as sorrowful."
Then he set out, and I moved on behind him. 136

I·2

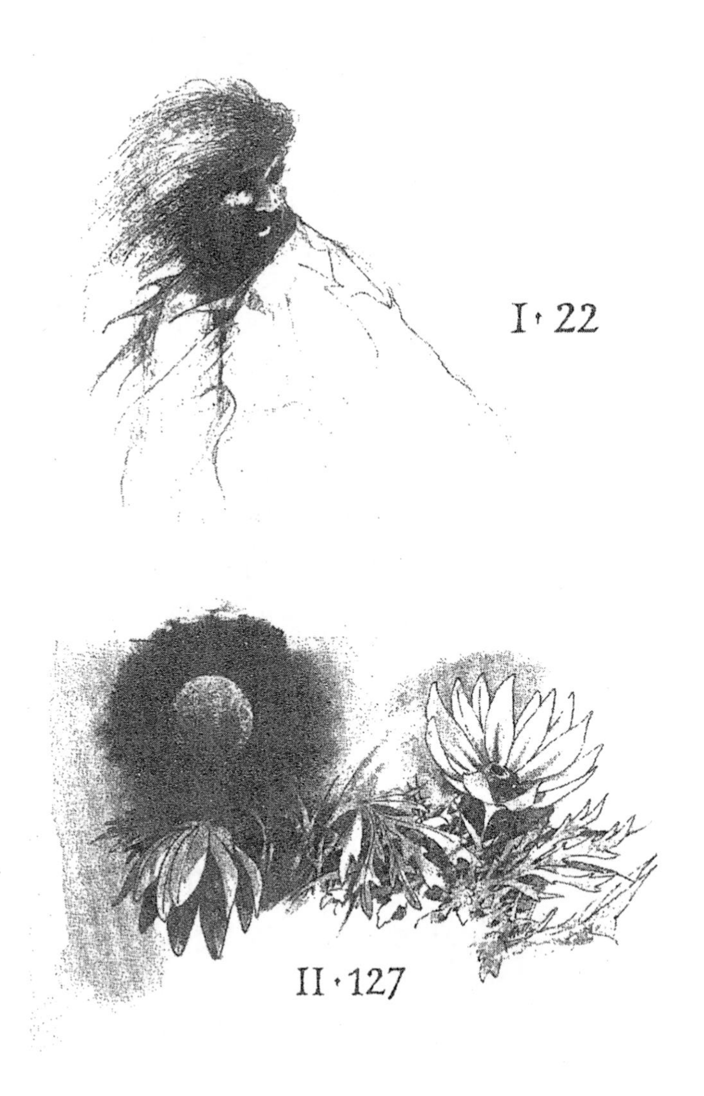
I • 22
II • 127

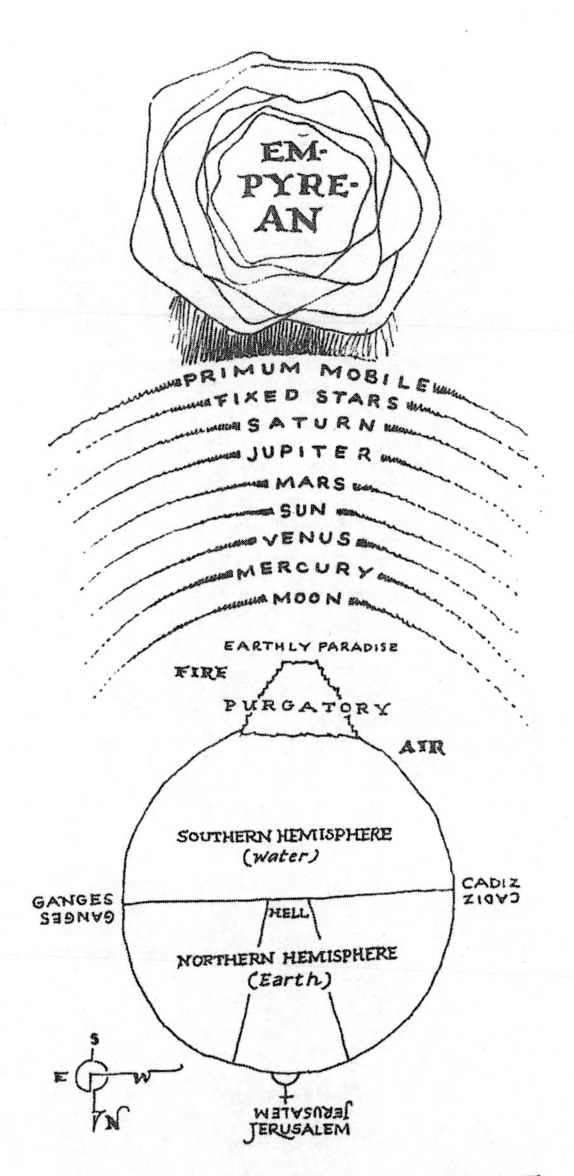

THE UNIVERSE OF DANTE

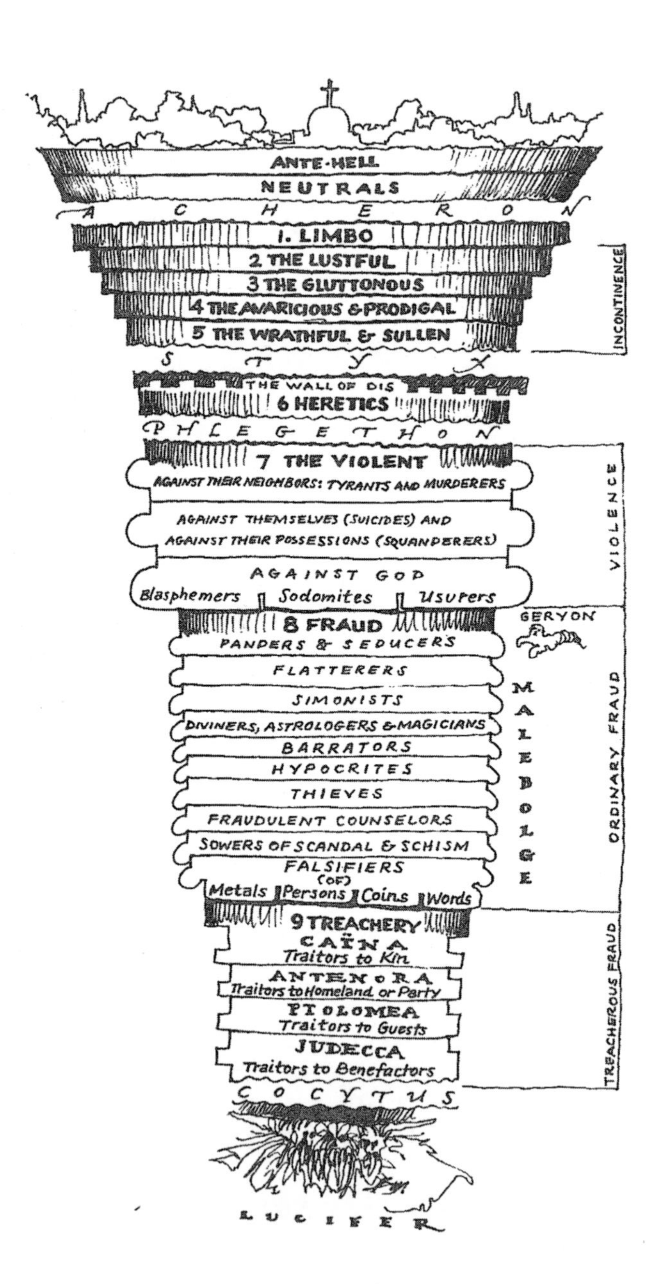
ANTE-HELL
NEUTRALS
A C H E R O N
1. LIMBO
2 THE LUSTFUL
3 THE GLUTTONOUS
4 THE AVARICIOUS & PRODIGAL
5 THE WRATHFUL & SULLEN
INCONTINENCE
S T Y X
THE WALL OF DIS
6 HERETICS
P H L E G E T H O N
7 THE VIOLENT
AGAINST THEIR NEIGHBORS: TYRANTS AND MURDERERS
AGAINST THEMSELVES (SUICIDES) AND
AGAINST THEIR POSSESSIONS (SQUANDERERS)
AGAINST GOD
Blasphemers
Sodomites
Usurers
VIOLENCE
GERYON
8 FRAUD
PANDERS & SEDUCERS
FLATTERERS
SIMONISTS
DIVINERS, ASTROLOGERS & MAGICIANS
BARRATORS
HYPOCRITES
THIEVES
FRAUDULENT COUNSELORS
SOWERS OF SCANDAL & SCHISM
FALSIFIERS
(OF)
Metals
Persons
Coins
Words
M A L E B O L G E
ORDINARY FRAUD
9 TREACHERY
CAÏNA
Traitors to Kin
ANTENORA
Traitors to Homeland or Party
PTOLOMEA
Traitors to Guests
JUDECCA
Traitors to Benefactors
TREACHEROUS FRAUD
C O C Y T U S
LUCIFER

Notes

CANTO I

1–3 It is not known exactly when Dante began to write the *Inferno*. But he was surely writing while in exile from Florence; and he was constructing a fiction dated before both his exile and his act of writing began. This predating gives him some advantage in "foreseeing" events that occurred between the date of the tale and the date of the telling.

Dante delays the chief indication of the possible date of his fictive voyage until Canto XXI, 112–114 (see note there for a fuller account). That latter passage allows most commentators to define the night in the dark wood as the night of Maundy Thursday, the night before Good Friday, the evening of April 7 in the year 1300. The day of Good Friday is then spent with the three beasts and Virgil in Canto I, so that the entry into Ante-Hell at the beginning of Canto II takes place on the evening of Good Friday, April 8.

"*Our* life"—with its "possessive of human solidarity" (Spitzer)—links the particularity of Dante the wayfarer to the universality of everyman. In the *Convivio* (IV, xxiii, 6–10), Dante fixes 35 years as the midpoint of man's life, following Psalm 89:10 (90:10 in the King James), which sets 70 years as the length of man's days. Thus, for Dante himself, who was born in 1265, the year 1300 accords well with the cited texts and with the passage in Isaiah (38:10), "In the middle of my days, I shall go to the gates of Hell."

2 The "shadowed" or dark forest is our way station to many images of darkness, blindness, and obscurity that obsess Hell—that realm in which the sun never appears, as it does throughout Purgatory—though Virgil, somewhat clairvoyantly, will refer to the movement of the unseen skies on the earth above "starless" (III, 23) Hell. (While *Inferno* begins at night, *Purgatorio* begins at dawn and *Paradiso* at noon.)

But the forest precedes the journey through Hell. It is the dark wood of life on earth when lived in sin; it is Dante's interior wood; and it is the wood of political darkness, of Florence, of Italy, of papal corruption, of the absence of imperial authority.

5 In accord with most commentators, this translation sees *forte* as "difficult" (that is, difficult to traverse—or, perhaps better, to escape from).

8 The "good discovered there" has a host of probable meanings, but it certainly anticipates Dante's rescue by Virgil and the beginning of the long journey to salvation.

13–18 At this point Dante sees the alternative to the dark forest: the "hill"—that is, the path to virtue, which leads upward. The hill is illuminated by the sun, which Dante does not see directly but whose rays stand for the light of God's illuminating grace. Dante's access to the hill, however, is blocked by the three beasts he encounters—beasts symbolic of different aspects of human sinfulness (see 31–60).

17 In the Ptolemaic system, the sun is a "planet" revolving around the earth. For the cosmos of Dante see the diagram on p. 343.

21 In terms of the physiology of Dante's time, "the lake of my heart" refers to that inner chamber of the heart thought to be the physical seat of the emotion of fear.

22–25 This first simile of the poem already draws on an important theme of imagery throughout the *Comedy*: the sea. It is not unrelated to the Red Sea of the Exodus (Singleton) and, given Dante's use of *pelago* here for "sea," to the exhausted Trojan survivors of the storm in *Aen.* I, 242; 251–252 (Hollander) or to the landing from the *pelago* that precedes Aeneas's own entry into the underworld *(Aen.* VI, 1–3).

30 The difficulty of interpreting this line has given pause to many commentators. Boccaccio's literal reading was that those who climb always tend to support themselves more on that foot which remains below. This translation is compatible with his reading—and with the view that the firm foot may, alternately, be the left, then the right. Recent allegorists (Freccero, Mazzoni) identify the firm foot as *one* foot, the left—the foot weighed down by appetites, concupiscence, limping will—as against the right—the foot of the intellect. For them, *fermo* means "halting, dragging, inhibiting."

31–60 For most early commentators—and, after many alternate proposals, for many moderns—the leopard represents lust; the lion, pride; the she-wolf, avarice or cupidity. Whatever specific area of sin is assigned to each animal, the Italian certainly links them alliteratively to each other—*lonza—leone—lupa* (Ragonese in the *E.D.)* (which this translation cannot do)—and to Lucifer of Canto XXXIII (Sarolli). The translation's "leopard" keeps the text close, as early commentators do, to Jer. 5:6, which speaks of a lion, a wolf, and a leopard. But *lonza* may be a lynxlike animal (see *Aen.* I, 458) or a strange hybrid.

37–40 The world was believed to have been created in spring, with the sun in the constellation of Aries; and Dante's own voyage takes place in the springtime.

60 Dante's use of synesthesia—the merging of the visual ("the sun") and the auditory ("speechless")—recurs in line 63.

63 This translation's "faint" for *fioco* echoes the auditory and visual connotations of the Italian, though leaning here to the visual: Dante sees Virgil indistinctly—in a shadowed space where the "sun is speechless." This initiates and reinforces Dante's uncertainty, which gives rise to the "whatever you may be" of line 66. But this shadowed space also resonates as time—the long ages in which Virgil did not have the full voice he will now find again through and in Dante.

70–72 Virgil (70–19 B.C.) was born *sub Julio,* in the time of Julius Caesar, though too late to win Caesar's esteem. Though "false and lying gods" is close indeed to Augustine's *"deos falsos fallacesque" (City of God* II, xxix, 2), Dante's own use of pagan gods in the machinery of the *Comedy* would reframe this assertion: the pagan gods were "false and lying" when seen as sufficient ends in themselves, but they carried some truth as prefigurations of the Christian God.

73–75 "The righteous son of Anchises" is Aeneas, hero of the *Aeneid,* to which Dante refers repeatedly in the *Inferno.*

82–87 "The noble style" is the tragic style, the style of epic narrative and of the exalted, spacious, ethically-intellectually committed lyric. Dante can claim to "have been honored" for his achievement in the latter category before 1300, but Virgil was hardly his chief mentor then. This passage seems, rather, to carry wishful meaning, the force and weight of desire, as if Dante were saying, "You, Virgil, using the ancient but ever-living tongue of the Latins, gave full life to the stately tragic style, the noble upper register, in epic; my mixed, comic style, drawing on all three styles—the upper, the middle, the lower—for this my modern, Christian, prophetic epic in the maternal tongue of the Italians, the modern Latins, needs you as exemplary inspiration and would achieve honor comparable to yours."

Boccaccio, glossing "for which I have been honored" with "here he uses the past tense for the future, producing a solecism," senses the same intention.

101 The Greyhound of this prophetic passage, the redeemer who "will restore low-lying Italy" (106), has been identified in very diverse ways: as an ecclesiastic; as a secular political figure; as Christ; as Dante himself; as Cangrande della Scala of Verona, Dante's benefactor and an Imperial viceroy; and as others. Most probably the term connotes a political prophecy; almost as probably it foretells and hopes for a Holy Roman Emperor or his viceroy; and possibly it may refer to Henry VII, who was elected Holy Roman Emperor on November 27, 1308.

103–104 Earthly goods and nourishment are represented by "land or pewter" (which here would stand for "money"); spiritual goods by the attributes of the Trinity—wisdom, the Son; love, the Holy Ghost; virtue, the Father. This is not, however, a necessary argument for reading the Greyhound as a papal or ecclesiastical figure: for Dante elsewhere in his works, temporal authority, too, has its direct source in God.

105 Those who opt for Cangrande della Scala as the Greyhound capitalize the two *Feltros,* referring them to Feltre and Montefeltro, towns that mark the rough limits of Cangrande's domains. But this translation renders a lowercase *feltro* as "felt": the "two felts" would be the two felt-lined urns in which "Yes" and "No" ballots, respectively, were deposited in elections in Dante's time; such urns could call up the image of electing a Holy Roman Emperor. In that case, the "place of birth" would refer, not to the Greyhound's physical birth, but to his birth in and his assumption of office.

106 Virgil's *humilemque videmus Italiam,* "we sight... the low coastline of Italy" *(Aen.* III, 681–682), is a geographic observation: Dante's *umile Italia,* "low-lying Italy," on the other hand, has moral overtones.

106–107 Those mentioned in these lines are all figures in Virgil's *Aeneid* who died in the war between the Trojans and the Latins. Camilla was a faithful woman warrior who aided Turnus, King of the Rutulians, in the war of the Latins against Aeneas *(Aen.* VII, 1055–1072; XI, 854–1126). Nisus and Euryalus were close friends who died together after a night attack on a Rutulian camp *(Aen.* IX, 232–597). Turnus was killed in the single combat with Aeneas that is placed at the end of the *Aeneid* (XII, 928–1271). This is one point where Dante shares Virgil's overarching compassion, which embraces the victors and the vanquished; Dante alternates Latin, Trojan, Latin, Trojan—and cites two Trojans who were, themselves, sacrificed in the course of the Trojans' victorious campaign.

117 This translation sees "the second death" as the state of damned souls rejoined with their bodies after the Last Judgment, and translates *grida* as "laments"—a use of this word that presents some difficulty. But as F. Mazzoni, who is followed here, notes: this line is "more tormented and disputed than, in itself, it deserves to be."

118–120 The souls in Purgatory.

121 "These" are "the blessed people" in Paradise.

122 "A soul more worthy than I am" is Beatrice, born in 1266, the year after Dante's birth, loved by Dante from his boyhood, and celebrated by him—after her death in 1290—in his *Vita Nuova.* Boccaccio and other 14th-century commentators, including Dante's son Pietro, identify her as one of the daughters of Folco Portinari; Boccaccio also mentions her marriage to a Simone de' Bardi. Folco Portinari's will of 1288 confirms this last detail for Beatrice Portinari. In the *Comedy,* the historical Beatrice is spokeswoman for the divine science of theology.

125–126 Because, as a pagan, Virgil did not worship God, he is not allowed entry to His city. For a fuller explanation of pagans' status in the Christian scheme of the afterlife, see Canto IV, 24; 52–61, and notes.

Virgil's description of Heaven as a city makes explicit the analogy drawn throughout the *Comedy,* and especially in the *Inferno,* between the Roman Empire (see II, 13–24, and note) and the heavenly City of God.

134 Since Virgil is to lead Dante through, but not beyond, Purgatory, it is best to read "the gateway of St. Peter" as the gate of Purgatory, where the vicar of St. Peter is custodian, rather than the entry to Paradise (which, in any case, in Dante's account, has no gate).

from *Revelations of Divine Love*

Julian of Norwich

This is a vision shown, through God's goodness, to a devout woman, and her name is Julian, and she is a recluse at Norwich and is still alive in the year of our Lord 1413; in this vision there are many comforting and very moving words for all those who wish to be lovers of Christ.

1

I asked for three graces of God's gift. The first was vivid perception of Christ's Passion, the second was bodily sickness and the third was for God to give me three wounds. I thought of the first as I was meditating: it seemed to me that I could feel the Passion of Christ strongly, but yet I longed by God's grace to feel it more intensely. I thought how I wished I had been there at the crucifixion with Mary Magdalene and with others who were Christ's dear friends, that I might have seen in the flesh the Passion of our Lord which he suffered for me, so that I could have suffered with him as others did who loved him. Nevertheless, I firmly believed in all the torments of Christ as Holy Church reveals and teaches them, and also in the paintings of crucifixes that are made by God's grace in the likeness of Christ's Passion, according to the teaching of Holy Church, as far as human imagination can reach.

In spite of all this true faith, I longed to be shown him in the flesh so that I might have more knowledge of our Lord and Saviour's bodily suffering and of our Lady's fellow-suffering and that of all his true friends who have believed in his pain then and since; I wanted to be one of them and suffer with him. I never wished for any other sight or showing of God until my soul left my body, for I faithfully trusted that I would be saved, and my intention was this: that afterwards, because of the showing, I would have a truer perception of Christ's Passion.

As for the second gift, there came to me with contrition, freely, without any effort on my part, a strong wish to have of God's gift a bodily sickness. And I wanted this bodily sickness to be to the death, so that I might in that sickness receive all the rites of Holy Church, that I might myself believe I was dying and that everyone who saw me might believe the same, for I wanted no hopes of fleshly or earthly life. I longed to have in this sickness every kind of suffering both of body and soul that I would experience if I died, with all the terror and turmoil of the fiends, and all other kinds of torment, except for actually giving up the ghost, because I hoped that it might be to my benefit when I died, for I longed to be soon with my God.

I longed for these two things—the Passion and the sickness—with one reservation, for it seemed to me that they went beyond the common course of prayers; and therefore I said, 'Lord, you know what I would have, If it is your will that I should have it, grant it to me. And if it is not your will, good Lord, do not be displeased, for I only want what you want.' I asked for this sickness in my youth, to have it when I was thirty years old.

As for the third gift, I heard a man of Holy Church tell the story of Saint Cecilia; from his description I understood that she received three sword wounds in the neck from which she slowly and painfully died. Moved by this I conceived a great longing, praying our Lord God that he would grant me three wounds in my lifetime: that is to say, the wound of contrition, the wound of compassion and the wound of an earnest longing for God. Just as I asked for the other two with a reservation, so I asked for the third with no reservation.

The first two of the longings just mentioned passed from my mind, and the third stayed with me continually.

2

And when I was thirty and a half years old, God sent me a bodily sickness in which I lay for three days and three nights; and on the fourth night I received all the rites of Holy Church and did not believe that I would live until morning. And after this I lingered on for two days and two nights. And on the third night I often thought that I was dying, and so did those who were with me. But at this time I was very sorry and reluctant to die, not because there was anything on earth that I wanted to live for, nor because I feared anything, for I trusted in God, but because I wanted to live so as to love God better and for longer, so that through the grace of longer life I might know and love God better in the bliss of heaven. For it seemed to me that all the short time I could live here was as nothing compared with that heavenly bliss. So I thought, 'My good Lord, may my ceasing to live be to your glory!' And I was answered in my reason, and by the pains I felt, that I was dying. And I fully accepted the will of God with all the will of my heart.

So I endured till day, and by then my body was dead to all sensation from the waist down. Then I felt I wanted to be in a sitting position, leaning with my head back against the bedding, so that my heart could be more freely at God's disposition, and so that I could think of God while I was still alive; and those who were with me sent for the parson, my parish priest, to be present at my death. He came, and a boy with him, and brought a cross, and by the time he came my eyes were fixed and I could not speak. The parson set the cross before my face and said, 'Daughter, I have brought you the image of your Saviour. Look upon it and be comforted, in reverence to him that died for you and me.' It seemed to me that I was well as I was, for my eyes were looking fixedly upwards into heaven, where I trusted that I was going. But nevertheless I consented to fix my eyes on the face of the crucifix if I could, so as to be able to do so for longer until the moment of my death; because I thought that I might be able to bear looking straight ahead for longer than I could manage to look upwards. After this my sight began to fail and the room was dim all around me, as dark as if it had been night, except that in the image of the cross an ordinary, household light remained—I could not understand how. Everything except the cross was ugly to me, as if crowded with fiends. After this I felt as if the upper part of my body was beginning to die. My hands fell down on either side, and my head settled down sideways for weakness. The greatest pain that I felt was shortness of breath and failing of life. Then I truly believed that I was at the point of death. And at this moment all my suffering suddenly left me, and I was as completely well, especially in the upper part of my body, as ever I was before or after. I marvelled at this change, for it seemed to me a mysterious work of God, not a natural one. And yet, although I felt comfortable, I still did not expect to live, nor did feeling more comfortable comfort me entirely, for I felt that I would rather have been released from this world, for in my heart I was willing to die.

3

And it suddenly occurred to me that I should entreat our Lord graciously to give me the second wound, so that he would fill my whole body with remembrance of the feeling of his blessed Passion, as I had prayed before; for I wanted his pains to be my pains, with compassion, and then longing for God. Yet in this I never asked for a bodily sight or any kind of showing of God, but for fellow-suffering, such as it seemed to me a naturally kind soul might feel for our Lord Jesus, who was willing to become a mortal man for love. I wanted to suffer with him, while living in my mortal body, as God would give me grace.

And I suddenly saw the red blood trickling down from under the crown of thorns, all hot, freshly, plentifully and vividly, just as I imagined it was at the moment when the crown of thorns was thrust on to his blessed head—he who was both God and man, the same who suffered for me. I believed truly and strongly that it was he himself who showed me this, without any intermediary, and then I said, 'Benedicite dominus!' Because I meant this with such deep veneration, I said it in a very loud voice; and I was astounded, feeling wonder and admiration that he was willing to be so familiar with a sinful being living in this wretched flesh. I supposed at that time that our Lord Jesus of his courteous love would show me comfort before the time of my temptation. For I thought it might well be, by God's permission and under his protection, that I would be tempted by fiends before I died. With this sight of the blessed Passion, along with the Godhead that I saw in my mind, I saw that I, yes, and every creature living that would be saved, could have strength to resist all the fiends of hell and all spiritual enemies.

4

And at the same time that. I saw this bodily sight, our Lord showed me a spiritual vision of his familiar love. I saw that for us he is everything that is good and comforting and helpful. He is our clothing, wrapping and enveloping us for love, embracing us and guiding us in all things, hanging about us in tender love, so that he can never leave us. And so in this vision, as I understand it, I saw truly that he is everything that is good for us.

And in this vision he showed me a little thing, the size of a hazel-nut, lying in the palm of my hand, and to my mind's eye it was as round as any ball. I looked at it and thought, 'What can this be?' And the answer came to me, 'It is all that is made.' I wondered how it could last, for it was so small I thought it might suddenly disappear. And the answer in my mind was, 'It lasts and will last for ever because God loves it; and in the same way everything exists through the love of God.' In this little thing I saw three attributes: the first is that God made it, the second is that he loves it, the third is that God cares for it. But what does that mean to me? Truly, the maker, the lover, the carer; for until I become one substance with him, I can never have love, rest or true bliss; that is to say, until I am so bound to him that there may be no created thing between my God and me. And who shall do this deed? Truly, himself, by his mercy and his grace, for he has made me and blessedly restored me to that end.

Then God brought our Lady into my mind. I saw her spiritually in bodily likeness, a meek and simple maid, young of age, in the same bodily form as when she conceived. God also showed me part of the wisdom and truth of her soul so that I understood with what reverence she beheld her God who is her maker, and how reverently she marvelled that he chose to be born of her, a simple creature of his own making. For what made her marvel was that he who was her Maker chose to be born of the creature he had made. And the wisdom of her faithfulness, and knowledge of the greatness of her Maker and the littleness of her who was made, moved her to say very humbly to the angel Gabriel, 'Behold, the handmaid of the Lord.' With this sight I really understood that she is greater in worthiness and fullness of grace than all that God made below her; for nothing that is made is above her except the blessed Manhood of Christ. This little thing that is made that is below our Lady Saint Mary, God showed it to me as small as if it had been a hazel-nut. It was so small I thought it might have disappeared.

In this blessed revelation God showed me three nothings. Of these nothings this was the first I was shown, and all men and women who wish to lead the contemplative life need to have knowledge of it: they should choose to set at nothing everything that is made so as to have the love of God who is unmade. This is why those who choose to occupy themselves with earthly business and are always pursuing worldly success have nothing here of God in their hearts and souls: because they love and seek their rest in this little thing where there is no rest, and know nothing of God, who is almighty, all wise and all good, for he is true rest. God wishes to be known, and is pleased that we should rest in him; for all that is below him does nothing to satisfy us. And this is why, until all that is made seems as nothing, no soul can be at rest. When a soul sets all at nothing for love, to have him who is everything that is good, then it is able to receive spiritual rest.

5

And during the time that our Lord was showing in spiritual sight what I have just described, the bodily sight of the plentiful bleeding from Christ's head remained, and as long as I could see this sight I kept saying, 'Benedicite dominus!' In this first showing from our Lord I saw six things in my understanding: the first is the signs of Christ's blessed Passion and the plentiful shedding of his precious blood; the second is the Maiden who is his beloved mother; the third is the blessed Godhead that ever was, is and ever shall be, almighty, all wisdom and all love. The fourth is all that he has made; it is vast and wide fair and good, but it looked so small to me because I saw it in the presence of him that is Maker of all things; to a soul that sees the Maker of all, all that is made seems very small. The fifth thing I understood is that he made everything that is made for love; and the same love sustains everything, and shall do so for ever, as has been said before. The sixth is that God is everything that is good, and the goodness that is in everything is God. And all these our Lord showed me in the first vision, and gave me time and space to contemplate it. And when the bodily vision stopped, the spiritual vision remained in my understanding. And I waited with reverent fear, rejoicing in what I saw, and longing, as far as I dared, to see more if it was his will, or else to see the same vision for longer.

6

All that I saw concerning myself, I mean to be applied to all my fellow Christians, for I am taught by our Lord's spiritual showing that this is what he means. And therefore I beg you all for God's sake and advise you all for your own advantage that you stop paying attention to the poor, worldly, sinful creature to whom this vision was shown, and eagerly, attentively, lovingly and humbly contemplate God, who in his gracious love and in his eternal goodness wanted the vision to be generally known to comfort us all. And you who hear and see this vision and this teaching, which come from Jesus Christ to edify your souls, it is God's will and my desire that you should receive it with joy and pleasure as great as if Jesus had shown it to you as he did to me.

I am not good because of the showing, unless I love God better, and so may and should everyone that sees it and hears it with good will and true intention; and so my desire is that it should bring everyone the same advantage that I desired for myself, and this is how God moved me the first time I saw it. For it is universal and addressed to all because we are all one, and I am sure I saw it for the advantage of many others. Indeed it was not shown to me because God loved me better than the lowest soul that is in a state of grace, for I am sure that there are very many who never had a showing or vision, but only the normal teaching of Holy Church, and who love God better than I do. For if I look solely at myself, I am really nothing; but as one of mankind in general, I am in oneness of love with all my fellow Christians; for upon this oneness of love depends the life of all who shall be saved; for God is all that is good, and God has made all that is made, and God loves all that he has made.

And if any man or woman ceases to love any of his fellow Christians, then he loves none, for he does not love all; and so at that moment he is not saved, for he is not at peace; and he who loves all his fellow Christians loves all that is; for in those who shall be saved, all is included: that is all that is made and the Maker of all; for in man is God, and so in man is all. And he who loves all his fellow Christians in this way, he loves all; and he who loves in this way is saved. And thus I wish to love, and thus I love, and thus I am saved. (I am speaking in the person of my fellow Christians.) And the more I love with this kind of love while I am here, the more like I am to the bliss that I shall have in heaven without end, which is God, who in his endless love was willing to become our brother and suffer for us. And I am sure that whoever looks at it in this way will be truly taught and greatly comforted if he needs comfort.

But God forbid that you should say or assume that I am a teacher, for that is not what I mean, nor did I ever mean it; for I am a woman, ignorant, weak and frail. But I know well that I have received what I say from him who is the supreme teacher. But in truth, I am moved to tell you about it by love, for I wish God to be known and my fellow Christians helped, as I wish to be helped myself, so that sin shall be more hated and God more loved. Just because I am a woman, must I therefore believe that I must not tell you about the goodness of God, when I saw at the same time both his goodness and his wish that it should be known? And you will see that clearly in the chapters which follow, if they are well and truly understood. Then you must quickly forget me, a paltry creature, you must not let me hinder you, but look directly at Jesus, who is teacher of all. I speak of those who will be saved, for at this time God showed me no others. But in all things I believe what Holy Church teaches, for in all things I saw this blessed showing of our Lord as one who is in the presence of God, and I never perceived anything in it that bewilders me or keeps me from the true teaching of Holy Church.

7

All this blessed teaching of our Lord God was shown me in three parts: that is, by bodily sight, and by words formed in my understanding, and by spiritual sight. But I neither can nor may show you the spiritual vision as openly or as fully as I would like to. But I trust that our Lord God almighty will, out of his own goodness and love for you, make you receive it more spiritually and more sweetly than I can or may tell you; and so may it be, for we are all one in love. And in all this I was much moved with love for my fellow Christians, wishing that they might see and know what I was seeing; I wanted it to comfort them all as it did me, for the vision was shown for everyone and not for any one particular person. And what comforted me most in the vision was that our Lord is so familiar and courteous. And this was what gave me most happiness and the strongest sense of spiritual safety. Then I said to the people who were with me, 'For me, today is the Day of Judgement.' And I said this because I thought I was dying; for on the day that someone dies, he receives his eternal judgement. I said this because I wanted them to love God better and set a lower value on the vanity of the world, to remind them that life is short, as they might see by my example; for all this time I thought I was dying.

8

And after this I saw with my bodily sight in the face of Christ on the crucifix which hung before me, which I was looking at continuously, a part of his Passion: contempt and spitting, which soiled his body, and blows on his blessed face, and many lingering pains, more than I can tell, and frequent changes of colour, and all his blessed face covered at one time in dry blood. I saw this bodily in distress and darkness, and I wished for better bodily light to see it more clearly. And I was answered in my reason that if God wanted to show me more he would, but I needed no light but him.

And after this I saw God in an instant, that is in my understanding, and in seeing this I saw that he is in everything. I looked attentively, knowing and recognizing in this vision that he does all that is done. I marvelled at this sight with quiet awe, and I thought, 'What is sin?' For I saw truly that God does everything, no matter how small. And nothing happens by accident or luck, but by the eternal providence of God's wisdom. Therefore I was obliged to accept that everything which is done is well done, and I was sure that God never sins. Therefore it seemed to me that sin is nothing, for in all this vision no sin appeared. So I marvelled no longer about this but looked at our Lord to see what he would show me; and at another time God showed me what sin is, in its naked essence, as I shall recount later.

And after this I saw, as I watched, the body of Christ bleeding abundantly, hot and freshly and vividly, just as I saw the head before. And I saw the blood coming from weals from the scourging, and in my vision it ran so abundantly that it seemed to me that if at that moment it had been natural blood, the whole bed would have been blood-soaked and even the floor around. God has provided us on earth with abundant water for our use and bodily refreshment, because of the tender love he has for us, yet it pleases him better that we should freely take his holy blood to wash away our sins; for there is no liquid created which he likes to give us so much, for it is so plentiful and it shares our nature.

And after this, before God revealed any words, he allowed me to contemplate longer all that I had seen, and all that was in it. And then, without any voice or opening of lips, there were formed in my soul these words: 'By this is the Fiend overcome.' Our Lord said these words meaning overcome by his Passion, as he had shown me earlier. At this point our Lord brought into my mind and showed me some part of the Fiend's wickedness and the whole of his weakness, and to do so he revealed how with his Passion he defeats the Devil. God showed me that he is still as wicked as he was before the Incarnation and works as hard, but he continually sees that all chosen souls escape him gloriously, and that grieves him; for everything that God allows him to do turns into joy for us and into pain and shame for him; and that is because he may never do as much evil as he would wish, for God holds fast all the Devil's power in his own hand. I also saw our Lord scorn his wickedness and set him at nought, and he wants us to do the same.

At this revelation I laughed heartily and that made those who were around me laugh too, and their laughter pleased me. I wished that my fellow Christians had seen what I saw, and then they would all have laughed with me. But I did not see Christ laughing. Nevertheless, it pleases him that we should laugh to cheer ourselves, and rejoice in God because the Fiend has been conquered. And after this I became serious, and said, 'I can see three things: delight, scorn and seriousness. I see delight that the Fiend is defeated; I see scorn because God scorns him and he is to be scorned; and I see seriousness because he is defeated by the Passion of our Lord Jesus Christ and by his death, which took place in all seriousness and with weary hardship.'

After this our Lord said, 'I thank you for your service and your suffering, especially in your youth.'

9

God showed me three degrees of bliss which every soul who has willingly served God shall have in heaven, whatever his degree on earth. The first is the glorious gratitude of our Lord God, which he will receive when he is freed from his sufferings; the gratitude is so exalted and so glorious that it would seem to fill the soul, even if there were no greater bliss; for I thought that all the pain and trouble that could be suffered by all living men could not have deserved the gratitude which one man shall have who has wittingly served God. The second degree is that all the blessed beings who are in heaven will see that glorious gratitude of our Lord God, and all heaven will know about his service. And the third degree is that this pleasure will for ever seem as new and delightful as it did when it was first felt. I saw that this was said and revealed to me sweetly and in kind terms: every man's age shall be known in heaven, and he will be rewarded for his willing service and for the time he has served; and more especially the age of those who willingly and freely offered their youth to God is surpassingly rewarded and they are wonderfully thanked.

And our Lord's next showing was a supreme spiritual pleasure in my soul. In this pleasure I was filled with eternal certainty, strongly anchored and without any fear. This feeling was so joyful to me and so full of goodness that I felt completely peaceful, easy and at rest, as though there were nothing on earth that could hurt me. This only lasted for a while, and then my feeling was reversed and I was left oppressed, weary of myself, and so disgusted with my life that I could hardly bear to live. There was no ease or comfort for my feelings but faith, hope and love, and these I had in reality, but I could not feel them in my heart. And immediately after this God again gave me the spiritual rest and comfort, certainty and pleasure so joyful and so powerful that no fear, no sorrow, no bodily or spiritual pain that one might suffer could have distressed me. And then the sorrow was revealed to my consciousness again, and first one, then the other, several times, I suppose about twenty times. And in the moments of joy I might have said with Paul, 'Nothing shall separate me from the love of Christ.' And in the moments of sorrow I might have said with Saint Peter, 'Lord save me, I perish.'

This vision was shown to me, as I understand, to teach me that it is necessary for everybody to have such experiences, sometimes to be strengthened, sometimes to falter and be left by himself. God wishes us to know that he safely protects us in both joy and sorrow equally, and he loves us as much in sorrow as in joy. And to benefit his soul, a man is sometimes left to himself, though not because of sin; for at this time I did not deserve by sinning to be left alone, neither did I deserve the feeling of bliss. But God gives joy generously when he so wishes, and sometimes allows us sorrow; and both come from love. So it is God's will that we should hold on to gladness with all our might, for bliss lasts eternally, and pain passes and shall vanish completely. Therefore it is not God's will that we should be guided by feelings of pain, grieving and mourning over them, but should quickly pass beyond them and remain in eternal joy, which is God almighty, who loves and protects us.

10

After this Christ showed me the part of his Passion when he was near death. I saw that dear face as if it were dry and bloodless with the pallor of death; and then it went more deathly, ashen and exhausted, and still nearer to death it went blue, then darker blue, as the flesh mortified more completely; all the pains that Christ suffered in his body appeared to me in the blessed face as far as I could see it, and especially in his lips; there I saw these four colours, though before they appeared to me fresh and red-tinted, vivid and lovely. It was a sorrowful change to see this extreme mortification; and, as it appeared to me, the nose shrivelled and dried. This long agony made it seem to me that he had been dead for a full week, always suffering pain. And I thought that the drying of Christ's flesh was the greatest agony, and the last, of his Passion. And in this dryness the words that Christ spoke were brought to my mind: 'I thirst'; and I saw in Christ a double thirst, one bodily, the other spiritual. In these words was revealed to me the bodily thirst, and the spiritual thirst was revealed to me as I shall say later. And I understood that the bodily thirst was caused by the body's loss of moisture, for the blessed flesh and bones were left altogether without blood and moisture. The blessed body was drying for a long time, becoming distorted because of the nails and the heaviness of the head and its own weight, with the blowing of the wind from without that dried him more and tormented him with cold more than I can imagine, and all other torments. I saw such pains that everything I could say would be quite inadequate, for they were indescribable. But every soul, as Saint Paul says, should feel in himself what was in Jesus Christ. This showing of Christ's pain filled me with pain, though I knew well he only suffered once, yet he wanted to show it to me and fill me with awareness of it as I had wished previously.

My mother, who was standing with others watching me, lifted her hand up to my face to close my eyes, for she thought I was already dead or else I had that moment died; and this greatly increased my sorrow, for in spite of all my suffering, I did not want to be stopped from seeing him, because of my love for him. And yet, in all this time of Christ's presence, the only pain I felt was the pain of Christ. Then I thought to myself, 'I little knew what pain it was that I asked for'; for I thought that my pain was worse than bodily death. I thought, 'Is any pain in hell like this pain?', and I was answered in my mind that despair is greater, for that is spiritual pain, but no bodily pain is greater than this. How could any pain be greater to me than to see him who is my whole life, all my bliss and all my joy, suffering? Here I truly felt that I loved Christ so much more than myself that I thought bodily death would have been a great relief to me.

Here I saw part of the compassion of our Lady Saint Mary, for Christ and she were so united in love that the greatness of her love caused the intensity of her pain; for just as her love for him surpassed that of anyone else, so did her suffering for him; and so all his disciples, and all those who truly loved him, suffered greater pain than they would for their own bodily death; for I am certain, from my own feelings, that the humblest of them loved him much better than themselves.

Here I saw a great union between Christ and us; for when he was in pain, we were in pain. And all creatures who were capable of suffering, suffered with him. And as for those who did not know him, their suffering was that all creation, sun and moon, withdrew their service, and so they were all left in sorrow during that time. And thus those that loved him suffered for love, and those that did not love him suffered from a failure of comfort from the whole of creation.

At this point I wanted to look away from the cross, but I dared not, for I well knew that while I contemplated the cross I was safe and sound; therefore I was unwilling to imperil my soul, for beside the cross there was no safety, but the ugliness of fiends. Then a suggestion came from my reason, as though a friendly voice had spoken, 'Look up to his Father in heaven.' Then I saw clearly with the faith that I felt, that there was nothing between the cross and heaven which could have distressed me, and either I must look up or I must answer. I answered and said, 'No, I cannot, for you are my heaven.' I said this because I did not wish to look up, for I would rather have suffered until Judgement Day than have come to heaven otherwise than by him; for I well knew that he who redeemed me so dearly would unbind me when he wished.

11

Thus I chose Jesus as my heaven, though at that time I saw him only in pain. I was satisfied by no heaven but Jesus, who will be my bliss when I am there. And it has always been a comfort to me that I chose Jesus for my heaven in all this time of suffering and sorrow. And that has been a lesson to me, that I should do so for evermore, choosing him alone for my heaven in good and bad times. And thus I saw my Lord Jesus Christ lingering for a long time; for union with the Godhead gave his Manhood the strength to suffer for love more than anyone could. I do not mean only more pain than any man could suffer, but also that he suffered more pain than all men who ever existed from the very beginning until the very last day. No tongue may tell, nor heart fully imagine, the pains that our Saviour suffered for us, considering the majesty of the highest, most worshipful King and the shameful, insulting and painful death; for he who was highest and most majestic was brought lowest and most truly despised. But the love that made him suffer all this is as much greater than his pain as heaven is above the earth; for the Passion was a deed performed at one particular time through the action of love, but the love has always existed, exists now and will never end. And suddenly I saw, while looking at the same cross, his expression changed into one of bliss. The changing of his expression changed mine, and I was as glad and happy as it was possible to be. Then our Lord made me think happily, 'What is the point of your pain or your sorrow?' And I was very happy.

12

Then our Lord spoke, asking, 'Are you well pleased that I suffered for you?' 'Yes, my good Lord,' I said. 'Thank you, my good Lord, blessed may you be!'

'If you are pleased,' said our Lord, 'I am pleased. It is a joy and a delight and an endless happiness to me that I ever endured suffering for you, for if I could suffer more, I would suffer.' As I became conscious of these words my understanding was lifted up into heaven, and there I saw three heavens, a sight which caused me great amazement, and I thought, 'I saw three heavens, and all of them of the blessed Manhood of Christ; and none is greater, none is lesser, none is higher, none is lower, but they are all equally full of supreme joy.'

For the first heaven Christ showed me his Father, in no bodily likeness, but in his nature and his action. This is how the Father acts: he rewards his son, Jesus Christ. This gift and this reward give Jesus such great joy that his Father could have given no reward that pleased him better. The first heaven, that is the pleasing of the Father, appeared to me like a heaven, and it was full of great joy, for he is greatly pleased with all the deeds he has done to promote our salvation; because of these we do not just belong to Jesus by redemption, but also by his Father's generous gift. We are his joy, we are his reward, we are his glory, we are his crown. What I am describing causes Jesus such great pleasure that he thinks nothing of all his hardship and his bitter suffering and his cruel and shameful death. And in these words, 'If I could suffer more, I would suffer more', I saw truly that if he might die once for each man who shall be saved as he died once for all, love would never let him rest until he had done it. And when he had done it, he would still think nothing of it out of love; for everything seems a trifle to him in comparison with his love. And he showed me this very seriously, saying these words, 'If I could suffer more'. He did not say, 'If it were necessary to suffer more', but 'If I could suffer more'; for if he could suffer more, he would, even if it were not necessary. This deed and this action for our salvation was ordered as well as he could order it, it was done as gloriously as Christ could do it. And here I saw complete joy in Christ, but this joy would not have been as complete if it could have been done any better than it was done.

And in these three sayings, 'It is a joy, a delight and an endless happiness to me', three heavens were shown to me, as follows: by the joy I understood the pleasure of the Father; by the delight, the glory of the Son; and by the endless happiness, the Holy Ghost. The Father is pleased, the Son is glorified, the Holy Ghost rejoices. Jesus wishes us to consider the delight which the Holy Trinity feels in our salvation, and wishes us to delight as much, through his grace, while we are on earth. And this was shown in these words, 'Are you well pleased?' In the other words that Christ spoke, 'If you are pleased, I am pleased', he revealed the meaning, as if he had said, 'It is joy and delight enough to me, and I ask nothing more of you for my hardship but that I give you pleasure.' This was shown to me abundantly and fully. Think hard too about the deep significance of the words 'That I ever endured suffering for you', for in those words was a great sign of love and of the pleasure that he took in our salvation.

13

Very happily and gladly our Lord looked into his side, and gazed, and said these words, 'Look how much I loved you'; as if he had said, 'My child, if you cannot look at my Godhead, see here how I let my side be opened, and my heart be riven in two, and all the blood and water that was within flow out. And this makes me happy, and I want it to make you happy.' Our Lord revealed this to make us glad and joyful.

And with the same mirth and joy he looked down to his right and brought to my mind the place where our Lady was standing during the time of his Passion; and he said, 'Would you like to see her?' And I answered and said, 'Yes, my good Lord, thank you, if it is your will. ' I prayed for this repeatedly and I thought I would see her in bodily likeness, but I did not do so. And with these words Jesus showed me a spiritual vision of her; just as I had seen her low and humble before, he now showed her to me high, noble and glorious, and more pleasing to him than any other creature. And so he wants it to be known that all those who rejoice in him should rejoice in her and in the joy that he has in her and she in him. And in these words that Jesus said, 'Would you like to see her?', it seemed to me I had the greatest pleasure that he could have given me, with the spiritual vision of her; for our Lord gave me no special revelation except of our Lady Saint Mary, and he showed her to me three times: the first when she conceived, the second as if she were in her sorrow under the cross and the third as she is now, in delight, honour and joy.

And after this our Lord showed himself to me in even greater glory, it seemed to me, than when I saw him before, and from this revelation I learned that each contemplative soul to whom it is given to look for God and seek him, shall see her and pass on to God through contemplation. And after this friendly and courteous teaching of true and blessed life, our Lord Jesus said to me repeatedly, 'It is I who am highest; it is I you love; it is I who delight you; it is I you serve; it is I you long for; it is I you desire; it is I who am your purpose; it is I who am everything; it is I that Holy Church preaches and teaches you; it is I who showed myself to you before.' I only make these utterances known so that, according to the powers of understanding and loving which are given by the grace of God, everyone may receive them as our Lord intended.

Afterwards, our Lord reminded me of the longing I had had for him; and I saw that nothing kept me from him but sin, and I saw that this is so with all of us. And I thought that if sin had never existed, we should all have been pure and like himself, as God made us; and so I had often wondered before now in my folly why, in his great foreseeing wisdom, God had not prevented sin; for then, I thought, all would have been well. I ought certainly to have abandoned these thoughts, and I grieved and sorrowed over the question in great pride, with no reason or judgement. Nevertheless, Jesus, in this vision, informed me of all that I needed to know. I am not saying that I do not need any more teaching, for our Lord, in this revelation, has left me to Holy Church; and I am hungry and thirsty and needy and sinful and frail, and willingly submit myself to the teaching of Holy Church, with all my fellow Christians, until the end of my life.

He answered with this assurance: 'Sin is befitting.' With this word 'sin' our Lord brought to my mind the whole extent of all that is not good: the shameful scorn and the utter humiliation that he bore for us in this life and in his dying, and all the pains and sufferings of all his creatures, both in body and spirit—for we are all to some extent brought to nothing and should be brought to nothing as our master Jesus was, until we are fully purged: that is to say until our own mortal flesh is brought completely to nothing, and all those of our inward feelings which are not good. He gave me insight into these things, along with all pains that ever were and ever shall be; all this was shown in a flash, and quickly changed into comfort; for our good Lord did not want the soul to be afraid of this ugly sight.

But I did not see sin; for I believe it has no sort of substance nor portion of being, nor could it be recognized were it not for the suffering which it causes. And this suffering seems to me to be something transient, for it purges us and makes us know ourselves and pray for mercy; for the Passion of our Lord supports us against all this, and that is his blessed will for all who shall be saved. He supports us willingly and sweetly, by his words, and says, 'But all shall be well, and all manner of things shall be well.' These words were shown very tenderly, with no suggestion that I or anyone who will be saved was being blamed. It would therefore be very strange to blame or wonder at God because of my sins, since he does not blame me for sinning.

Thus I saw how Christ feels compassion for us because of sin. And just as I was earlier filled with suffering and compassion at the Passion of Christ, so was I now also partly filled with compassion for all my fellow Christians; and then I saw that whenever a man feels kind compassion with love for his fellow Christian, it is Christ within him.

14

But you must apply yourself to this: contemplating these things in general, sad and grieving, in my mind I said to our Lord with great reverence, 'Ah, my good Lord, how could all be well, given the great harm that has been done to humankind by sin?' And here I prayed, as much as I dared, for some clearer explanation to ease my mind over this. And our blessed Lord answered most compassionately and in a very friendly way, and showed me that Adam's sin was the greatest harm that ever was done, or ever shall be, until the end of the world; and he also showed me that this is publicly acknowledged through all Holy Church on earth. Furthermore he taught me that I should consider the glorious atonement; for this atonement is incomparably more pleasing to God and more glorious in saving mankind than Adam's sin was ever harmful.

So what our blessed Lord's teaching means is that we should take heed of the following: 'Since I have turned the greatest possible harm into good, it is my will that you should know from this that I shall turn all lesser evil into good.'

He made me understand two aspects of this. One of them is our Saviour and our salvation; this aspect is blessed and is clear and bright, light and beautiful and abundant, for all men who are or shall be of good will are included in it; we are bidden to it by God, and drawn to it, admonished and taught inwardly by the Holy Ghost and outwardly by Holy Church by the same grace; our Lord wishes our minds to be filled with this, rejoicing in him because he rejoices in us; and the more abundantly we are filled with this, reverently and humbly, the more we deserve his thanks and the more we benefit ourselves, and thus we may say, rejoicing, our Lord is our portion.

The second aspect is closed to us and hidden (that is to say, everything which is not necessary for our salvation); for it is our Lord's privy counsel and it is proper to the royal lordship of God that his privy counsel should be undisturbed, and it is proper for his servants, out of obedience and reverence, not to know his counsel too well. Our Lord feels pity and compassion for us because some people are so anxious to know about it; and I am sure that if we knew how much we would please him and set our own minds at rest by leaving the matter alone, then we would do so. The saints in heaven do not want to know anything except what our Lord wants to reveal to them, and their love and their desires are directed by our Lord's will. We should desire to be like them: then, like the saints, we should wish and desire nothing that is not the will of our Lord; for God's purpose for us all is the same.

And here I was taught that we must rejoice only in our blessed Saviour Jesu and trust in him for everything.

15

And thus our good Lord answered all the questions and doubts I could put forward, saying most comfortingly as follows: 'I will make all things well, I shall make all things well, I may make all things well and I can make all things well; and you shall see for yourself that all things shall be well.' I take 'I may' for the words of the Father, I take 'I can' for the words of the Son and I take 'I will' for the words of the Holy Ghost; and where he says 'I shall', I take it for the unity of the Holy Trinity, three persons in one truth; and where he says, 'You shall see for yourself', I understand it as referring to the union with the Holy Trinity of all mankind who shall be saved. And with these five sayings God wishes to be surrounded by rest and peace; and thus Christ's spiritual thirst comes to an end; for this is the spiritual thirst, the love-longing that lasts and ever shall do until we see that revelation on Judgement Day.

For we that shall be saved, and shall be Christ's joy and his bliss, are still here on earth, and shall be until that last day. Therefore this is the thirst, the incompleteness of his bliss, that he does not have us in himself as wholly as he will have then. All this was shown me as a revelation of compassion, and his thirst will cease on Judgement Day. Thus he has pity and compassion for us, and he has longing to have us, but his wisdom and love do not permit the end to come until the best time.

And thus I understand the five sayings mentioned above—'I may make all things well', etc.—as a powerful and comforting pledge for all the works of our Lord which are to come; for just as the Holy Trinity made all things from nothing, so the Holy Trinity shall make all well that is not well. It is God's will that we should pay attention to all the deeds he has done, for he wants us to know from them all he will do; and he showed me that when he said, 'And you shall see yourself that all manner of things shall be well.' I understand this in two ways: first, I am well pleased that I do not know it; second, I am glad and happy because I shall know it. It is God's wish that we should know in general terms that all shall be well; but it is not God's wish that we should understand it now, except as much as is suitable for us at the present time, and that is the teaching of Holy Church.

16

God showed me the very great pleasure he takes in men and women who strongly and humbly and eagerly receive the preaching and teaching of Holy Church; for he is Holy Church; he is the foundation, he is the substance, he is the teaching, he is the teacher, he is the goal, he is the prize which every true soul works hard to win; and he is known and shall be known to every soul to whom the Holy Ghost reveals it. And I am sure that all those who are seeking this will succeed, for they are seeking God. All that I have now said, and more that I shall say afterwards, gives strength against sin; for first, when I saw that God does all which is done, I did not see sin, and then I saw that all is well. But when God gave me a revelation about sin, then he said, 'All shall be well.'

And when almighty God had shown his great goodness so fully and abundantly, I requested to know how it would be with a certain person whom I loved. And in this request I stood in my own way, for I was not answered immediately. And then I was answered in my reason as though by a friendly man, 'Take these showings generally, and consider the kindness of your Lord God as he gives them to you; for it honours God more to consider him in all things than in any particular thing.' I assented, and with this I learned that it honours God more to have knowledge of everything in general than to take pleasure in any one thing in particular. And if I were to follow this teaching faithfully I should not rejoice over any one special thing, nor be distressed over anything of any kind, for 'All shall be well.'

God reminded me that I would sin; and because of my pleasure in contemplating him, I was slow to pay attention to that showing. And our Lord very courteously waited till I paid attention; and then our Lord, along with my own sins, reminded me of the sins of all my fellow Christians, in general and not in particular.

17

Although our Lord showed me that I would sin, by me alone I understood everyone. At this I began to feel a quiet fear, and to this our Lord answered me as follows; 'I am keeping you very safe.' This promise was made to me with more love and assurance and spiritual sustenance than I can possibly say, for just as it was previously shown that I would sin, the help was also shown to me: safety and protection for all my fellow Christians. What could make me love my fellow Christians more than to see in God that he loves all who shall be saved as though they were one soul? For just as there is an animal will in our lower nature which can have no good impulses, there is a godly will in our higher nature which, no less than the persons of the Holy Trinity, can will no evil, but only good. And this is what our Lord showed in the completeness of love in which he holds us: yes, that he loves us as much now while we are here as he will do when we are there in his blessed presence.

God also showed me that sin is not shameful to man, but his glory; for in this revelation my understanding was lifted up into heaven; and then there came truly into my mind David, Peter and Paul, Thomas of India and the Magdalene—how they are famous in the Church on earth with their sins as their glory. And it is no shame to them that they have sinned, any more than it is in the bliss of heaven, for there the badge of their sin is changed into glory. In this way our Lord God showed them to me as an example of all others who shall come there.

Sin is the sharpest scourge that any chosen soul can be struck with; it is a scourge which lashes men and women so hard, and batters them and destroys them so completely in their own eyes, that they think they only deserve to sink down into hell. But when the touch of the Holy Ghost brings contrition, it turns the bitterness into hope of God's mercy; and then their wounds begin to heal and the soul begins to revive into the life of Holy Church. The Holy Ghost leads a man on to confession, and he earnestly shows his sins, nakedly and truly, with great sorrow and great shame that he has so befouled the fair image of God. Then, in accordance with the basic teaching which the Church has received from the Holy Ghost, his confessor imposes a penance on him for each sin. By this medicine every sinful soul needs to be healed, especially of sins that are in themselves mortal. Although a man has the scars of healed wounds, when he appears before God they do not deface but ennoble him. And as on the one hand sin is punished here with sorrow and suffering, on the other it shall be rewarded in heaven by the generous love of our Lord God almighty, who does not want the toils and troubles of any who come there to be wasted. The reward we are going to receive there will not be a small one, but great, splendid and glorious. And so all shame will be turned into glory and into greater joy. And I am sure, by what I feel myself, that the more every well-natured soul sees this in the kind and generous love of God, the more loath he is to sin.

18

But if you are moved to say or think, 'Since this is true, then it would be a good idea to sin in order to have the greater reward', beware of this impulse, for it comes from the Enemy, for any soul that chooses to follow this impulse can never be saved until he has been healed of this as if it were a mortal sin. For if there were laid out before me all the sufferings of hell and of purgatory and of earth—death and everything else—and sin, I would choose all those sufferings rather than sin, for sin is so vile and so very hateful that it cannot be compared to any suffering other than the suffering of sin itself. For all things are good but sin, and nothing is wicked but sin. Sin is neither a deed nor a pleasure, but when a soul deliberately chooses to sin (which is punishment in God's eyes), in the end he has nothing at all. That punishment seems to me the hardest hell, for he does not have his God. A soul can have God in all sufferings except sin.

And God is as eager to save man as he is strong and wise; for Christ himself is the foundation of the whole law of Christian men, and he taught us to return good for evil. Here we can see that he himself is love, and he treats us as he wishes us to treat others, for he wants us to be like him in completeness of unending love for ourselves and our fellow Christians. Just as his love for us does not fail because of our sin, he does not want our love for ourselves and our fellow Christians to fail; we must feel naked hatred for sin and unending love for the soul, as God loves it. This assertion of God's is an endless help and comfort, which keeps us very safe.

19

After this our Lord gave a revelation about prayer. I saw two qualities in those who pray, like those I have felt in myself. One is that they do not wish to pray for anything that may be, but only for things which are God's will and his glory. The second thing is that they set themselves strongly and continually to pray for things which are his will and his glory. And that is what I have understood from the teaching of Holy Church. And in this our Lord gave me the same teaching, to have as God's gift faith, hope and love, and hold to them until our lives' end. And so we say 'Pater noster', 'Ave' and the Creed, with devotion, as God may grant. And so we pray for all our fellow Christians, and for all manner of men, according to God's will, for we wish that all manner of men and women were in the same state of virtue and grace that we ought to desire for ourselves. But yet, for all this, often we do not trust God almighty fully for it seems to us that, because of our unworthiness, and because we are feeling absolutely nothing, we cannot be certain that he is hearing our prayers. For often we are as barren and as dry after our prayers as we were before, and so we feel our folly is the cause of our weakness; I have felt like this myself.

And our Lord brought all this suddenly into my mind, strongly and vividly, and, as a comfort to me against this kind of weakness in prayers, he said, 'I am the foundation of your prayers: first it is my will that you should have something, and then I make you desire it, and then I make you pray for it; and if you pray, then how could it be that you should not have what you pray for?' And thus in his first statement, along with the three which follow, our good Lord shows us something immensely helpful. Where he begins by saying, 'If you pray for it', there he reveals the very great joy and unending reward that our prayer will receive from him. And where he says next, 'Then how could it be that you should not have what you pray for?', there he gives a serious rebuke, because we do not trust as strongly as we should.

Thus our Lord wants us both to pray and to trust, for the purpose of the preceding statements is to strengthen us against weakness in our prayers. For it is God's will that we should pray, and he moves us to do so in these preceding words. He wants us to pray with sure trust, for prayer pleases him. Prayer gives man pleasure in himself, and makes him calm and humble, where before he was contentious and troubled. Prayer unites the soul to God; for though the soul is always like God in nature and substance, yet because of sin on man's part, it is often in a state which is unlike God. Prayer makes the soul like God; when the soul wills what God wills, it is then in a state like God, as it is like God in nature. And so God teaches us to pray, and to trust firmly that we shall obtain what we pray for, though everything which is done would be done, even if we never prayed for it. But the love of God is so great that he considers us sharers in his good deed, and therefore he moves us to pray for what it pleases him to do; and for these prayers and for the good will which he grants us, he will reward us and give us an everlasting recompense. And this was shown in these words, 'If you pray for it'. In this statement God revealed to me such great pleasure and so much delight that it seemed as if he was deeply grateful to us for every good deed that we do—and yet it is he who does them—and because we entreat him earnestly to do everything that pleases him; as if he said, 'Then what could please me more than to he entreated earnestly, truly and eagerly to do what I wish to do?' And thus prayer makes accord between God and man's soul, though while man's soul is near to God, there is no need for him to pray, but reverently to contemplate what he says. For during all the time of my showing, I was not moved to pray, but always to have this good in mind for my comfort, that when we see God, we have what we desire, and then we do not need to pray. But when we do not see God, then we need to pray because we lack something, and to make ourselves open to Jesus; for when a soul is tempted, troubled and isolated by distress, then it is time to pray and to make oneself pliable and submissive to God. Unless we are submissive, no kind of prayer can make God bend to us, though his love is always alike; but while man is in a state of sin, he is so enfeebled, so unwise and so unloving, that he can love neither God nor himself.

His worst trouble is blindness, for he cannot see all this. Then the whole love of God almighty, which is ever one, gives him eyes to see himself, and then he supposes that God is angry with him for his sin. And then he is moved to contrition, and by confession and other good deeds to allay God's anger, until he finds rest of soul and ease of conscience. And then it seems to him that God has forgiven his sins, and it is true. And then it seems to the soul that God turns towards it, as though it had been in pain or in prison, saying this: 'I am glad you have come to rest, for I have always loved you, and love you now, and you love me.' And thus with prayers, as I have said before, and with other good works that are customarily taught by Holy Church, is the soul united to God.

20

Before this time I often had a great longing, and desired that as a gift from God I should be delivered from this world and this life, so as to be with my God in bliss where, through his mercy, I hope to be surely for ever. For I often saw the grief which is here and the well-being and bliss which is existence there. And even if there had been no sorrow in this life except for the absence of our Lord, I sometimes thought it more than I could bear, and this made me grieve and earnestly yearn. Then God said to me, to bring me comfort and patience, 'You shall suddenly be taken from all your suffering, from all your pain and from all your woe. And you shall come up above, and you shall have me as your reward, and you shall be filled with joy and with bliss. And you shall have no kind of suffering, no kind of sickness, no kind of displeasure, no unfulfilled desires, but always joy and bliss without end. Why should you fret about suffering for a while, since it is my will and my glory?' And at these words, 'You shall suddenly be taken', I saw how God rewards man for the patience he shows in awaiting God's will in his lifetime, and I saw that man's patience extends throughout the time he has to live, because he does not know the time of his passing. This is a great advantage, for if a man knew his time, he would not have patience over that time. And God wishes that while the soul is in the body it should seem to itself always about to die, for all this life of distress which we have here is only a moment, and when we are suddenly taken from suffering into bliss, then it will be nothing. And this is why our Lord said, 'Why should you fret about suffering for a while, since it is my will and my glory?' It is God's will that we accept his promises and his comfort in as broad and strong a sense as we can take them. And he also wants us to take our waiting and our distress as lightly as we can and to consider them nothing; for the more lightly we take them, the less importance we give them for love, the less we shall suffer from feeling them and the more thanks we shall have for them.

In this blessed revelation I was truly taught that the people who in this life willingly choose God may be sure that they are chosen. Remember this faithfully, for truly it is God's will that we should hope as securely for the bliss of heaven while we are here, as we shall enjoy it securely while we are there. And the more pleasure and joy we take in this security, with reverence and humility, the more it pleases him. For I am sure that if there had been none but I that would be saved, God would have done all that he has done for me. And every soul, knowing how God loves him, should think the same, forgetting if he can all other people, and thinking that God has done for him all that he has done. And it seems to me that this should inspire a soul to love and hold him dear, and fear only him, for he wants us to understand that all the strength of our Enemy is held fast in our Friend's hand. And therefore a soul that knows this truly will fear none but him that he loves, and set all other fears among sufferings and bodily sickness and mental apprehensions.

And therefore if a man is suffering so much pain, so much woe and so much distress, that it seems he can think of nothing but the state he is in and what he is feeling, he should pass over it lightly and set it at nought as soon as he can. And why? Because God wishes to be known. For if we knew him and loved him, we should have patience and be completely at rest, and everything that he does should be pleasing to us. And our Lord revealed this to me in these words: 'Why should you fret about suffering for a while, since it is my will and my glory?' And that was the end of all that our Lord revealed to me that day.

21

And after this I soon returned to myself and to my bodily sickness, understanding that I would live, and like a wretch I tossed and moaned with the feeling of bodily pain, and I thought it a great weariness that I should live longer; and I was as barren and dry, through the return of my pain and my loss of spiritual feeling, as if I had received little comfort. Then a man belonging to a religious order came to me and asked me how I was. And I said that I had been delirious today, and he laughed loud and heartily. And I said, 'The cross which stood at the foot of my bed, it was bleeding hard.' And as soon as I said this, the person to whom I was speaking became very serious and marvelled. And I was immediately very ashamed at my heedlessness, and I thought, 'This man takes my least word seriously, saying nothing in reply.' And when I saw that he took it so seriously and so reverently, I became very ashamed, and wanted to be given absolution; but I did not feel I could tell any priest about it, for I thought, 'How could a priest believe me? I did not believe our Lord God. ' I had truly believed while I was seeing him, and had then wanted and intended to do so for ever, but, like a fool, I let it slip from my mind. What a wretch I was! This was a great sin and very ungrateful, that I, through stupidity, just because I felt a little bodily pain, should so foolishly lose for the time being the comfort of all this blessed showing of our Lord God.

Here you can see what I am of myself; but our kind Lord would not leave me like this. And I lay still till night, trusting in his mercy, and then I went to sleep. And as soon as I fell asleep it seemed the Fiend was at my throat, and he tried to strangle me, but he could not. Then I woke out of my sleep, and I was barely alive. The people who were with me noticed and bathed my temples, and my heart began to take comfort. And immediately a little smoke came in through the door with a great heat and a foul stench. I said, 'Benedicite dominus! Everything here is on fire!' And I supposed it was a physical fire and would burn us all to death. I asked those who were with me if they smelled any stench. They said no, they smelled none. I said, 'Blessed be God!' for then I knew well it was the Fiend that had come to torment me. And I had recourse at once to all that our Lord had shown me that same day, along with the faith of Holy Church, for I consider both as one, and fled to that as my comfort. And immediately it all vanished completely, and I was brought to a state of great rest and peace without sickness of the body or terrors of the mind.

22

And I was still awake, and then our Lord opened my spiritual eyes and showed me my soul in the middle of my heart. I saw my soul as large as if it were a kingdom; and from the properties that I saw in it, it seemed to me to be a glorious city. In the centre of that city sits our Lord Jesu, true God and true man, glorious, highest Lord; and I saw him dressed imposingly in glory. He sits in the soul, in the very centre, in peace and rest, and he rules and protects heaven and earth and all that is. The Manhood and the Godhead sit at rest, and the Godhead rules and protects without any subordinate or any trouble; and my soul was blissfully filled with the Godhead, which is supreme power, supreme wisdom, supreme goodness. In all eternity Jesus will never leave the position which he takes in our soul; for in us is his most familiar home and his favourite dwelling. This was a ravishing and restful sight, for it is truly so everlastingly. And it is very pleasing to God and extremely helpful to us that we should see this while we are here. And the soul which sees it in this way makes itself like the one seen and unites itself to him in rest and peace. And it was a very great joy and bliss to me that I saw him sitting, for the sight of this sitting gave me certainty that he dwells there eternally. And I knew for certain that it was he who had shown me all that went before. And when I had considered this carefully, our Lord gently revealed words to me, without any voice or opening of his bps, as he had done before, and he said very seriously, 'Know well that what you saw today was no delirium; accept and believe it, and hold to it, and you shall not be overcome.' These last words were said to me to prove with frill assurance that it is our Lord Jesu who showed me everything. For just as in the first phrase which our Lord revealed, referring to his blessed Passion—'By this is the Fiend overcome'—in just the same way he said his last phrase with very great certainty, 'You shall not be overcome.'

And this teaching and true comfort applies without exception to all my fellow Christians, as I said before, and it is God's will that it should be so. And these words, 'You shall not be overcome', were said very loudly and clearly, for security and comfort against all the tribulations that may come. He did not say, 'You shall not be tormented, you shall not be troubled, you shall not be grieved', but he said, 'You shall not be overcome.' God wants us to pay attention to his words and wants our certainty always to be strong, in weal and woe; for he loves and is pleased with us, and so he wishes us to love and be pleased with him and put great trust in him; and all shall be well.

And soon after this it was all over and I saw no more.

23

After this the Fiend came again with his heat and his stench and distressed me greatly, the stench was so vile and so agonizing and the physical heat was terrifying and tormenting. And I also heard a human jabbering as if there were two people, and it seemed to me that both of them were jabbering at once, as if they were having a very tense discussion; and it was all quiet muttering, and I could understand nothing they said. But I thought that all this was to drive me to despair. And I trusted firmly in God and comforted my soul by speaking aloud as I would have done to another person who was distressed like this. I thought that this anxiety could not be compared to any other human anxiety. I set my bodily eyes on the same cross in which I had seen comfort before, and my tongue to speaking of Christ's Passion and reciting the faith of Holy Church, and I fixed my heart on God with all my trust and with all my strength. And I thought to myself, 'You must now be very careful to hold to the faith; if only from now on you could always be so careful to keep yourself from sin, it would be a beneficial and good way of life'; for I truly thought that if I were safe from sin I would be quite safe from all the fiends of hell and enemies of my soul. And so they kept me occupied all that night and in the morning until it was just after sunrise. And then at once they were all gone and passed away, leaving nothing but a stench; and that persisted for a while. And I thought of them with contempt. And thus I was delivered from them by the power of Christ's Passion, for that is how the Fiend is overcome, as Christ said to me before.

Ah, wretched sin! What are you? You are nothing. For I saw that God is all things: I saw nothing of you. And when I saw that God has made all things, I saw nothing of you; and when I saw that God is in all things, I saw nothing of you; and when I saw that God does all things that are done, greater and lesser, I saw nothing of you. And when I saw our Lord Jesu sitting so gloriously in our souls, and loving and liking and ruling and guiding all that he has made, I saw nothing of you. And so I am certain that you are nothing; and all those who love you, and like you, and follow you, and choose you at the end, I am certain that they shall be brought to nothing with you, and endlessly overthrown. God protect us all from you. Amen, for the love of God.

And I will say what vileness is, as I have been taught by the revelation of God. Vileness is all things that are not good: the spiritual blindness which we fall into with our first sin, and all that follows from that vileness: passions and pains of spirit or body, and all that is on earth or in any other place which is not good. And this leads to the question: what are we? And to this I answer: if all that is not good were taken from us, we should be good. When vileness is taken from us, God and the soul are all one, and God and man all one.

What is there on earth which separates us from God? I answer and say: in that it serves us, it is good, and in that it shall perish, it is vile, and for a man to consider it in any other way is sinful. And during the time that a man or woman loves sin, if there are any who do, his suffering is beyond all suffering. And when he does not love sin, but hates it and loves God, all is well. And he who truly does this, though he may sometimes sin through frailty or inexperience, he does not fall, for he will strongly rise again and behold God, whom he loves with all his might. God has made the world to be loved by him or her who is a sinner, but he always loves us, and always longs to have our love. And when we love Jesu strongly and truly, we are at peace.

All the blessed teaching of our Lord God was shown to me in three ways, as I have said before; that is to say, by bodily sight, by words formed in my understanding and by spiritual sight. I have described what I saw with bodily sight as truly as I can; and I have said the words exactly as our Lord revealed them to me; but so far as the spiritual sight is concerned, I have said something about it, but I could never recount it all, and so I am moved to say more if God will give me grace.

24

God showed me that we suffer from two kinds of sickness, of which he wishes us to be cured: one of them is impatience, because we find our trouble and suffering a heavy burden to bear, and the other is despair, or doubtful fear, as I shall explain later. And these two are the ones which most trouble and torment us, according to what our Lord showed me, and the ones it most pleases him if we reform. I am talking of those men and women who for the love of God hate sin and are anxious to do God's will. And these are the two secret sins which threaten us most, so it is God's will that they should be recognized and then we shall reject them as we do other sins.

And our Lord very humbly revealed to me the patience with which he bore his terrible Passion and also the joy and delight which that Passion gave him because of his love. And he showed by his example that we should bear our sufferings gladly and lightly, because that pleases him greatly and benefits us for ever. And we are troubled by them because we do not recognize love. Though the persons of the Holy Trinity are all equal in nature, what was shown me most clearly was that love is nearest to us all. And this is the knowledge of which we are most ignorant; for many men and women believe that God is almighty and has power to do everything, and that he is all wisdom and knows how to do everything, but that he is all love and is willing to do everything—there they stop. And this ignorance is what hinders those who most love God; for when they begin to hate sin, and to mend their ways under the laws of Holy Church, there still remains some fear which moves them to think of themselves and their previous sins. And they take this fear for humility, but it is foul ignorance and weakness. And we cannot despise it, though if we knew it we should immediately despise it, as we do some other sin that we recognize, for it comes from the Enemy, and it is contrary to truth. So, of all the properties of the Holy Trinity, it is God's wish that we should place most reliance on liking and love; for love makes God's power and wisdom very gentle to us; just as through his generosity God forgives our sin when we repent, so he wants us to forget our sin and all our depression and all our doubtful fear.

25

For I saw four kinds of fear. One is fear of attack which suddenly comes to a man through weakness. This fear does good, for it helps to purify, just like bodily sickness or other sufferings which are not sinful; for all such suffering helps if it is endured patiently.

The second fear is that of punishment, whereby someone is stirred and woken from the sleep of sin; for those who are deep in the sleep of sin are for the time being unable to perceive the gentle comfort of the Holy Ghost, until they have experienced this fear of punishment, of bodily death and of spiritual enemies. And this fear moves us to seek the comfort and mercy of God; and this fear serves as an entrance and enables us to be contrite through the blessed teaching of the Holy Ghost.

The third is doubtful fear; for though it may be small in itself, if it were recognized it would be seen as a sort of despair. For I am sure that God hates all doubtful fear, and he wishes us to separate ourselves from it by gaining true knowledge of life.

The fourth is reverent fear; the only fear we can have which pleases God is reverent fear; and it is very sweet and gentle because of the greatness of love. And yet this reverent fear and love are not one and the same. They are two in their nature and their way of working, yet neither of them may be had without the other. Therefore I am certain that those who love also fear, though they may only feel it a little.

Even though they may appear to be holy, all the fears which face us, apart from reverent fear, are not truly so; and this is how we can tell which is which. For reverent fear, the more we have it, the more it softens and comforts and pleases and rests us; and the false fear disquiets, distresses and disturbs. This is the remedy then, to recognize them both and reject the false fear, just as we would a wicked spirit that appeared in the likeness of a good angel. However attractive his company and his behaviour appear to be, he first disquiets and distresses and disturbs the person he speaks with, and hinders him and leaves him thoroughly upset; and the more he has to do with him, the more he disturbs him, and the further he is from peace. Therefore it is God's will and our gain that we should know them apart; for God always wants us to be secure in love, and peaceful and restful, as he is towards us. And in the same way as he is disposed towards us, so he wishes us to be disposed towards ourselves and towards our fellow Christians. Amen.

The Wife of Bath's Tale

Geoffrey Chaucer

The Prologue of the Wife of Bath's Tale

Experience, even if there were no other authority
in this world, would be grounds enough for me
to speak of the woe that is in marriage;
for, my lords, since I was twelve years old,
thanks be to eternal God, 5
I have had five husbands at the church door—
if I may have been legally married so often;
and all were worthy men in their different ways.
But I was definitely told, not long ago,
that since Christ went but once 10
to a wedding, in Cana of Galilee,
by that example he taught me
that I should not be married more than once.
Also, consider what sharp words
Jesus, God and man, spoke beside a 15
well in reproof of the Samaritan:
'Thou hast had five husbands,' he said,
'and he whom thou now hast
is not thy husband'; thus he spoke, certainly;
what he meant by it, I cannot say. 20
But I ask this, why was the fifth man
no husband to the Samaritan?
How many was she allowed to have in marriage?
Never yet in my life have I heard
this number defined. 25
People may guess and interpret the text up and down,
but I know well, without a doubt, God bade
us expressly to increase and multiply;

that pleasant text I can well understand.
And also I well know that he said my husband 30
should leave father and mother, and take me;
but he made no mention of number—
of bigamy or of octogamy;
why should men speak evil of it?
"Look at the wise king, Lord Solomon; 35
I think he had more than one wife; I would to God
I could be refreshed half so often as he!
What a gift from God he had with all his wives!
No man living in this world has such. 40
God knows this noble king to my thinking
had many a merry bout with each of them
the first night; he had a good life.
Blessed be God that I have married five!
Welcome the sixth, whenever he comes along. 45
For indeed, I don't want to keep myself entirely chaste;
when my husband has gone from the world,
some Christian man shall wed me soon.
for the Apostle says that then I am free
to marry in God's name where I please. 50
He says it's no sin to be married;
it is better to marry than to burn.
What do I care if folk speak evil
of cursed Lamech and his bigamy?
I know very well that Abraham was a holy man, 55
and Jacob too, as far as I can see;
and each of them had more than two wives,
and so did many another holy man.
Tell me, where, in any time,
did God on high expressly prohibit marriage? 60
I pray you, tell me;
or where did he command virginity?
I know as well as you do—not a doubt!—
that the Apostle, when he spoke of maidenhood,
said that he had no commandment for it. 65
One may counsel a woman to be a virgin,
but counseling is not commandment;
he left it to our own judgment.

For if God had decreed maidenhood, then
he would have condemned marriage in effect; 70
and certainly if there were no seed sown,
then where should virginity grow from?
Paul did not dare in the least to decree
a thing for which his master gave no order.
The prize is set up for virginity; 75
grab it who may, let's see who wins the race.
"But this saying does not apply to every man,
but only where it pleases God to give it, of his might.
I very well know that the Apostle was a virgin;
but nevertheless, although he wrote and said 80
that he wished that everyone were such as he,
all this is only advice in favor of virginity;
and he gave me, as an indulgence, leave
to be a wife; so it is no reproach
for me to marry if my mate dies; 85
it is without any taint of bigamy—
although it may be good not to touch a woman
(he meant in a bed or couch;
for it is dangerous to assemble fire and tow—
you know what this example means). 90
This is the sum of the matter, he held virginity to be
more perfect than marrying in the frailty of the flesh.
It is frailty, that is, unless the man and woman
intend to live all their lives in chastity.
"I grant it freely; I'm not envious, 95
although maidenhood be preferred to bigamy.
It pleases some to be pure, body and soul;
I won't make any boast about my own estate.
As you well know, a lord doesn't have every
vessel in his household made of gold; 100
some are made of wood, and are serviceable to their lord.
God calls people to him in sundry ways,
and each one has an appropriate gift of God,
some this, some that—as it pleases him to provide.
"Virginity is a great perfection, 105
and also devoted continence,
but Christ, who is the well of perfection,

did not bid every man to go and sell
all that he had and give it to the poor,
and in that way to follow in his footsteps; 110
He spoke to them that wished to live perfectly:
and by your leave, my lords, that isn't me.
I will bestow the flower of my whole life
in the acts and fruits of marriage.
"Tell me also, to what end 115
were reproductive organs made,
why are people made so perfectly?
Believe me, they were not made for nothing.
whoever wants to, let him enlarge on the matter
and argue to
and fro that they were made for the purgation 120
of urine, and that both our private parts
were made to distinguish a female from a male,
and for no other cause—do you say no?
Experience knows well it is not so;
So that the clerics won't be angry with me, 125
I'll say this: they were made for both;
that is to say, for necessary business and for pleasure
in engendering, when we do not displease God.
Why else should men set it down in their books
that a man shall yield his wife her debt? 130
Now how shall he make his payment
unless he uses his simple instrument?
Then, they were given to creatures
for purging urine and also for propagation.
"But I don't say that everyone who has 135
such equipment as I mentioned is bound
to go and use it in engendering;
then we wouldn't care about chastity.
Christ, who was formed as a man, was a virgin,
and many a saint since the world began 140
lived always in perfect chastity.
I won't envy them virginity:
let them be white bread of finest wheat,
and let us wives be called barley bread;
and yet, with barley bread, as Mark tells us, 145
Our Lord Jesus refreshed many a man.

In such estate as God has called us to
I'll persevere; I'm not particular.
In marriage I'll use my equipment
as freely as my maker sent it; 150
If I should be grudging, God give me sorrow!
My husband shall have it both evening and
  morning,
whenever he wants to come forth and pay his debt.
I'll have a husband—I won't make it difficult—
who shall be both my debtor and my slave, 155
and have his trouble
in the flesh while I'm his wife.
All through my life I have the power
over his own body, and not he.
Just so the Apostle explained it to me, 160
and he bade our husbands to love us well.
Every bit of this lesson pleases me—"
  Just then the Pardoner started up;
"Now, dame," he said, "by God and by Saint John,
you are a noble preacher in this matter! 165
I was about to wed a wife; alas,
why should I purchase it so dearly with my flesh?
I'd rather not wed a wife this year!"
  "Wait," said she, "my tale is not begun;
no, you'll drink from another barrel 170
before I am through—one that shall taste worse
  than ale.
And when I have told you my tale
of the tribulation of marriage,
in which I have been an expert all my life—
that is to say, I myself have been the whip— 175
then you may choose whether you wish to sip
of the tun that I shall broach.
Be wary of it, before you approach too near;
for I shall tell more than ten examples.
By him who won't be warned by other men 180
shall other men be warned.
These same words were written by Ptolemy;
read in his *Almagest*, and find it there."

"Dame, I pray you, if it be your will,"
said this Pardoner, "tell your tale 185
as you began; leave off for no man,
and teach us young men some of your practice."
"Gladly" said she, "since it may please you.
But yet I pray all this company
that if I speak according to my fancy, 190
you do not take what I say amiss;
for I only intend to amuse you.
"Now, sirs, I'll go on with my tale.—
As ever I hope to drink wine or ale,
I'll tell the truth; of those husbands that I had, 195
three of them were good and two were bad.
The first three men were good, and rich, and old;
they were scarcely able to keep the statute
by which they were bound to me—
you know quite well what I mean by this, by heaven! 200
So help me God, I laugh when I think
how pitifully I made them work at night;
and by my faith I set no store by it.
They had given me their land and their treasure;
I no longer needed to be diligent 205
to win their love, or show them reverence.
They loved me so well, by God above,
that I didn't prize their love!
A wise woman will concentrate on getting
that love which she doesn't possess; 210
but since I had them wholly in my hand,
and since they had given me all their land,
why should I take pains to please them,
unless it should be for my own profit and
pleasure?
I so set them to work, by my faith, 215
that many a night they sang 'alas!'
The prize of bacon some people have in
Essex at Dunmow was never brought to them, I know.
I governed them so well in my way
that each of them was most happy and eager 220
to bring me gay things from the fair.

They were glad indeed when I spoke pleasantly
to them;
for God knows I chided them cruelly.
"'Now hear how suitably I behaved myself,
you wise wives who can understand. 225
You should speak thus and put them in the wrong;
for no man can perjure himself and lie
half so boldly as a woman can.
I don't say this for wives that are wise,
except when they have made a mistake. 230
A wise wife, if she knows what is good for her,
will convince her husband that the chough is mad,
and call as a witness her own maid,
who conspires with her; but listen to how I spoke:
"'Old sluggard, is this the way you dress me? 235
Why is my neighbor's wife so smart?
She is honored everywhere she goes;
I sit at home, I have no decent clothes.
What do you do at my neighbor's house?
Is she so fair? Are you so amorous? 240
What are you whispering to our maid, for
heaven's sake?
Old sir, lecher, stop your tricks!
Why, if I have a friend or acquaintance
in all innocence, you chide like a fiend
if I walk to his house and visit! 245
You come home as drunk as a mouse
and preach from your bench, bad luck to you!
You tell me it is a great misfortune
to marry a poor woman, as far as cost is concerned;
and if she is rich and of high lineage, 250
then you say that it is a torment
to suffer her pride and her melancholy.
And if she is fair, you knave,
you say that every lecher wants to have her;
she who is assaulted on every side 255
can't remain chaste very long.
"'You say some men desire us for wealth,
some for our shapeliness, and some for our beauty;

some want a woman because she can sing or dance,
some because she is well-bred and flirtatious; 260
some like her hands and her graceful arms;
thus we all go to the devil by your account.
You say no one can keep a castle wall
when it is assailed all around for so long a time.
"'And if she is ugly, you say that she 265
covets every man she sees;
for she will leap on him like a spaniel
until she finds some man who will buy her wares;
there is no goose swimming in the lake, you say,
that is so gray it cannot find a mate. 270
And you say it is very hard to manage
a thing that no man will willingly keep.
You say this, you wretch, as you go to bed,
and that no wise man needs to marry,
nor any man who aspires to heaven. 275
May wild thunderbolts and fiery lightning
break your withered neck!
"'You say that leaking houses and smoke
and nagging wives make men flee
out of their own houses; bless us, 280
what ails such an old man to scold so?
You say we wives will hide our vices
until we are safely married, and then we will show them;
that's certainly a fit proverb for a scolding curmudgeon!
You say that oxen, asses, horses, and hounds 285
are tested at various times;
and so are basins and washbowls, before people
buy them—
spoons and stools and all such household goods,
and so are pots, clothes and adornments;
but men don't try out wives 290
until they are married; scolding old dotard!
And then, you say, we'll show our vices.
"'You also say that I am displeased
unless you praise my beauty,
and pore constantly on my face, 295
and call me "fair dame" everywhere;
and unless you hold a feast on my

birthday, and give me gay new clothing,
and unless you honor my nurse
and my chambermaid, 300
and my father's relatives and connections;—
you say all this, old barrel full of lies!
"'Moreover, you have caught a false
suspicion of our apprentice Jankin,
because he has curly hair, shining like purest gold, 305
and squires me everywhere;
I wouldn't want him even if you died tomorrow.
"'But tell me this, why do you hide—sorrow to you!—
the keys of your chest away from me?
It is my property as well as yours, by heaven. 310
Do you think you can make an idiot of the mistress of the
house? Now by the lord who is called Saint James,
you shall not be master of both my body and my goods,
even if you rage with anger;
you'll go without one of them, like it or not. 315
What use is it to snoop and spy on me?
I think you'd like to lock me in your chest!
You should say, "Wife, go where you like;
amuse yourself, I won't believe any gossip.
I know you for a true wife, Dame Alice." 320
We don't love a man who carefully watches
where we go; we want to be at large.
"'Beyond all other men, may the wise
astrologer Lord Ptolemy be blessed,
for in his *Almagest* he speaks this proverb: 325
"The wisest of all men is he
that never cares who has the world in his hand."
You should understand by this proverb
that if you have enough, why should you care
how merrily other folks fare? 330
For certainly, old dotard, by your leave,
you'll have quite sex enough at night.
He who forbids another man to light a candle
at his lantern is too great a niggard;
he'll have none the less light, by heaven; 335

if you have enough, you needn't complain.
"'You also say that if we make ourselves attractive
with fine clothing and adornments
it imperils our chastity;
and further—sorrow take you—you must back
yourself up 340
by saying these words in the Apostle's name:
"You women shall adorn yourselves
in shamefastness and sobriety," said he,
"and not in braided hair and gay jewels,
as pearls or gold, or rich array"; 345
I won't conform to this text and
rubric one gnat's worth!
You said this: that I was like a cat;
for if someone singes a cat's fur,
then the cat will stay in its dwelling; 350
and if the cat's fur is sleek and attractive,
she won't stay in the house half a day,
but out she'll go, before the break of day,
to show her fur and go a-caterwauling;
this is to say, sir grouch, that if I'm gaily dressed, 355
I'll run out to show off my clothes.
"'You old fool, what use is it for you to spy?
Even if you ask Argus, with his hundred eyes,
to be my bodyguard (as he can do it best),
in faith, he can't guard me unless I please; 360
I still could deceive him, as I hope to thrive.
"'You also said that there are three things
which trouble all this earth,
and that no man can endure a fourth;
O dear sir tartar, Jesus shorten your life! 365
Still you preach and say that a hateful wife
is reckoned as one of these misfortunes.
Are there no other kind of comparisons
you can apply your parables to—
must a poor wife be one of them? 370
"'You compare a woman's love to hell,
to barren land where water can't remain.
You compare it also to wild fire:

the more it burns, the more it wants
to consume everything that will burn. 375
You say that just as worms destroy a tree,
just so a wife destroys her husband; and
that all who are bound to wives know this.'
"My lords, just so, as you have learned,
I boldly accused my old husbands 380
of speaking in their drunkenness;
and all was false, but I called on
Jankin and my niece as witnesses.
Oh Lord, the pain and woe I gave them,
though they were guiltless, by God's sweet suffering! 385
For I could bite and whinny like a horse;
I could complain, though I was the guilty one;
else many time I would have been ruined.
Whoever comes first to the mill, grinds first;
I complained first, and so our fight was ended. 390
They were quite glad to excuse themselves quickly
for things they had never been guilty of in their lives.
"I would accuse them about wenches
when they were so sick they could hardly stand.
Yet it tickled a husband's heart, since he 395
thought I showed such great fondness for him.
I swore that all my walking out by night
was to spy out the wenches he lay with;
under this pretense I had many a merry time,
for all such wit is given us at our birth; 400
God has given women by nature deceit, weeping,
and spinning, as long as they live.
And thus I can boast of one thing:
in the end I got the better of them in every case,
by trick, or force, or by some kind of method, 405
such as continual complaining or whining;
in particular, they had misfortune in bed,
where I would chide and give them no pleasure;
I would no longer stay in the bed
if I felt my husband's arm over my side 410
until he had paid his ransom to me;
then I'd allow him to do his bit of business.

Therefore I tell this moral to everyone—
profit whoever may, for all is for sale:
you cannot lure a hawk with an empty hand; 415
for profit I would endure all his lust,
and pretend an appetite myself;
and yet I never had a taste for aged meat—
that's what made me scold them all the time.
For even if the pope had sat beside them, 420
I wouldn't spare them at their own board;
I swear I requited them word for word.
So help me almighty God,
even if I were to make my testament right now,
I don't owe them a word which has not been repaid. 425
I brought it about by my wit
that they had to give up, as the best thing to do,
or else we would never have been at rest.
For though he might look like a raging lion,
yet he would fail to gain his point. 430
"Then I would say, 'Dear friend, notice
the meek look on Wilkin, our sheep;
come near, my spouse, let me kiss your cheek!
You should be quite patient and meek,
and have a scrupulous conscience, 435
since you preach so of the patience of Job.
Always be patient, since you preach so well;
for unless you do, we shall certainly teach you
that it is a fine thing to have a wife in peace.
One of us two must bend, without a doubt; 440
and since a man is more reasonable
than a woman is, you must be patient.
What ails you to grumble and groan so?
Is it because you want to have my thing to yourself?
Why take it all, then, have every bit of it! 445
Peter! I swear you love it well!
Now if I would sell my *belle chose*,
I could walk as fresh as a rose;
but I will keep it for your own taste.
You're to blame, by God, I tell you the truth.' 450
"We would have words like this.

Now I will speak of my fourth husband.
   "My fourth husband was a reveller—
that is to say, he had a paramour;
and I was young and full of wantonness, 455
stubborn and strong and merry as a magpie.
How gracefully I could dance to a harp,
and sing just like a nightingale,
when I bad drunk a draught of sweet wine!
Metellius, the foul churl, the swine, 460
who took his wife's life with a staff
because she drank wine—if I had been his wife
he wouldn't have daunted me from drink;
and after wine I must needs think of Venus:
for just as surely as cold brings hail, 465
a lickerish mouth must have a lecherous tail.
A drunken woman has no defense;
this, lechers know by experience.
   "But Lord Christ! When I remember
my youth and my gaeity, 470
it tickles me to the bottom of my heart;
to this day it does my heart good
that I have had my world in my time.
But age, alas, that poisons everything,
has robbed me of my beauty and my pith; 475
let it go, farewell, the devil with it!
The flour is gone, there is no more to say:
now I must sell the bran, as best I can;
but still I will contrive to be right merry.
Now I'll tell about my fourth husband. 480
   "I tell you I was angry in my heart
that he had delight in any other.
But he was repaid, by God and by Saint Joce!
I made him a staff of the same wood—
not with my body in a filthy way, 485
but indeed my manner with other men was such
that I made him fry in his own grease
for anger and pure jealousy.
By God, I was his purgatory on earth,
by which help I hope his soul is in glory. 490

For God knows he often sat and sang out
when his shoe pinched him bitterly.
No one but God and he knew
how sorely I wrung him in many ways.
He died when I came back from Jerusalem, 495
and lies buried under the rood-beam,
although his tomb is not so elaborate
as the sepulchre of that Darius was
which Appelles wrought so skillfully;
it would have been just a waste to bury him expensively. 500
Farewell to him, may God rest his soul;
he is now in his grave and in his coffin.
"Now I will tell of my fifth husband:
God never let his soul go down to hell!
And yet he was the most brutal to me; 505
that I can feel on my ribs, all down the row,
and always shall, to my dying day.
But in our bed he was so tireless and wanton,
and moreover he could cajole me so well
when he wanted to have my *belle chose*, 510
that even if he had beaten me on every bone,
he could soon win my love again.
I think I loved him best because
he was so cool in his love to me.
We women have, to tell the truth, 515
an odd fancy in this matter;
whatever we cannot easily get
we will cry after and crave all day.
Forbid us a thing, and we desire it;
press it upon us, and then we will flee. 520
Faced with coyness we bring out all our wares;
a great crowd at the market makes wares expensive,
and what is too cheap is held to be worth little;
every wise woman knows this.
"My fifth husband, God bless his soul, 525
whom I took for love and not money,
was at one time a scholar at Oxford,
and had left school, and went home to board
with my close friend, who dwelt in our town:

God bless her soul! Her name was Alison. 530
She knew my heart and private affairs
better than our parish priest, as I may thrive!
To her I revealed all my secrets.
For whether my husband had pissed on a wall
or done something which should have cost him his life, 535
to her, and to another worthy wife,
and to my niece, whom I loved well,
I would have betrayed every one of his secrets.
And so I did often enough, God knows,
and that often made his face red and hot 540
for very shame, so that he blamed himself
for having told me so great a confidence.
"And so it happened that once, in Lent
(thus many times I went to my friend's house,
for I always loved to be merry, 545
and to walk, in March, April, and May,
from house to house, to hear various tidings),
that Jankin the clerk and my dear friend Dame Alice
and I myself went into the fields.
My husband was at London all that Lent; 550
I had the better leisure to enjoy myself
and to see, and be seen by,
lusty people; how could I know how my favor
was destined to be bestowed, or where?
Therefore I made my visits 555
to feast-eves and processions,
to sermons and these pilgrimages,
to miracle plays and to marriages,
and wore my gay scarlet clothes:
on my life, worms or moths or mites 560
never ate a bit of them;
and do you know why? Because they were
used constantly.
"Now I'll tell what happened to me.
As I was saying, we walked in the fields, 565
until truly this clerk and I enjoyed
such dalliance that in my foresight
I spoke to him and told him that

if I were a widow he should marry me.
For certainly (I don't say it as a boast)
I was never yet unprovided for 570
in marriage, and other matters too;
I hold that a mouse that has but one hole
to run to has a heart not worth a leek;
for if that should fail, then all is finished.
"I made him believe he had enchanted me; 575
my mother taught me that trick.
And also I said I had dreamed of him all night:
he wanted to slay me as I lay on my back,
and all my bed was full of blood;
but yet I expected that he would bring me luck; 580
for blood signifies gold, as I was taught.
And all this was false, I had dreamed none of it;
I was just following my mother's lore, as I
always did, in this as well as in other matters.
"But now sir, let me see, what am I talking about? 585
Aha! By God, I have my tale back again.
"When my fourth husband was on his bier,
I wept, all the same, and acted sorrowful,
as wives must, for it is customary,
and covered my face with my handkerchief; 590
but since I was provided with a mate,
I wept but little, that I guarantee.
"My husband was brought to church in the morning,
with neighbors who mourned for him;
and Jankin our clerk was one of them. 595
So help me God, when I saw him walk
behind the bier, it seemed to me he had a pair
of legs and feet so neat and handsome
that I gave all my heart into his keeping.
He was, I think, twenty years old, 600
and I was forty, if the truth be told;
but yet I always had a colt's tooth.
I was gap-toothed, and that became me well;
I had the print of St. Venus's seal.
So help me God, I was a lusty one, 605
and fair and rich and young and well off;

and truly, as my husbands told me,
I had the best *quoniam* that might be.
For certainly, my feelings all come
from Venus, and my heart from Mars: 610
Venus gave me my lust, my lecherousness,
and Mars gave me my sturdy hardiness,
because Taurus was in the ascendant when I was
born, and
Mars was in that sign. Alas, alas, that ever love was sin!
I always followed my inclination 615
according to the stellar influences at my birth;
I was so made that I could not withhold
my chamber of Venus from a good fellow.
I still have the mark of Mars on my face,
and also in another private place. 620
For, as surely as God is my salvation,
I never had any discrimination in love,
but always followed my appetite,
be he short or tall, dark or fair;
I didn't care, so long as he pleased me, 625
how poor he was, nor of what rank.
"What should I say, except that at the end of the
month
this gay clerk Jankin, that was so pleasant,
wedded me with great ceremony,
and to him I gave all the lands and property 630
that had ever been given to me before;
but afterward I repented this sorely:
he would not allow anything I wanted.
By God, he hit me once on the ear
because I had torn a leaf out of his book; 635
as a result of that stroke, my ear became totally deaf.
I was stubborn as a lioness,
and as for my tongue, an absolute ranter;
and I'd walk, as I'd done before,
from house to house, although he'd sworn I wouldn't; 640
because of this he would often preach
and teach me of the deeds of ancient Romans:
how Simplicius Gallus left his wife

and forsook her for the rest of his life
just because he saw her looking out 645
of his door bareheaded one day.
"He told me by name of another Roman
who also, because his wife was at a summer
game without his knowledge, forsook her.
And then he would seek in his Bible 650
for that proverb of Ecclesiasticus
where he makes a command strictly forbidding
a man to allow his wife to go roaming about;
then you could be sure he would say this:
'Whoever builds his house of willows, 655
and rides his blind horse over plowed land,
and allows his wife to visit shrines,
is worthy to be hanged on the gallows.'
But all for nought; I didn't care a berry
for his proverbs and old saw, 660
nor would I be corrected by him.
I hate that man who tells me my vices,
and so, God knows, do more of us than I.
This made him utterly furious with me;
I wouldn't give in to him in any case. 665
"Now I'll tell you truly, by Saint Thomas,
why I tore a leaf out of his book,
for which he hit me so that I became deaf.
He had a book that he always loved to read
night and day to amuse himself. 670
He called it Valerius and Theophrastus;
at which book he was always laughing heartily;
and also there was at some time a clerk at Rome,
a cardinal, that was called St. Jerome,
who wrote a book against Jovinian; 675
in this book there was also Tertulian,
Chrysippus, Trotula, and Heloise,
who was an abbess not far from Paris;
and also the Parables of Solomon,
Ovid's *Art of Love*, and many other books, 680
and all these were bound in one volume.
And every day and night it was his custom,

when he had leisure and could rest
from other worldly occupation,
to read in this book of wicked wives. 685
He knew more legends and lives of them
than there are of good wives in the Bible.
For believe me, it is an impossibility
for any clerk to speak good of wives—
unless it be of the lives of holy saints, 690
but never of any other woman.
Who painted the lion, tell me who?
By God, if women had written stories,
as clerks have in their oratories,
they would have written more of men's wickedness 695
than all of the sex of Adam can redress.
The children of Mercury and of Venus
are quite contrary in their ways;
Mercury loves wisdom and learning,
and Venus loves revelry and expenditure. 700
And, because of their diverse dispositions,
each loses power when the other is dominant;
and thus, God knows, Mercury is powerless
in the Sign of the Fish, where Venus is dominant;
and Venus falls when Mercury ascends; 705
therefore no woman is praised by any clerk.
The clerk, when he is old, and unable to do
any of Venus's work worth his old shoe,
then sits down and writes in his dotage
that women cannot keep their marriage vows! 710
"But now to the purpose, as to why I was beaten,
as I told you, because of a book, for heaven's sake.
One night Jankin, who was the head of the household,
read in his book as he sat by the fire,
first, concerning Eve, that all mankind was brought 715
to wretchedness by her wickedness,
for which Jesus Christ himself was slain,
who redeemed us with his heart's blood.
Here you can expressly find this of woman:
that woman caused the fall of all mankind. 720
"Then he read to me how Samson lost his hair:

while he was sleeping, his mistress cut it with her shears;
through this treason he lost both his eyes.
  "Then he read to me, and this is no lie,
about Hercules and his Dejanira, 725
who caused him to set himself on fire.
"He forgot none of the sorrow and woe
  that Socrates had with his two wives;
how Xantippe cast piss upon his head;
this poor man sat as still as if he were dead; 730
he wiped his head; he dared to say no more
than, 'Before the thunder stops, comes the rain.'
  "The tale of Pasiphaë, who was the queen of Crete,
he maliciously thought sweet;
fie, speak no more—it is a grisly thing— 735
about her horrible lust and her preference.
"Of Clytemnestra, who because of her lechery
with falseness caused her husband's death,
he read with great devotion.
  "He told me also why 740
Amphiaraus lost his life at Thebes;
my husband had a story about his wife,
Eriphyle, who for a trinket of gold
secretly told the Greeks
where her husband had hidden himself, 745
which is why he had sad luck at Thebes.
  "He told me of Livia and of Lucilla;
they both caused their husbands to die,
one for love and the other for hate;
Livia, late one night, poisoned 750
her husband, because she was his foe.
Lustful Lucilla loved her husband so
that in order to make him think of her always
she gave him a love potion of such a kind
that he was dead before morning; 755
and thus husbands always suffer.
  "'Then he told me how one Latumius
complained to his friend Arrius
that in his garden there grew a tree
on which, he said, his three wives 760

had spitefully hanged themselves.
"'O dear brother,' said this Arrius,
'give me a cutting of that blessed tree,
and it shall be planted in my garden.'
"He read of wives of a later date 765
some of whom had slain their husbands in their beds,
and let their lechers make love to them all the night
while the corpse lay flat on the floor.
And some have driven nails into their husband's brain
while they slept, and thus slain them. 770
Some have given them poison in their drink.
He told of more evil than the heart can imagine;
and along with that, he knew more proverbs
than there are blades of grass or herbs in the world.
"'It is better,' said he, 'to dwell 775
with a lion or a foul dragon
than with a woman accustomed to scold.
It is better,' said he, 'to stay high on the roof
than with an angry wife down in the house;
they are so wicked and contrary 780
they always hate what their husbands love.'
He said, 'A woman casts her shame away
when she casts off her smock,' and furthermore,
'A fair woman, unless she is also chaste,
is like a gold ring in a sow's nose.' 785
Who would suppose or imagine
the woe and pain that was in my heart?
"And when I saw he would never stop
reading in this cursed book all night,
suddenly I plucked three leaves 790
out of his book, right as he was reading, and also
I hit him on the cheek with my fist, so
that he fell down into our fire backward.
He started up like a raging lion
and hit me on the head with his fist 795
so that I lay on the floor as if I were dead.
And when he saw how still I lay,
he was aghast, and would have fled away,
until at last I awoke from my swoon:

'Oh! Have you slain me, false thief?' I said, 800
'And have you murdered me thus for my land?
Before I die, I yet want to kiss you.'
"He came near, and kneeled down gently,
and said, 'Dear sister Alisoun,
so help me God, I shall never hit you again; 805
what I have done, you are to blame for yourself.
Forgive me for it, I beseech you.'
But yet again I hit him on the cheek,
and said, 'Thief, this much I am avenged;
now I shall die, I can speak no longer.' 810
But at last, after much care and woe,
we fell into accord between ourselves.
He gave the bridle completely into my hand
to have control of house and land,
and also of his tongue and hand; 815
and I made him burn his book right then.
And when I had got for myself,
through superiority, all the sovereignty,
and he had said, 'My own true wife,
do as you wish the rest of your life, 820
preserve your honor, and my public position, too,'
after that day we never argued.
So God help me, I was as kind to him
as any wife from Denmark to India,
and as true, and so was he to me. 825
I pray to God who sits in majesty
to bless his soul, for his dear mercy's sake!
Now I'll tell my tale; if you will listen."

Behold the words between the Summoner and the Friar

The Friar laughed when he had heard all this:
"Now, dame," said he, "as I may have joy or bliss, 830
this is a long preamble to a tale!"
And when the Summoner heard the Friar exclaim,
"Lo!" said the Summoner, "By God's two arms!
A friar will always be butting in.
See, good people, a fly and a friar 835
will fall into every dish and also every matter.

What do you mean, talking about perambulation?
Oh, amble or trot or pace, or go sit down;
you're spoiling our fun by behaving in this manner."
"Oh, is that so, sir Summoner?" said the Friar, 840
"Now by my faith, before I go, I'll
tell such a tale or two about a summoner
that everyone here shall laugh."
"Now, Friar, damn your eyes,"
said this Summoner, "and damn me 845
if I don't tell two or three tales
about friars before I get to Sittingbourne,
so that I shall make your heart mourn;
I can easily see that your patience is gone."
Our Host cried "Peace! And that at once!" 850
And said, "Let the woman tell her tale.
You behave like people who have got drunk on ale.
Tell your tale, dame; that is best."
"All ready, sir," said she, 'just as you wish,
if I have the permission of this worthy Friar." 855
"Yes, dame," said he, "tell on and I will listen."

Here begins the Wife of Bath's Tale

In the old days of King Arthur,
of whom Britons speak great honor,
this land was all filled with fairies.
The elf queen with her jolly company
danced often in many a green meadow— 5
this was the old belief, as I have read;
I speak of many hundred years ago.
But now no one can see elves anymore,
for now the great charity and prayers
of limiters and other holy friars, 10
who search every field and stream,
as thick as specks of dust in a sunbeam,
blessing halls, chambers, kitchens, bedrooms,
cities, towns, castles, high towers,
villages, barns, stables, dairies: 15
this is the reason that there are no fairies.
For where an elf was wont to walk,

there now walks the limiter himself,
in afternoons and in mornings,
and says his Matins and his holy things, 20
as he goes about within his limits.
Women may go up and down safely;
in every bush or under every tree
there is no other incubus but he—
and he won't do anything but dishonor to them. 25
It so happened that this King Arthur
had in his house a lusty bachelor,
who one day came riding from the river;
and it happened that he saw a maiden
walking before him, alone as she was born. 30
And from this maiden then, against her will,
and by pure force, he took her maidenhood.
Because of this violation, there was such a clamor
and such petitioning to King Arthur
that this knight was condemned to die 35
according to law, and should have lost his head—
it happened that such was the statute then—
except that the queen and various other ladies
prayed to the king for grace so long
that he granted him his life on the spot, 40
and gave him to the queen, completely at her will,
to choose whether she would save or destroy him.
The queen thanked the king heartily,
and then spoke thus to the knight,
one day, when she saw a fitting time: 45
"You are still in such a position," said she,
"that you have no guarantee of your life as yet.
I will grant you life if you can tell me
what thing it is that women most desire.
Be wary, and keep your neck from the ax. 50
And if you cannot tell it to me now,
I will still give you leave to go
a year and a day to seek and learn
a sufficient answer in this matter.
And I want a guarantee, before you go, 55
that you will yield up your person in this place."

The knight was woeful, and he sighed sorrowfully;
but then, he could not do as he pleased.
And in the end he decided to go off,
and to come back again just at the end of the year, 60
with such an answer as God would provide for him;
he took his leave and went forth on his way.
He sought in every house and every place
where he hoped to find favor,
in order to learn what thing women most love; 65
but he reached no land where he could find
two people who were in agreement
with each other on this matter.
Some said women love riches best;
some said honor; some said amusement; 70
some, rich apparel; some said pleasure in bed,
and often to be widowed and remarried.
Some said that our hearts are most soothed
when we are flattered and pampered:
he came near the truth, I will not lie; 75
a man can win us best with flattery,
and with constant attendance and assiduity
we are ensnared, both high and low.
And some said that we love best
to be free, and do just as we please, 80
and to have no man reprove us for our vice,
but say that we are wise and not at all foolish.
For truly, if anyone will scratch us
on a sore spot, there is not one of us
who will not kick for being told the truth; 85
try it, and he who does shall find this out.
No matter how full of vice we are within,
we wish to be thought wise and clean from sin.
And some said that we take delight
in being thought reliable and able to keep a secret 90
and hold steadfast to a purpose
and not betray anything that people tell us.
But that idea isn't worth a rake handle;
by heaven, we women can't conceal a thing;
witness Midas; would you hear the tale? 95

Ovid, among other brief matters,
said Midas had two ass's ears growing
on his head under his long hair;
which evil he hid from everyone's sight
as artfully as he could, 100
so that no one knew of it except his wife.
He loved her most, and also trusted her;
he prayed her not to tell anyone
of his disfigurement.
She swore to him that not for all the world 105
would she do such villainy and sin
as to give her husband so bad a name;
out of her own shame she wouldn't tell it.
But nonetheless she thought that she would die
for having to keep a secret so long; 110
it seemed to her that her heart swelled so painfully
some word must needs burst from her;
and since she dared not tell it to anybody,
she ran down to a marsh close by—
her heart was on fire until she got there— 115
and, as a bittern booms in the mire,
she laid her mouth down to the water:
"Betray me not, you water, with your sound,"
said she. "To you I tell it, and to no one else:
my husband has two long ass's ears! 120
Now my heart is all cured, for the secret is out!
I simply couldn't keep it any longer."
In this you can see that though we wait a time,
yet out it must come: we cannot hide a secret.
If you wish to hear the rest of the tale, 125
read Ovid, and there you can learn of it.
When this knight whom my tale specially concerns
saw that he couldn't come by it—
that is to say, what women love most—
his spirit was very sorrowful within his breast; 130
but home he went, he might not linger:
the day was come when he must turn homeward.
And on his way, burdened with care, he happened
to ride by the edge of a forest,

where he saw more than twenty-four 135
ladies moving in a dance;
he drew eagerly toward that dance
in the hope that he might learn something.
But indeed, before he quite got there,
the dancers vanished, he knew not where. 140
He saw no living creature,
except a woman sitting on the green:
no one could imagine an uglier creature.
This old woman rose before the knight
and said, "Sir knight, no road lies this way. 145
Tell me, by your faith, what you seek for.
Perhaps it may be the better;
these old folks know many things," said she.
"Dear mother," said this knight, "certainly
I am as good as dead unless I can say 150
what thing it is that women most desire;
if you could tell me, I would repay your trouble well."
"Give me your promise, here upon my hand," said she,
"that you will do the next thing I require
of you, if it lies in your power, 155
and I will tell it to you before nightfall."
"Here is my promise," said the knight, "I grant it."
"Then," said she, "I dare to boast
that your life is safe, for I'll swear
upon my life that the queen will say as I do. 160
Let's see whether the proudest of all those
that wear a coverchief or headdress
dares deny what I shall teach you;
let's go on without any more talk."
Then she whispered a message in his ear, 165
and told him to be glad and not afraid.
When they had come to the court, this knight
said he had kept his day as he had promised,
and his answer, he said, was ready.
Many a noble wife and many a maiden, 170
and many a widow (since widows are so wise),
were assembled to bear his answer
with the queen herself sitting as judge;

and then the knight was ordered to appear.
Everyone was commanded to keep silence, 175
and the knight was commanded to tell in open assembly
what thing it is that secular women love best.
This knight did not stand in beastlike silence,
but answered to his question at once
with manly voice, so that all the court heard it: 180
"My liege lady," he said, "generally
women desire to have dominion
over their husbands as well as their lovers,
and to be above them in mastery;
this is your greatest desire, though you may kill me; 185
do as you please, I am at your will here."
In all the court there was neither wife nor maiden
nor widow who contradicted what he said,
but all said he deserved to have his life.
And at that word up jumped the old woman 190
whom the knight had seen sitting on the green:
"Mercy," said she, "my sovereign lady queen!
Before your court depart, do right by me,
I taught this answer to the knight;
for this he gave me his promise there 195
that he would do the first thing
I required of him, if it lay in his power.
Before the court, then, I pray you, sir knight,"
said she, "to take me as your wife;
for well you know that I have saved your life. 200
If I say false, deny me, on your faith!"
The knight answered, "Alas and woe is me!
I know quite well that such was my promise.
For the love of God ask for something else;
take all my property and let my body go." 205
"No then," said she. "Curse the two of us!
For though I am ugly and old and poor,
I wouldn't want all the metal or ore
that is buried under the earth or lies above
unless I were your wife and your love as well." 210
"My love?" said he; "No, my damnation!
Alas, that any of my birth

should ever be so foully disgraced!"
But it was all for nothing; the end was this, that he
was forced to accept the fact that he must needs wed her; 215
and he took his old wife and went to bed.
Now some people might say, perhaps,
that out of negligence I am not bothering
to tell you about the joy and the pomp
at the feast that day, 220
to which objection I shall answer briefly:
I am telling you that there was no joy or feast at all,
there was nothing but gloom and much sorrow;
for he married her privately in the morning
and afterward hid himself like an owl all day— 225
he was so dejected because his wife looked so ugly.
Great was the woe in the knight's mind
when he was brought with his wife to bed;
he tossed and he turned to and fro.
His old wife lay smiling all the time, 230
and said, "O dear husband, bless my soul!
Does every knight behave with his wife as you do?
Is this the law of King Arthur's house?
Is every one of his knights so cold?
I am your own love and your wife; 235
I am she who saved your life;
and certainly I never yet did wrong to you.
Why do you act thus with me the first night?
You act like a man who has lost his mind.
What am I guilty of? For God's sake, tell me, 240
and it shall be corrected, if I can manage it."
"Corrected?" said this knight, "Alas, no, no!
It will never be corrected!
You are so loathsome and so old,
and what is more, of such low birth, 245
that it is little wonder if I toss and turn.
I wish to God my heart would break!"
"Is this," said she, "the cause of your unrest?"
"Yes, certainly," said he, "it's no wonder."
"Now, sir," said she, "I could rectify all this, 250
if I wanted to, before three days were up,

if you behaved yourself to me well.
"But in the matter of your speaking of such nobility
as descends from ancient wealth,
claiming that because of it you are supposed to be — 255
noblemen—such arrogance is not worth a hen.
Find the man who is always the most virtuous,
privately and publicly, and who always tries hardest
to do what noble deeds he can,
and consider him the greatest nobleman. — 260
Christ wants us to claim our nobility from him,
not from our ancestors because of their ancient wealth:
for though they give us all their heritage,
on the strength of which we claim to be of noble descent,
yet they cannot bequeath by any means — 265
or to any of us their virtuous manner of life
which made them be called noblemen;
and which summoned us to follow them at the
same level.
"Well can the wise poet of Florence
who is called Dante speak on this subject; — 270
in this sort of rhyme is Dante's tale:
'Not oft by branches of a family tree
Does human prowess rise; for gracious God
Wants us to claim from him nobility.'
For from our elders we may claim nothing — 275
but perishable matter, to which man may do hurt
and injury. And everyone knows as well as I that
if nobility were implanted by nature
in a certain lineage, down the line of descent,
they would never cease, in private or public, — 280
to do the fair offices of nobility;
they could do nothing shameful or evil.
"Take fire, and bear it into the darkest house
from here to the Mount of Caucasus,
and let men shut the doors and go away; — 285
yet the fire will blaze and burn as well
as if twenty thousand men were looking at it;
it will maintain its natural function always
until it dies, I'll stake my life.

"By this you can easily see that nobility 290
is not tied to possessions,
since people do not perform their function
without variation as does the fire, according to
its nature.
For, God knows, men may very often find
a lord's son committing shameful and vile deeds; 295
and he who wishes to have credit for his nobility
because he was born of a noble house,
and because his elders were noble and virtuous,
but will not himself do any noble deeds
or follow the example of his late noble ancestor, 300
he is not noble, be he duke or earl;
for villainous, sinful deeds make him a churl.
This kind of nobility is only the renown
of your ancestors, earned by their great goodness,
which is a thing apart from yourself. 305
Your nobility comes from God alone;
then our true nobility comes of grace,
it was in no way bequeathed to us with our station
in life.
"Think how noble, as Valerius says,
was that Tullius Hostilius 310
who rose out of poverty to high nobility.
Read Seneca, and read Boethius, too;
there you shall see expressly that there is no doubt
that he is noble who does noble deeds.
And therefore, dear husband, I thus conclude 315
even if my ancestors were low,
yet God on high may—and so I hope—
grant me grace to live virtuously;
then I am noble, from the time when I begin
to live virtuously and avoid sin. 320
"And as for the poverty you reprove me for,
high God in whom we believe
chose to live his life in willing poverty;
and certainly every man, maiden, or wife
can understand that Jesus, heaven's king, 325
would not choose a vicious way of life.

Contented poverty is an honorable thing, indeed;
this is said by Seneca and other learned men.
Whoever is content with his poverty
I hold to be rich, even if he hasn't a shirt. 330
He who covets anything is a poor man,
for he wants to have something which is not in
his power.
But he who has nothing and desires nothing is rich,
although you may consider him nothing but a
lowly man.
"True poverty sings of its own accord; 335
Juvenal says of poverty, 'Merrily can
the poor man sing and joke before the
thieves when he goes by the road.'
Poverty is a good that is hated, and, I guess,
a great expeller of cares; 340
a great amender of knowledge, too,
to him that takes it in patience.
Poverty is this, although it seem unhealthy:
possession of that which no man will challenge.
Poverty will often, when a man is low, 345
make him know his God and himself as well.
Poverty is a glass, it seems to me,
through which he can see his true friends.
And therefore, sir, since I do not harm you by it,
do not reprove me for my poverty anymore. 350
"Now, sir, you reprove me for age;
but certainly, sir, aside from bookish
authority, you nobles who are honorable
say that one should honor an old person,
and call him father, for the sake of your nobility; 355
and I can find authors to that effect, I imagine.
"Now as to the point that I am ugly and old—
then you need not dread being a cuckold;
for ugliness and age, as I may thrive,
are great wardens of chastity. 360
But nevertheless, since I know what pleases you,
I shall fulfill your fleshly appetite.
"Choose now," said she, "one of these two things:

to have me ugly and old until I die,
and be a faithful, humble wife to you, 365
and never displease you in all my life;
or else to have me young and fair,
and take your chances on the flocking
of people to your house because of me—
or to some other place, it may well be. 370
Now choose yourself, whichever you like."
The knight considered and sighed sorely,
but at last he spoke in this manner,
"My lady and my love, and wife so dear,
I put myself under your wise control; 375
you yourself choose which may be most pleasurable
and most honorable to you and to me also.
I don't care which of the two I get;
for whatever pleases you suffices for me."
"Then have I got mastery over you," said she, 380
"since I may choose and rule as I please?"
"Yes, certainly, wife," said he, "I consider that best."
"Kiss me," said she, "we won't be angry anymore;
for I swear I will be both these things to you;
that is to say, both fair indeed and good. 385
I pray to God that I may die mad
if I am not just as good and true to you
as ever was wife since the world began.
And, if I am not tomorrow as fair to see
as any lady, empress, or queen 390
between the east and the west,
do with the question of my life and death just as
you wish.
Raise the curtain, and see how it is."
And when the knight actually saw all this—
that she was so fair and so young, too, 395
he seized her in his two arms for joy,
his heart was bathed in bliss;
he kissed her a thousand times in a row.
And she obeyed him in everything
that might give him pleasure or joy. 400
And thus they lived to the end of their lives

in perfect joy; and Jesus Christ sends us
husbands who are meek, young, and lively in bed,
and grace to outlive those that we marry.
And also I pray Jesus to shorten the lives 405
of those that won't be governed by their wives;
and as for old and angry niggards with their money,
God send them soon a true pestilence.